I've Claimed the Promi.

Original Healing 3 John II

Because there are:

NO

"HEALING MEDICINES!"

Jeremiah 30:13, 46:11

Rick L. Lee, N.D., D.D.
Missionary Health Restoration Practitioner

ℵO "HEALING MEDICINES!"

Based upon Jeremiah 30:13, 46:11

No rights reserved. All parts of this publication may be reproduced or utilized without written permission from the Author.

Editor: Rick L. Lee

Printed in the United States of America

Seventh Edition January, 2018

TABLE OF CONTENTS

Chapter VI: *With True Knowledge Comes Personal Responsibility*

Chapter VII: *The Ultimate Goal is Population Reduction*

Chapter VIII: *True Education & Faith in God is the Answer*

Colporteurs please contact us at office@originalhealing.org for pricing of book purchases in bulk and their break points.

About the Author

In 1982, a co-worker's observation of certain behavioral abnormalities of mine (impatience, irritability, and confrontational attitude at times to name a few) prompted me to make an appointment with his naturopathic physician. On completion of a six-hour Glucose Tolerance Test (see appendix A), I was diagnosed with hypoglycemia. Afterward, I realized how accurate my co-worker's description was as he expressed exactly how I felt - much like I wanted to climb right out of my own skin. This incident began a 15 month-long odyssey that resulted in the complete healing of my pancreas. To this day, I have no blood sugar issues and realize that it was no coincidence that led me to a naturopathic physician. This was the beginning of my journey for truth in God's word.

As a Naturopathic doctor, I implement "Christian Natural Healing" methodologies, which are based upon God's way of healing as found in His Holy Word. I graduated from the Institute of Alternative Medicine, Philosophy and Research in 1998. I received training and certification in the principles of Low Level Laser Therapy from the American Society of Laser Therapy in 2002. In July 2006 I became a Diplomate of the National Board (D.N.B.), through the National Board of [Traditional] Naturopathic Examiners (NBNE). The NBNE is the first and original Naturopathic Board in the United States, registered in Washington, D.C.

Personal Experience

Like the majority of you, I have personal experience with family member(s) that have died from cancer, and another one that died as a result of the chemotherapy and radiation treatments she was administered. It is a helpless and sad feeling watching family members pass away, but to then find out the system has lied to you and them, causes righteousness indignation within. This book is dedicated to Nathaniel James and Betty Jean Lee that their deaths were not in vain, and to give you and your loves ones, hope to believe in God's saving health, Ps. 67:2. In late 2014 my sister was diagnosed with colon rectal cancer and the medical established pressured her to get a colon resection. Against the advice of her medical doctors, her husband and many well meaning and genuine family members and friends, including members of her church, she declined and traveled approximately five thousand miles to her younger brother for God's healing. After she made a decided commitment to change her diet and lifestyle, to keep the way of the Lord, I put her on a program based upon God's way of healing and not mans. Today, she is alive and healthy, with her complete colon praising God.

With much Christian love, I pray that the message in this book inspires you to research for yourself and discover the "Truth". Then seek out God's way of healing and leave the outcome of life or death in His hands. Whether therefore ye eat, or drink, or whatsoever ye do, do all to the glory of God, 1Cor. 10:31. The [whatsoever ye do] includes how we choose to die. God never intended His true children to be cut, burned or poisoned. In fact, Psalms 37:37 says: "Mark the perfect *man,* and behold the upright: for the end of *that* man *is* peace.
"And now abideth faith, hope, charity, these three; but the greatest of these is charity". I Cor. 13:13.

As Christians, when it comes to life or death, we should trust God and be at peace with His decision. We must do all that is humanly possible to do, which are God's Ten Natural Laws of health, and not be frightened into accepting, as our only hope; toxic chemicals, surgery, and radiation. Like King Ahaziah inquired of Baal-zebub the god of Ekron; II Kings 1:2, many of us go and inquire of the god of Modern Medicine. The question begs to be asked; 'Is there no God in heaven that ye go inquire of the god of Modern Medicine? II Kings 1:3. Modern medicine has its place, if I was in a car accident and need a life saving surgery, I would go to a medical doctor, but not for lifestyle diseases, which I and you have the power to avoid or heal ourselves from. It is my intention to enlighten health care consumers of the medical deception and fraud perpetrated upon scared and misinformed believers, Hosea 4:6.

The only source of true healing that encompasses the healing of the whole person, i.e. mental, physical, emotional and spiritual, comes from God in His living Word and those trained in Hygienic agencies and the Ten Laws of Health, Psalms 107:20.
Dr. Rick L. Lee, N.D., D.D. Director of Original Healing Ministries
office@originalhealing.org
The statements in this book are not meant to reflect badly on the dedicated staff employed within the sick-care industry, which daily renders compassionate service to the unfortunate sick.
The fault and blame clearly lies with The Catholic church, John D. Rockefeller, Andrew Carnegie, The American Medical Association, the Pharmaceutical industry and the many governmental agencies and employees of these organizations that turn a blind eye to maintain and up hold a failed system. The Rockefellers', Rothchilds' and Carnegies of the world incorporated health care as one of the sectors of the U.S.

economy, insuring their families' wealth at the expense of the masses. As you will learn, this was done out of greed and loyalty to the secret societies they belonged to. There are those also on the European side of the Atlantic like I.G. Farben, Bayer, etc. that are equally responsible.

Do not take my word for it, read the following words from a medical doctor. *"Very few know that the birth hour of the pharmaceutical industry is actually a deliberate decision by a handful of people on this side (Europe) and the other side (America) of the Atlantic Ocean to define disease as a marketplace, and build what has now become the largest investment industry upon that simple thought."*

-Dr. Matthias Rath, M.D.

"The thief cometh not, but for to steal, and to kill, and to destroy"… John10:10.

Preface

In our quest for health we often rely on other people who we consider to be skilled in the healing arts. Sometimes these are orthodox medical doctors; other times chiropractic or naturopathic physicians and sometimes we even include friends and relatives whom we respect. However, this relationship often begins with a wrong question which almost always leads to a wrong approach to health restoration. We often ask, "what can I do to treat my illness" or "will taking this substance make me get well". What Rick Lee will explain in this book is how to start with the right question, "how can I have the exuberant health God wants to give me" and begin a lifelong journey of health and fitness.

Dr. Lee first explains the pitfalls of many healing systems, including orthodox allopathic medicine, and explains the origins and premises that have caused it to develop into a system that may preserve life in the short term, but offers little assistance in obtaining optimal health. Unfortunately, this may often be true for "natural healing" programs as well. Instead of asking what drug I need, the question may be what herb or vitamin will cure my illness. This is a fundamentally flawed approach to healing. Only rarely is an illness simply due to a deficiency of a single vitamin or mineral, therefore, rarely will taking one cure the illness. Of course, illness is never due to a deficiency of a drug, drugs usually provide short-term relief from symptoms without providing true healing. Health is obtained and illness avoided by following just a few basic principles which you will learn in this book. If you learn nothing else from this book, learn how to incorporate the 10 basic principles of health into your daily routine.

1. Trust in divine power
2. Breathe fresh air
3. Pure water, inside and out
4. Proper nutrition
5. Avoid harmful substances (temperance)
6. Regular Exercise
7. Rest
8. Regular exposure to sunlight
9. Attitude of Gratitude
10. Benevolence

Dr. Lee will help you learn how to apply these principles to your everyday life until they become routine and habitual.

It is unfortunate that so many people will follow several of these principles and find themselves to be sickly and wonder why. I personally speak with people almost every day who describe their excellent eating habits, supplement use, and who would never touch tobacco, sugar, coffee etc, but still complain of feeling tired and weak all the time. I have yet to find one who can honestly say that they are not violating any of the above principles – most often they are not getting enough rest. In this fast-paced high stress world we must have proper rest to survive. As you study this book, make notes on how you can apply each of these principles to your daily life and look forward to a renewed vitality experienced by only a few.

Jim Daily III, Ph.D.
Daily Manufacturing, Inc.
Rockwell, NC 28138
www.daily-mfg.com

"Modern Medicine never calls itself a church. You will never see a medical building dedicated to the religion of medicine; it always says the medical arts, or medical science.

Modern medicine relies on FAITH to survive. All religions do. So heavily does the Church of Modern Medicine rely on FAITH that if everyone somehow simply forgot to believe in it for just one day, the whole system would collapse. For how else could any institution get people to do the things Modern Medicine gets people to do, without introducing a profound suspension of doubt? Would people allow themselves to be artificially put to sleep then cut to pieces in a process they couldn't have the slightest notion about – if they didn't have faith? Would people swallow the thousands of tons of pills a year - again without the slightest knowledge what these chemicals were going to do - if they didn't have faith?

Common to all religions is the claim that reality is not limited to or dependent upon what can be seen, felt, tasted, or smelled. You can easily test modern medical religion on this characteristic by simply asking your doctor WHY enough times. Why are you prescribing this drug? Why is this operation going to do me any good? Why do I have to do that? Why do you have to do that to me?

Just ask WHY and sooner or later you will get to the Chasm of Faith. Your doctor will retreat into the fact that you have no way of knowing or understanding all the wonders he has at his command, and will say "Just Trust Me"!

[1]Confessions of a Medical Heretic, Robert S. Mendelson, M.D. pp, 16, 17.

Foreword

In spite of the thousands of books that have been written on health and the seemingly endless stream of conventional medication flooding the market, the world is still in dire need of better health; virtually millions are in poor health. People are sick and dying who might be well if they could learn how to live. The common allopathic procedures are largely unnatural, artificial, expensive and worst; sadly they do not cure but only treat the symptoms of the ailment. God's Word is clear, He says in Jeremiah 46:11: "...in vain shalt thou use many medicines; [for] thou shalt not be cured."

The philosophy of this book is to make use of those God-given foods and herbs which aid in restoring a measure of the body's natural immunity to disease. God has revealed in His word where healing can be obtained. He says in Revelation 22:2 "and the leaves of the tree [were] for the healing of the nations." The author of this well-written book outlines some of the recent research that clearly proves that God's methods for restoring and maintaining health is superior to the practices of the AMA and other medical establishments.

Rick Lee takes his readers back to study Satan's counterfeit health methodologies with a look at the historical and biblical evidences of the Chaldean (Babylonian) system of healing. Mr. Lee challenges Christians everywhere to rethink their perceptions of current allopathic practices versus the healing methods of our wonderful Creator God.

Finally, he ends by expounding upon the principles of health as set forth in the Word of God. These principles have been tested and proven. Through faith in God and obedience to His precepts we can obtain not only physical health but healing for the whole man. "And [Moses] said, If thou wilt diligently hearken to the voice of the LORD thy God, and wilt do that which is right in his sight, and wilt give ear to his commandments, and keep all his statutes, I will put none of these diseases upon thee, which I have brought upon the Egyptians: for I [am] the LORD that healeth thee." Exodus 15:26.

Mamon Wilson, Director
Centurion Bible School of Health Ministry

Definition of a "Quack"

"One who professes knowledge concerning subjects of which he is ignorant." …Oxford Universal Dictionary

According to the FDA: "Quackery encompasses both people and products --- broadly speaking, quackery is misinformation about health."

FDA "Fact Sheet" dated November, 1971.

As far as allopathic medicine is concerned, I am indeed a "unlicensed quack." However, as far as NUTRITION is concerned, the FDA and M.D.'s are likewise "quacks".

True Ott, Ph.D.

Nature's Definition of a "Quack"
Quack: A highly evolved clarion call that has evolved to signal others to a safe haven full of good nutritious food; also in many cases issued as a loud trumpet, alerting the flock to possible mortal dangers.

It is your inalienable right to decide which "Quack" you wish to follow.

True Ott, Ph.D.

A Definition of Medicine:

Medicine (měd' ĭ-sĭn), *n.*
3. A drug or the like used for a purpose <u>not curative</u>, as a poison, the alchemist's elixir, etc.   …Webster's Collegiate Dictionary 1916.

Disclaimer:

The information presented in this book has been obtained from authentic and reliable sources. Although great care has been taken to ensure the accuracy of the information presented, the author and the publisher cannot assume responsibility for the validity of all the materials or the consequences of their use. Before starting a regimen of nutritional supplementation, and/or exercise, you should consult a Health Restoration Practitioner proficient in God's Ten Natural Laws of Health.

While it is true that nutrition is the foundation of health, and will again be the leading edge of disease prevention, the information in this book is not intended to tell people to take or stop taking prescription medication. This book is intended to equip the health care consumer with knowledge to be used in conjunction with the advice of a knowledgeable Christian professional health restoration practitioners.

It is to this end I pray, that all God fearing peoples but especially Christians will wake up and throw off the cloak of darkness and modern day superstitions and trust God with their lives. As Abraham trusted God and was willing to sacrifice Isaac, counting God faithful even unto raising Isaac from the dead. That we will follow God's way of healing even unto the closing of our lives in Christ Jesus and counting God faithful to awake us from our sleep at His second coming.

Only because of the current medical laws, I make the following statement: The material contained in this book, is not intended to replace professional medical advice or care. However, it is intended to direct Christians to the correct health care discipline for your health restoration needs. Remember, the religion of modern medicine continues to "practice medicine" with you as the subject in their test tubes. Before deciding upon any treatment, medical procedure, etc. obtain two or more professional opinions and then seek God for wisdom.

God has sent you His Word, too heal you and deliver you from destruction (Psalms 107:20); both physically and spiritually, from the cut (surgery), burn (chemotherapy) and poison (prescription drugs) system of so called modern medicine.

-Rick L. Lee, N.D.

Introduction

In order to achieve and/or maintain optimal health, a person has to work at it. Most people know more about the latest fashions, or how the engine in their automobile runs than they do about how their body functions.

The human body is made up of individual cells. These cells make up our organs, such as the heart and kidneys, which in turn make up the body's systems such as the digestive and circulatory systems. The human body is a very complicated, intricate, complex, electrical/chemical factory. Many of the organs are controlled electrically and chemically through mineral salts and hormones, and these hormones control many of the body functions. Organ malfunction is often a combination of faulty electrical, chemical, and hormonal interaction. I believe it is an electrical and/or chemical imbalance that causes a low or unbalanced hormone level, which cannot support health. This is a process that could take years to develop in diseases like cancer. An out-of-balance body chemistry, I believe, is a major factor in allowing disease to overwhelm the immune system.

When God formed man from the dust of the ground, as recorded in Genesis 2:7, we see man was made up of elements. Remember the "Periodic Table of Elements" from high school chemistry, see appendix B. The human body needs approximately 88 of these 110 elements in order to maintain or achieve optimal health. Dr. James Balch, M.D. and Phyllis Balch, in their book Rx Prescription for Cooking on pages 18-26, list the organs of the human body and the nutrients needed to keep each organ healthy. By volume, the brain uses more potassium than any other organ, the liver more calcium, the reproductive organs magnesium, etc. Not once does Dr. Balch list toxins, poisons or inorganic minerals. For many years, scientists laughed at the apparent simplicity of the scriptural account that God used the "dust of the ground" to construct the complex elements and molecules that make up a human being. However, after a century of scientific examination of the elements within the human body, scientists have been startled to discover that clay and earth have every single element found in the human body. A Readers Digest article entitled, "How Life began on Earth," in November 1982, describes a fascinating discovery by the researchers at NASA's Ames Research Center which confirmed the Bible's account that every single element found in the human body exists within the soil.

The scientists concluded, "The biblical scenario for the creation of life turns out not to be far off the mark." Bottom line: it has been scientifically proven that the nutrition of the human body is organic minerals, not inorganic minerals or toxic chemicals.

The logical conclusion drawn from the discovery of the researchers at NASA's Ames Research Center is that it takes nutrition, proper nutrition to keep us healthy and/or restore health. Modern food processing began in the U.S. during the 1940's, to extend the shelf life of food products. Food processors seem more concerned with shelf life than with human life. By removing the bran and germ of wheat, flour can be made into bread that won't spoil as quickly. This process, however, removes 22 vitamins and other nutrients. (Matthew 19:6 tells us, "What therefore God hath joined together, let not man put asunder"). Most Christians only apply this passage of scripture to marriage. However, the passage says "what God hath joined together" includes food. Because man has chosen to separate nutrients, for shelf life and profits, scientists soon discovered that this processed flour was causing B1, B2, B3 and iron deficiencies in the American population. Therefore, Congress passed the Enrichment Act of 1948 that forced food processors to add these four nutrients back into the flour they "refined." The word *refined* means *free from impurities*. God created a whole grain called *wheat* containing the bran, wheat germ, and 22 vitamins and other nutrients, which man calls *impurities* and removes! The labels on their brands read "enriched." How can processors enrich something they have robbed and perverted? The foods that we put into our bodies have been processed or, more accurately, "destroyed by the arrogance of man who takes the foods of God and alters them to suit his taste, whims, and greed." These refined or *destroyed* foods also destroy our bodies. "The thief cometh not, but for to steal, and to kill, and to destroy: I am come that they might have life, and that they might have *it* more abundantly." John 10:10.

There is a very simple yet profound scriptural fact concerning health, and once you understand it, you will have an epiphany! In Matthew 28:19 we read, Go ye therefore, and teach *all nations*, baptizing them in the name of the Father, and the Son, and of the Holy Ghost... We know this as the great commission, the gospel of the New Testament. In Psalms 67:2 we read, "thy way may be known upon the earth, thy saving health among *all nations*." There are two things that are commissioned to go to all nations, the gospel of Jesus Christ and God's saving health!

Chapter One: Acknowledge the Source of Life, Knowledge & Love

What is God's Saving Health?

We think we know the gospel when God has said there is one Lord, one faith, one baptism...Eph 4:5. If we are confused concerning the gospel with so many different denominations, religions, and beliefs, then how can we be so arrogant to think we know God's healing way, Psalms 67:2? III John 2 says, "Beloved, I wish above all things that thou mayest prosper and be in health, even as thy soul prospereth." What is the soul? In Genesis 2:7 we read "And the LORD God formed man [of] the dust of the ground, and breathed into his nostrils the breath of life; and man became a living soul". Job 33:4 confirms and clarifies this fact. Then, how does your soul prosper? First, in order for the soul to prosper, it has to be born again of the Spirit of God. Jesus answered and said unto him, "Verily, verily, I say unto thee, except a man be born again, he cannot see the kingdom of God" John 3:3. "Being born again, not of corruptible seed, but of incorruptible, by the Word of God, which liveth and abideth forever"1 Peter 1:23. "Marvel not that I said unto thee, Ye must be born again" John 3:7.

The second aspect of the soul prospering has to do with our physical well being. Let us take a closer look at the 'dust of the ground'. N.A.S.A. scientists have already proven that every single element in the human body is in the soil. In other words, it takes approximately 88 elements (nutriments) found in the soil to be healthy. God's saving health is living by His ten laws of health in order to protect the body and especially the mind. It is very difficult to serve the Lord with a sick and feeble body, especially mind.

The gospel of truth, the gospel of righteousness, and the gospel of health are all part of the everlasting gospel of Jesus Christ. The truth of the matter is this "Ye cannot drink the cup of the Lord, and the cup of devils: ye cannot be partakers of the Lord's Table, and of the table of devils," 1. Corinthians 10:21. As a Christian you have to know and understand what is to be partaken of that is from God and abstain (temperance) from that of devils. Until we as Christians understand this, we will continue to die from the same diseases as the Egyptians.

It is the intent of this book to teach you the basic needs of the body and the simple and inexpensive tests you can do yourself at home to analyze, monitor, and determine your body's nutritional needs. You must actively participate in your own health in order to avoid sickness and maintain "Optimal Health."

Modern medicine is a pagan religion based upon the deception of a secondary process that is termed "symptoms" as the main cause of disease. It has as its god the test tube, or science so falsely called; 1 Timothy 6:20. Because man has ventured from God, while all the time believing that he is serving God, has accepted Satan's false science, false education, false day of worship, false medical practices. It is false science that is the foundation of satanic subtly that has the Church so weak.

"...We have a science that is above all human science. Many will grasp [false science], teaching it as truth. But we need not be led astray. God wants us to cherish the truth in the simplicity in which we have received it from Christ." RH, Lessons From the First Epistle of John, July 13, 1905.

The trend today is to rewrite history, religion and the sciences by so called revisionist, all leading to the one-world-government and the one-world Catholic-Ecumenical Church.

You have sincere Christian physicians using non-Christian methods, treatments, and prescribing poisons against the Word of God. The church has given many of its social responsibilities over to the state or cooperates with the state through a 501 (C) 3, making the church a created entity of the state. Therefore, the state becomes the church's god. If the church speaks out against an issue, the state simply threatens to revoke its tax-exempt status. A 501 (C) 3; along with "For all that [is] in the world, the lust of the flesh, and the lust of the eyes, and the pride of life, is not of the Father, but is of the world" 1 John 2:16, is why the church is called Laodicea, Rev. 3:14.
"Take heed, let no man deceive you".......Jesus Christ, Matthew 24:4

The Ultimate Goal Is Life Eternal
My desire is to share with everyone optimal health and how to maintain and/or restore health once wasted away. However, to accomplish this and to truly understand the laws of health and the cause of disease, one has to acknowledge the source of all life and the Creator of human life by intelligent design. It is God's love for you that leads Him to exclaim, "Beloved, I wish above all things that thou mayest prosper and be in health, even as thy soul prospereth, III John 2. The direct implication here is that as you accept and live by every word that proceedth out of the mouth of God, Matt 4:4, your soul goes

17

from death to life and you can have life more abundantly, e.g., optimal health.

God says, "Beloved, I wish above all things that thou mayest prosper and be in health." The word 'mayest' implies choice. True to His intelligent design of the human body, He leaves the power of decision within the sphere of human intellect, as with our choice of salvation. God knew when He spoke those words that the depravity of man would intentionally set up a system designed to cause pain, suffering and death to the human family. He also knew that through misinterpretation of the scriptures, the human family would try to eat and drink from "the cup of the Lord, and the cup of devils" 1 Corinthians 10:21. Finally, God foreknew that through ignorance that the human family would become slaves to our approximate 100,000 taste masters or taste buds causing us to become intemperate in diet and morality. Diet is discussed in detail in the chapter titled the Ten Natural Laws of Health.

As you read this book, please keep in mind that the ultimate goal of life is to achieve eternal life. There is a place for allopathic medicine in health care, just not in treating disease as the first line of defense. Sometimes, more often than not because of ignorance, our health deteriorates to the point where strong allopathic chemicals are necessary to keep a person alive, or to get a patient out of a life threatening condition. It is best to die trusting in Jesus with all of your faculties functioning properly than to live a poor quality of life, trusting in the arm of flesh. Any person, who believes in a Supreme Creator, has to rethink health care.

It is possible to achieve that which seems like health for a week, month, year, or even five years like chemotherapy cancer patients. Then the disease reappears in a more deadly form, then they die it seems without warning and very quickly as their immune system has been compromised. It is my desire to share with the reader an understanding of God's saving health. "Thy way may be known upon earth, thy saving health among all nations" Psalm 67:2, God is implying that there is a health unto death as there is a health unto life, and only God's way of healing gives life. God's way of healing encompasses the mental, physical, and spiritual to achieve salvation health.

I want to amplify four points, and then we will let history, science, and the Word of God speak to us. Then you, the reader, must "Choose you this day whom ye will serve; whether the gods which your fathers served that [were] on the other side of the flood: but as for me and my house, we will serve the LORD" Joshua 24:15.

Point number one: In Titus 1: 2 and Hebrews 6:18, we are told that God cannot lie. Do you believe this? If you do, you have a problem, and if you do not, you have a problem. If you do not, the problem is obvious. However, if you do believe, then why are you taking prescription drugs when God says; "There is none to plead thy cause, that thou mayest be bound up: thou hast "No Healing [Medicines]" Jeremiah 30:13. Also, "Go up into Gilead, and take balm, O virgin, the daughter of Egypt: in vain shalt thou use many [Medicines]; for thou shalt not be cured, Jeremiah 46:11. Now remember, God cannot lie.

So what is the deception that has been perpetrated upon us the American sheeple (people)? More importantly, why don't you trust God and take Him at His word and not get sick. Now remember, God cannot lie for He made you this promise, "And said, If thou wilt diligently hearken to the voice of the LORD thy God, and wilt do that which is right in his sight, and wilt give ear to his commandments, and keep all his statutes, I will put none of these diseases upon thee, which I have brought upon the Egyptians: for I [am] the LORD that healeth thee" Exodus 15:26. What were the diseases of the Egyptians? According to Modern Paleo-pathologist, which recently exhumed and examined the DNA of more than 100,000 Egyptian mummies, the Egyptians suffered from heart disease, cancer, diabetes, gout, arthritis, hemorrhoids, and tuberculosis, etc. Antiquity of Disease by R. Moodie, University of Chicago Press; J. Thorwald, Science and Secrets of early Medicine, (39); and D.P. Ucko, American Review of Respiratory Disease, (90). These are the same diseases Christians are suffering from today! Either God is a liar or His children do not understand the deceptive power of the enemy or the power of God, or both.

Point number two: "All true science is but an interpretation of the handwriting of God in the material world. Science brings from her research only fresh evidences of the wisdom and power of God," White, Patriarchs and Prophets, p. 599. Paul warns in his admonition, "O Timothy, keep that which is committed to thy trust, avoiding profane [and] vain babblings, and oppositions of [Science falsely] so called: 1Timothy 6:20. You measure science by the Word of God, not the word of God by science.

After 70 years of cancer research by the American Cancer Society and billions of federal and tax-payers' dollars, we are no closer to a man made cure for cancer. You see business is too good for secret societies, cartels and associations, etc, to close shop. As long as they can keep you believing that they are searching for a cure, or can keep you from dying from a disease, i.e. cancer, heart disease, diabetes, etc., hoping against hope, you will give them your last dime. "Thus saith the LORD; cursed [be] the man that trusteth in man, and maketh flesh his arm, and whose heart departeth from the LORD" Jeremiah 17:5. "There is a way which seemeth right unto a man, but the end thereof [are] the ways of death" Proverbs 14:12. When it came to the human eye, even Darwin had to admit, "The thought of the eye and how it could possibly be produced by natural selection, makes me ill." – Charles Darwin.

Science is but a perversion of itself unless it has, as its ultimate goal the betterment of humanity.   -Nikola Tesla – 1919

Point number three: Revelation 18:1-4, the fourth angel is calling God's true people out of the false Babylonian system which includes worship, health care, and any other system that is opposed to God's methods. The Babylonian system is aware of God's way of healing. That is why they pass laws and use strong-arm tactics to suppress natural healing modalities that are more effective than chemotherapy or radiation. Now, the big push is to pass laws that give control of vitamins, minerals and herbs to the pharmaceutical companies through the government.

I believe this is part of the reason why the Food and Drug Administration (FDA) is going to take control of natural supplements. *"Plans to extend Codex to U.S. and worldwide:* The United Nations *Codex Alimentarius Commission,* assisted by the U.S. *Food and Drug Administration* (FDA), views the European Union (EU) *Food Supplements Directive* as a basic pattern which should be followed in developing a global trade standard for dietary supplements!

FDA "harmonization" standards: The FDA is currently at work, preparing "directives" for "harmonization" of its dietary supplement laws, so they will fully agree with the excessively restrictive "international standard" set by the EU *Codex Alimentarius Commission.* http://www.cfsan.fda.gov/~dms/dscodex.html.

When you research the proposed takeover of natural supplements, one has to ask himself why? Yearly, there is not a single death directly related to vitamins, minerals, or herbs reported. Yet in 2003, a group of physicians and researchers calculated that medical treatments are actually the leading cause of death in America at 783,936. Food for Thought: With the public knowledge of Global 2000 "World Depopulation Initiative" and the United Nations "Population Control" programs, could it be with the takeover and control of natural supplements, the well-publicized "bird flu" or some other pandemic will finally be unleashed? How would you be able to help yourself and your family? With a strong immune system, knowledge of hydrotherapy treatments, and herbal remedies, most diseases including cancer, can be defeated. This is what one health professional has to say, *"If people understood how disease develops and what determines the severity of symptoms, they would not have an irrational fear of Bird Flu. They would know how to build their immunity through diet and lifestyle, and be confident that they could properly treat the flu if they got sick. They would also realize that vaccines do not prevent disease"* Dr. Sherri J. Tenpenny. D.O. Also, elimination of competition would be achieved, the same people that own and control the pharmaceutical industry would control the natural supplementation industry. It would be a travesty if we the Sheeple allow the FDA to take control of natural supplements in America.

Point number four: For prescription drugs to cure, they would have to overcome the bodies' natural resistance response or what is known as vital force. The most fundamental law of nature provokes this resistance response, which God has placed in all living creatures. Until allopathic medicine can prove to the public its ability to overcome resistance (life), without killing the patient, then the millions upon millions of dollars wasted on research should be better spent. I will discuss this law later in the book. The body has two types of energy, which I will compare to a checking and savings account. The checking account or ready-available energy is what we should live on every day and when we go to bed at night recharge that energy supply. The savings account or reserve energy (vital force), should only be used in emergencies or fight or flight situations. That is why the human body when experiencing distress for a prolong period of time will begin to breakdown. When the reserve energy drops below a certain level it will never come back, eventually the individual dies. This is usually what happens to cancer patients. They no longer have the energy to continue fighting the disease they grow weak, tired, and then die. Unfortunately, most people are daily living off their reserve energy unable to sustain a prolonged life saving battle against disease or accidental injury.

The True Object of Education

"The true object of education is to restore the image of God in the soul. The great work of life is character building, and the knowledge of God is the foundation of all true education." Mind, Character, and Personality, Volume 1, Southern Publishing Association, Nashville, TN, Ellen White, pp. 596.

Julius G. White in his book; The Christian's Experience, gives five reasons why Christians should lead in this field of knowledge, i.e. health care (pp. 168-176). First: we profess to believe in the Creator and His works of intelligent design more profoundly than any other people on earth; we are the most fundamental of all fundamentalist.
 Our profession to observe the Sabbath of the 4th Commandment, the day of rest and healing, as a memorial of creation and to be promoting such observance in the entire world, places us in that position and brands us and distinguishes us from all other people because of this belief and work. Therefore, when we study science of any sort, we approach it with awe, knowing that we are investigating arrangements of matter and laws governing it, which were fixed by the Creator at the time of creation week six thousand years ago. We regard God as the author of the facts and truths we are trying to learn and comprehend with our feeble intellects. If our interest is to understand the organs of the body and their miracle-like functions and mysteries, the secret process of life, we should be the keenest of all people, because our belief in the Creator is the most profound.

Furthermore, our advancement in such knowledge should be far beyond that of all other people because such a profession logically brings us within the pale of the Creator's influence and instruction. The position we profess to occupy should bring us into closer contact and communion with God than any other people. From God's side of the matter, He does wish in fact to be the teacher of His people in matters of science, medicine, health, and medical missionary work, as well as in all other lines of education and investigation of truth. He gives us promises if we will "Harken diligently unto His voice" in Deut. 28:1-6.

Secondly, we should know physiology because it is a study of ourselves. I should have a more intimate knowledge of myself than of any other thing in the world. I live by the well-being of my organs at the cellular level. I should be more interested in the functions of my heart and brain than in the engine of my car or the cut of my clothes. Popular ignorance in this matter is appalling; the lack of interest in this kind of information is shameful. Since the laws of nature are the laws of God, it is plainly our duty to give these laws careful study. We should study their requirements in regard to our own bodies, and conform to them. Ignorance to these things is death.

Thirdly, the preservation or loss of health is surely wrapped within physiology. The laws of nutrition, assimilation and metabolism are fixed; they cannot be reversed or changed; food is food and poison is poison; a blessing comes with one and a curse with the other. To eat of poor quality food slowly weakens the human machinery over time.

"Be not deceived; God is not mocked; for whatsoever a man soweth, that shall he also reap" Galatians 6:7.

The fourth reason God's children are concerned with health and physiology is for the sake of character development. The sort of character developed depends largely upon the knowledge and use of the five physical senses as they operate through the mind (smell, touch, taste, hearing, and sight). The exercise of the power of choice, which is the vital element in making character, is done through the use of these senses.

"The body is the only medium through which the mind and soul are developed for the up-building of character. Hence it is where the adversary of souls directs his temptations to the enfeebling and degrading of the physical powers. His success here means the surrender to evil of the whole being." The Ministry of Healing, Pacific Press Publishing Association, Mountain View, California, 1909, Mrs. E. G. White, pg. 130.

The fifth reason God's children should know and understand their body, is that "Man was created in the likeness of God, not only in character, but in form and feature." "And God said, Let us make man in our image, after our likeness...Gen. 1:26. This solemn view of man, consisting of parts and organs governed by laws, which in their entirety were a "specimen of Jehovah" exalts the study of physiology into the very heavens. When physiology is understood from the perspective that God designed us, created us, redeemed us, sanctifies us through His Word, and will glorify us at his second coming, then who would dare put a poisonous drug into "the counterpart of God" to leave its lingering evil effects for years to come, perhaps as long as life should last. The Christian Experience, Northwestern Publishing Association, Sacramento, Calif., 1945, Julius G. White, p. 168-176.

In the Hebrew language, when you number, you write, and when you write, you number. In the Word of God, numbers have meaning as well. For example the number seven stands for completion or perfection; five is the number of grace and redemption. The number ten represents ALL. In the book of Daniel 2:31-35, 41-46 we have an image, with [Ten] toes. What I want you to notice is verse 44: "But it shall break in pieces and consume [All] these kingdoms"… The image represents all the false systems, including allopathic medicine's managed death. Now turn to Matthew 25: 1-13 as we take a look at how God views His church. Verse 1 talks about [Ten] virgins. Notice God is talking about His church in these last days, as He likens it to Heaven. Please note very carefully that they [All] slumbered and slept. It is past time to wake up, for Peter says: "Wherefore gird up the loins of your mind, be sober, and hope to the end for the grace… I Peter 1:13. As a child of God, you must understand the battle that is taking place for your soul is waged in your mind. Allopathic medicine with prescription medication and toxic chemotherapy is putting you to sleep spiritually. The Frontal Lobe of the mind is the only location in the human body that God speaks to man. In the chapter "The Word of God Concerning Drugs," I share with you God's perspective concerning prescription drugs.

Chapter Two: How the Counterfeit Began

The Origin of Competing Health Care Philosophy
Modern medicine has made many necessary advances in lifesaving procedures. If I were in an accident and should require a lifesaving procedure, I would not go to a chiropractor, naturopath or any other health care discipline. This book deals specifically with disease, especially chronic disease. By chronic disease I mean cancer, arthritis, heart disease and diabetes, etc. As we compare man's methods to God's instructions given in His Word, we will see God's original healing methods are today still superior to drugs and New Age spiritualism. Natural healing is the earliest known healing system. Before surgery and synthetic isolation of chemical substances, food, water, and whole herbs were used by many cultures for a wide range of health problems. The ancient Egyptians used liver for night blindness. The Chinese, for example used kelp 3,000 years ago for thyroid health. Native Americans (as well as most other cultures) used various herbs to promote healing. Various forms of hydrotherapy have been used by many cultures (Egyptians, Chinese, Hebrews, Greeks,

Assyrians, Persians, Hindus, etc.) for thousands of years. "Excavation of ancient ruins, especially after the work carried on in Egypt, disclosed the fact that disease was treated by fasting, purging, emetics, sweats, etc, all with the very evident aim of assisting Nature to unload encumbering waste that was plainly causing the disorder. It seems that the accepted teachings in the manner of the care of the ill were very similar to our present methods of naturopathy, being in line with Nature's indicated efforts during illness." Combining Old and New: Naturopathy for the 21st Century, (Robert J. Thiel, Ph. D., N.H.D.

The Ancient History of Spiritualistic Healing

"And Cush begat Nimrod: he began to be a mighty one in the earth. He was a mighty hunter before the Lord: wherefore it is said, even as Nimrod the mighty hunter before the Lord. And the beginning of his kingdom was Babel (Babylon), and Erech (Assyria), and Accad, and Calneh, in the land of Shinar". Genesis 10:8-10.

"The early Sumerian inhabitants, whose religion was accepted later by the Babylonians and Assyrians, had an immense pantheon of nearly 4,000 deities. Six gods however formed the upper hierarchy, one of the six god's was Shamash the Sun god, who was presumed to have given the code to Hammurabi (which is the code of medicine in ancient Babylon). The number of the clergy was large and their power immense. All of the rulers were careful not to offend the Priest, who was the representative on earth of the various gods in the skies, in the waters and beneath the earth. Apparently the priests were also the judges, lawyers, and the physicians, which was quite logical because law and medicine were of divine origin" A History of Medicine; Ralph Major, pp. 28.

The priest taught the masses that sickness was outside of the individual's control. "It is said that astronomy is the oldest of the sciences and in all earliest civilizations we find it applied to the practical affairs of life as astrology. This trait, symbolized... with all of its zodiacal signs is the essence of Assyro-Babylon medicine. Wars, epidemics, famines and the succession of monarchs were studied in relation to... eclipses, comets, and changes in the moon, stars and other meteor- logical... events. Thus astrology and the interpretation of omens merged into prognosis... The first Babylonian physician was a priest or the first priest a physician... for the most part however, the Babylon physician regarded disease as a work of demons, which swarmed in the earth, air, water and against long litanies and incantations were recited." Fielding Garrison, MD. p. 61, 62.

Let me help you understand the significance of that last paragraph. Pre-modern science believed sickness was caused by demons; lifestyle and diet had nothing to do with it. In this modern scientific age, the cultured, educated, intellectual mind primarily does not ascribe disease to a demon, but rather to a germ that invades the body i.e. Louis Pasteur's Germ Theory. During the Dark Ages, the Catholic Church believed sickness was a direct result of sin in one's life. Today, a greedy few has substituted a demon and sin with a germ. However, as you will learn if you continue to read this book, that the microbe is the secondary cause of disease, not the primary as to why you get sick.

In recent years, five credible sources have clearly established the link between diet, lifestyle and disease. (1) Two time Nobel Prize winner Linus Pauling; (2) the 74th. Congress, second session, (3) C. Everett Koop, M.D., Sc.D, former two times Surgeon General of the United States, (4) the World Health Organization (WHO), and (5) The China Study, all scientifically confirm the correlation between diet and lifestyle and sickness and health. Remember, "The serpent was more subtle than any beast of the field which the Lord God had made"… Genesis 3:1. The name of the game then and now is still deception. Today, Christians don't even realize they are participating in the old Assyro-Babylonian philosophy of medicine. Let's begin with the ancient Babylonian empire and follow medicine unto today.

"Early Babylonian medicine was associated with religion and magic and belonged to the priesthood. In later times, a cast of lay-physicians and surgeons was formed to practice the profession according to definite and natural regulations. The priestly-doctor was known as the "assipu" priest. The lay-priest was known as the "asu". The Assuipu priest dealt primarily with internal diseases, and particularly with mental and nervous conditions which were generally contributed to demonic possession and cured largely by religious and magical means." Fielding Garrison, MD, pp. 161.

The Babylonian like primitive man believed, that everything that showed power and growth was alive and thus becomes [the unconscious originator of the modern Germ Theory], but he personified the germ by giving it a human or animal shape, or a combination of the two. The Babylonians and Assyrians also differentiated their demons just as we do our germs. [Jastrow] There was a demon for wasting diseases, for liver troubles, women diseases; every sick man was possessed by a demon. The obvious method to cure the disease in question was to drive out its particular demon, this being best accomplished by exorcism or incantations delivered by the priest-physician." A History of Medicine, Ralph Major, p. 28.

"Disease was largely of demonic origin, and consequently priests were best qualified to combat it. Demonic figures were set up at the gates or buried beneath the threshold of houses to frighten demons away." Fielding Garrison, MD, p. 162.

"Hordes of demons and devils were thought to cause disease and misfortune; each evil spirit tended to cause a particular disorder.

As in the case of folk medicine and so called primitive medicine, Mesopotamian (Babylonian) practitioners also attempted to rid their

patients of disease causing demons by the administration of remedies containing noxious ingredients. Enveloped in the aroma of burning feathers and liberally dosed with dog dung and pig's gall the patient hardly seemed an inviting abode for a discriminating demon." Lois N. Wagner, p. 19, 20,

Back then these priests actually carried a wand, which was a symbol of their power and religion. That wand was made out of a shaft and at the end of the shaft was a ball, solar orb. It had two wings and two snakes intertwined. This is a symbolic representation of their deified priest, whom they worshiped in the form of Hermes. Hermes would carry this wand which we know today is called the Cadeuces. The Secret Teachings of Occultism, by Manly P. Hall.

The Babylonian Cadeuces, through William Avery "Doc" Rockefeller (A Jesuit) has become the symbol of the American Medical Association and other health care organizations. Rockefeller was a member of a secret society

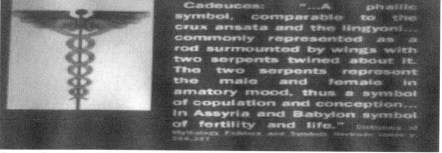

Gertrude Jobes, Dictionary of Mythology, Folklore and symbols, p.266, 267.

"Among the earliest seals of which we have recorded are the circula stamp and cylinder seals of the Uruk period in Mesopotamia, which is well before 3,000 B.C... Dr. H. Frankfort in his learned work on Cylinder Seals, in speaking of those in the Uruk period, suggests that on several seals we have the origin of the caduceus. He is referring to the symbols of the Tammiz, the god of corn, and the remarks that the 'the snake' emerging from Mother Earth with the sprouting corn was another of the god's symbols, sometimes elaborated... into a pair of copulating vipers, the origin of the caduceus." Symbols, Signs and their Meaning, by Arnold Whittick 1961, p. 40.

"The mathematician and the astronomer and the physician have founded their science on the lore of the Sumerian and Babylonians and Assyrians... Astrology, divination, the use of numbers and the SYSTEM OF MEDICINE which were in use in Mesopotamia in the third Millennium before Christ, are as much alive and as active in that country as ever... and in England and America in the present time large numbers of people are influenced by beliefs which were common in Babylonia four or five thousand years ago." E.A. Walls Budge, p. xxix.

As we will learn, germs are not the primary cause of disease, but rather secondary. Violation of God's Health Laws, changes the body's chemistry, which weakens the immune system, laying the foundation for the Internal Body Terrain to get out of balance (Homeostasis), which allows microbes to get a foot-hold, causing symptoms which are called disease. Today, there are many unsuspecting Christian physicians in the Babylonian-Assyrian-Egyptian-Greek-Western medical system that is unaware of the true cause of disease. On the next page, as you compare the similarities between ancient Babylonian society and today's society, you will see nothing has changed except they have modernized terminology so the system would be acceptable to an enlightened, sophisticated, intellectual, yet unsuspecting people.

	Ancient Babylon 	Modern Medicine
Cause of Disease	Primary cause of disease is an invisible, invading demon.	Primary cause of disease is an invisible, invading germ.
Object of Confidence	People taught to depend upon the witch-doctor priest	People taught to depend upon worldly physician
Primary Treatment	Use of gross and unnatural substances.	Use of unnatural and poisonous medications
Type of System	System of Healing tightly controlled by religious Monarchy.	System of Healing strictly monitored and regulated By Federal Government Obama care was an exam
Symbol	The Cadeuces	The Cadeuces

God's Health Restoration Plan vs. Spiritualistic Healing

The medical knowledge of man was very superficial until the beginning of the twentieth century. Yet, the first five books of the Bible, recorded by Moses approximately 1491-1451 B.C., reveal surprisingly advanced scientific principles. In addition, the Bible contains advanced scientific and medical knowledge about hygiene and sanitation. This advanced information in the Bible, written more than four millennia ago, is strong proof that a divine Creator inspired it. What other rational explanation is there for this precise medical knowledge in the five books of the law as Moses led the Israelites through the (hot) wilderness of Sinai. God inspired Moses to record these preventative health commandments to protect the health of His chosen people.

The book of Exodus reveals one of the most astonishing promises God ever made to mankind. "If thou will [diligently] hearken unto the voice of the Lord thy God and will do all that which is right in His sight and will give ear to His commandments and keep all His statutes, I will put none of these diseases upon thee that I have put upon the Egyptians, for I am the Lord thy God the [healeth] thee" Exodus 15:26. That promise is for spiritual Israel today. However, all God's promises are conditional, and because we eat like the Babylonians, we get sick like the Babylonians, which makes God's wonderful promise of non-effect.

God also tells of the effects of violating His Word "The Lord will smite thee with the botch of Egypt, and with the emerods (Hemorrhoids), and with the scab, and with the itch, whereof thou canst not be healed. The Lord shall smite thee with madness, and blindness, and astonishment of heart, Deut. 28:27-28.

We realize that gods of wood, gold, silver, etc, are powerless and not real, but have you ever stopped to consider that being overweight, or too underweight and sick with cancer, arthritis, diabetes, etc, the world is looking at you and thinking 'your God is just as weak as our god, so why should we serve Him?

As we look at the Egyptians, we find that "color pictographs on the walls of the tombs of the Egyptians furnish descriptions of their lifestyle. From the lowly slave to the Pharaoh on his throne, innumerable mummies have been preserved for thousands of years. Some of the mummies have been examined by autopsy. Since these initial autopsies in 1880 AD, 1900 more have been examined by X-ray. From these sources and the Bible, we gather considerable insight into the lifestyle of the Egyptians and know much about the maladies of ancient Egypt.

According to modern paleopathologists, obesity was a problem in ancient Egypt, as evidenced by the mummies. Degenerative arthritis was common. Ramses the II, in the 19th dynasty, had severe dental disease with abscesses in the jaw and severe degenerative arthritis of the hip joints. He had extensive arteriosclerosis of the major arteries of the lower extremities. His son, Mererpah, who is believed to be one of the Pharaoh of Egypt, was a partial bald, obese old man, who had severe degenerative arthritis of the cervical spine and evidence of arteriosclerosis. Antiquity of Disease, R. Moodie, University of Chicago, Science and Secrets of Early Medicine, p. 39; Thorwald, 1962, 2nd X-raying the Pharaohs; Harris, J.E. and K.R. Weeks; Charles Scribner & Son, New York, N.Y. 1973.

Know any children of God who have arthritis or arteriosclerosis? What about your belief that God cannot lie!? Obviously, someone has lied to you but it was not God. Consider the December 16, 1998, article in the

Journal of the American Medical Association, which reported Dr. Dean Ornish and his team conducted a "Lifestyle Heart Trial". The Lifestyle Heart Trial demonstrated that intensive lifestyle changes may lead to regression of coronary arteriosclerosis after one year. This study and its findings show just one of many examples of how diet impacts health.

Medical science did not know the existence of germs and their method of transmission of infection until the end of the 1900's. Medical doctors, until this century, believed that the presence and transmission of disease were entirely haphazard and governed by simple chance or bad luck.

Those who were sick with deadly diseases were cared for in the home, without any awareness of the contagious transmission of disease from one sick individual to others around them. People had no idea that invisible and deadly microscopic germs would exist on eating and cooking utensils. A famous medical book was written in Egypt called the Papyrus Ebers. This book lists scores of remedies or "cures" for a host of diseases, infections, and accidents. Although Egypt was the educational and cultural center of the world during Moses' lifetime, its medical knowledge and remedies were extremely primitive and dangerous.

As an example of the medical ignorance and primitive state of their medical knowledge, consider the Egyptian doctor's suggestion for healing a splinter wound. The prescription involved the application of an ointment mixture composed of blood of worms mixed with the dung of a donkey. The various germs, including tetanus, contained in donkey's dung must have assured that the patient would quickly forget the pain of his splinter as he died from an assortment of other diseases produced by his doctor's contaminated medicine. This is just one example out of several hundred prescriptions as quoted from the pages of the Papyrus Ebers manuscript as translated in S.E. Massengills, A Sketch in Medicine and Pharmacy.

You might ask, what does the medical practice of ancient Egypt have to do with modern medicine today? Just as we look at the ancient record of the Egyptians and other so-called cultural centers of the world, like the Babylonians, Greeks and Romans, we laugh at the ignorance with which these sincere peoples attempted to care for their sick and dying.

I want to suggest to you that within the next 100 years, if Jesus doesn't come before then, other cultures will look back on the American allopathic medicine system and laugh. They will truly be amazed as they discover how the American medical system, with its strong-arm tactics of threatening its citizens, and the American Medical Association (AMA) revoking the license of any doctor attempting to enlighten himself on the use of natural healing. What future societies will discover, which will both amaze and anger them, is how the AMA attempted to use a philosophy totally antagonistic to the Second Law of Thermodynamics and the physiology of the human body and call it healthcare. It is a sad commentary, but I believe they will view allopathic medicine as we presently view the Egyptian Papyrus Ebers.

Let's contrast the Papyrus Ebers with God's form of health care called Hygienic Healing Principles. In Leviticus 6:28, written more than four thousand years ago, reveals a clear commandment to discard broken pottery (because the cracks would contain harmful germs). "But the earthen vessel wherein it is sodden shall be broken: and if it be sodden in a brazen pot, it shall be both scourged and rinsed in water," indicating that a metal pot should be both disinfected by scouring and rinsing in water. How could Moses have known about the dangers of infectious germs in cooking and eating utensils thousands of years ago, unless God actually inspired him to write these words?

Moses did not receive this accurate medical knowledge from the Egyptians or any other pagan culture of that time. This advanced and accurate knowledge reveals a profound understanding of germs, infectious transmission routes, human sanitation needs, dietary principles, and many other medical advances unknown outside the Bible during the last thirty-six centuries. Moses abandoned the medical ignorance of the Egyptians when he left the palace in Egypt and spent the next eighty years of his life in the wilderness serving God.

An examination of the medical remedies of the ancient Egyptians and other pagan cultures of the Middle East reveals an appalling ignorance of the most rudimentary medical knowledge as we know it today. However the laws of Moses contained specific laws and sanitation procedures that, if faithfully followed, would eliminate the dreadful diseases that affected the Egyptians of that day and still affect most of mankind in the Third World today. The Black Death and leprosy were the two most terrible plagues of the middle ages. "The principles of public health or hygienic principles given by God and taught by Moses after the Exodus brought those scourges under control. Millions of lives were saved as doctors turned to the church for help during those plagues" History of Modern Health, George Rosen, M.D. pg. 63-65. Absolutely amazing! Does man now know more than God?

Every designer and manufacturer of a product, whether the product is a household product, an automobile, or a computer, provides an owner's manual for the user. The owner's manual contains specifics on how to maintain and operate the product. It is essential for the user to follow carefully the instructions in the owner's manual for the product to operate efficiently according to the manufacturer's specifications. Since God is the intelligent designer and manufacturer of our bodies He has given us an owner's manual, the Bible, the Greatest Medical Book ever written. He knows how we can avoid disease and keep our bodies at optimal performance. The presence of incredibly advanced and accurate knowledge of disease, sanitation and preventive healthcare in the ancient Scriptures is one more un-controvertible proof that the Bible is truly the inspired Word of God.

It is fascinating to note that a total of two hundred and thirteen (213) out of the six hundred and thirteen (613) biblical commandments found in the Torah were detailed medical regulations that ensure the good health of the children of Israel if they would obediently follow the laws of God. Please do not miss this very important fact. Could this be the lie, that allopathic medicine is based upon? 'Now the serpent was more subtle than any beast of the field which the Lord God had made'...Genesis 3:1. The science of what you call prescription medication of today was actually counterfeited by Satan from God's original purpose. First we have to define the word: a·poth·e·car·y [ə páwthə kèrree] (plural a·poth·e·car·ies) noun (archaic) 1. pharmacist: a pharmacist, 2. pharmacy: a pharmacy. [14th century. Via Old French from, ultimately, Greek apothēkē "storehouse" (source of English boutique), formed from apotithenai "to put away," from tithenai "to put."] Hebrew & Chaldee Dictionary #7543 raqach, *raw-kakh'* ; a prim. root; to perfume:--apothecary, compound, make [ointment], prepare, spice.

Moses was instructed of God to make holy anointing oil, Exodus 30:22-25. In verse 25 we read "...an ointment compound after the art of the apothecary..." Exodus 30:35, 37:29, and Ecc. 10:1. Please do not miss this Biblical fact. "Moses was learned in all the wisdom of the Egyptians, and was mighty in words and in deeds," Acts 7:22. Yet, when God instructed Moses to write the first five books of the Bible, not a single pagan, heathen, or spiritualistic health care principle was included. Why, because they do not heal and you could lose your soul salvation because of its affect upon the frontal lobe of the brain. Hippocrates is known as the founder of modern medicine and medical literature. Modern medicine is based upon the Hippocratic studies of Asclepius and not sound, unbiased science, which we will learn as we read the Hippocratic Oath, which doctors take upon completing medical school.

God used the apothecary form of art to make holy anointing oil for [external use only]. There is not a single example of God instructing any of the prophets in the Old Testament, or Jesus and the disciples in the New Testament, to use apothecary to heal or to administer to humans internally as medicine!

Pagan & Spiritualistic Medicine

As far back as 2500 B.C., there were three cradles of emerging Materia Medica, or medicine. The roots of New Age Holistic Health, Eastern Mysticism, and Modern Medicine can be traced to the ancient philosophical and religious beliefs of China, Egypt, and Greece. Reviewing these roots reveal that they are deeply embedded in the fertile soil of Eastern Mysticism and the Eastern Mystical Religions of Hinduism, Buddhism, Taoism, and other pagan and occult beliefs subscribing to non-biblical world views. The first of these three was on the Island of Cos, the birthplace of Hippocrates. He developed the Hippocratic Tradition of Medicine that spread from Greece to Egypt, to Persia in the east, and then on to Italy in the west. Secondly, the Yellow River of China, home to Chinese Medicine, and third the Indus Valley of India, which is the seat of Ayurvedic Medicine. These three branches of ancient traditional medicine were all different, yet the same in many ways, mainly by their cross-pollination by travelers and merchants. I will address the Yellow River of China, home to Chinese Medicine, and third the Indus Valley of India in the section on Spiritualist Medicine. Main Streaming of New Age, by Manuel Vasquez, pg. 130.

To understand modern western medicine, you have to understand the role the City of Pergamos played in promoting false healing. You will find the Church of Pergamos is "even where Satan's seat is…" Revelation 2:12-17.

The church in Pergamum (or Pergamos) represents the state church, which began with Emperor Constantine and ending with the church-state union of Rev. 13:13-17. "The Acropolis (the city on the edge of a cliff) crowned a steep hill that rose 1,000 feet above the plain on which there was an immense altar to Zeus, the chief of the mythological Greek gods. Pergamos means joined in marriage. It is important from many perspectives, but it is very important from the perspective of medicine. This temple was dedicated to Asclepius, the 'serpent god' or the 'god of healing' of the 'man-instructing serpent' who gave man the knowledge of good and evil. A live serpent was always kept in the temple of Zeus as an object of worship. A famous [school of medicine] was also located there, the emblem of which was the serpent of the caduceus twined around a pole. This came down to us today as the emblem of the medical profession."

Roy A. Anderson, Unfolding the Revelation, p. 24, 25.

This temple is where Asclepius lived, the legendary son of Apollo, who eventually became the prominent Greek and Roman god of healing. Asclepius was called the great physician, savior. Pergamos was a city of temples, Jupiter, Zeus, Athena, Dianesia, and Asclepius. The symbol of a snake on a pole, and sun god with wings was the symbol of Asclepius. Numerous temples were dedicated to Asclepius displaying this symbol on the outside; each temple contained a live snake on the inside and the people worshiped it. The symbol of a serpent on a pole is the symbol of the medical profession. The American Medical Association (AMA) has joined itself in marriage, via Rockefeller and Carnegie foundations, to the ancient Asclepius philosophy of healing.

"The Greek god Apollo was believed to bring on illness and plagues by shooting certain types of 'arrows'. He was addressed as the 'two-horned god' on Orphic hymns. But there was only one original two-horned god; Nimrod, who founded the Chaldean monarchy. Nimrod was the original Apollo. Apollo was the husband of Semiramis. Aesculapius, also called Ascelpios, the legendary son of Apollo, eventually became the predominant Greek and Roman god of healing. Numerous temples were dedicated to him throughout the kingdoms of Greece and Rome." Back to Eden, Jethro Kloss p. 49.

The name Aesculapius is not found in the Egyptian, Assyrian, Greek, or Hebrew languages, but is found in the Chaldean language. Three words make up the name Aesculapius- ashe, skul, aphe. The word ashe means man, skul means instruct, aphe means snake.
Aesculapius therefore, means man-instructing-snake. In the Bible, we are told that Satan, working through the serpent, was the only man instructing serpent, a menace to all mankind. ibid.

The Bible tells us in Genesis 10:8-10 that it was Nimrod, who built the city of Babel, which means "confusion." Nimrod was the Monarch of the Chaldean Dynasty. In Habakkuk 1:6, God calls the Chaldeans "that bitter and nasty nation."

In Daniel chapter 2:2, they are included with the magicians, the astrologers, and the sorcerers. Aesculapius, or Tammuz (Ezek. 8:13, 14) his Babylonian name, is derived from Nimrod. Even if the Hippocratic oath is not being administered today, it is important to understand that modern medicine is based upon the Hippocratic studies of Aesculapius and not the health, healing and prevention principles of God. The Hippocrates form of medicine spread from Greece to Egypt, to Persia in the east, and then to Italy in the west.

A second symbol of Babylonian Medicine is called the Staff of Aesculapius. Aesculapius was always depicted as a handsome man who always carried a stick with a snake coiled around it. This is not the symbol of the Caudeuces which has two serpents, wings and a solar orb at the top. The Staff of Aesculapius is not the staff which Moses made with a brass serpent on it in the wilderness as we are told in Numbers chapter, 21. Just look in any encyclopedia and it will say the "Staff of Aesculaplus." Please, do not confuse the two.

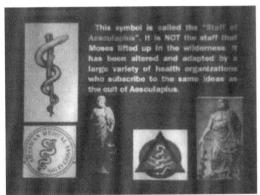

The symbol top left, is called the "Staff of Aesculapius." It is not the staff that Moses lifted up in the wilderness. It has been altered and adapted by a large variety of health organizations that subscribe to the same ideas as the cult of Aesculapius.

"The Aesclepieia, were large, sprawling groups of buildings, courtyards, groves, and watering places... Centrally of course, was the temple of Aescpelius, ornate with magnificent works of art, and other treasures, many of gold. Close by was a second important building, the abaton, where pilgrims retired to sleep and to be visited by the god in their dreams. Smaller temples devoted to the gods, might be found on the premises... A large corps of priest, helpers, choirboys, musicians, and others was required. Sacred animals, especially dogs and snakes, roamed about the grounds. Numerous stone tablets and steles, bearing stories of miraculous cures, were located on the grounds; and on the walls were many votive offerings of stones, terra cotta, or other materials... these votives reproduced in relief some part of the body that been healed, along with suitable prayers of thanks patients."

-George Bender, Robert Thorn, Great Moments in Medicine, p. 36.

"At night, patients went to places where they were supposed to wait for the god. Usually, these would be the abaton, although some Asclepieia patients were allowed to sleep in the temple...This practice, called incubation, was a standard custom. The god was seen by the pilgrim in his sleep, or in a strange state between sleeping and awaking... Aescpelius is reported to have come in the form in which he is portrayed in the statues... In his hand he held a rustic staff, about

which a serpent entwined. If the god did not visit the patient the first night, incubation was continued on following nights. Once personal contact was made, the god preceded either immediately to heal the disease or to advise treatment that was to be followed... Serpents, too, are reported to have appeared to patients in their dreams, and to have healed them by licking their wounds." Great Moments in Medicine, by George Bender & Robert Thorn p. 38.

Where Did This False System of Religion & Medicine Go?
"When the Persians overthrew Babylon (Daniel 7:4, 5; 8:3, 20), they gave the inhabitants of the city their freedom. The Babylonian priests later led a revolt and were driven from the city. The defeated Chaldeans fled to Asia Minor, Turkey today, and fixed their central college at Pergamos, and took the palladium of Babylon, the cubic stone, with them. Here independent of state control, they carried on the rites of their religion. Pergamos, Bergama Turkey today, became the seat of the satanic system of the Babylonian mysteries"
-Roy A. Anderson, Unfolding the Revelation, p. 23.

On the field of Arbela, in 331 B.C., Alexander the Great and the Grecian army defeated the Persians, taking complete control of the empire. Hippocrates a Grecian from the Isle of Cos, is known as the founder of modern medicine and medical literature.

Hippocrates developed an oath that has become known as the Hippocratic Oath that doctors upon completion of medical school were required to swear by. I do not believe this oath is required today, but the system is still the same. Part of the oath is as follows:

Hippocratic Oath

"I Hippocrates swear by Apollo the physician, and Aescpelius, and Health, and ALL Heal, and all the gods and goddesses, that according to my ability and judgment, I will keep the oath and this stipulation- to reckon him who taught me this art equally dear to me as my parents... to look upon his offspring... as my own brothers... and to teach them this art without fee. I will give no deadly medicine to anyone... I will not give a woman a pessary to produce abortion..." Please notice Hippocrates is swearing to Apollo, not the Most High God.

-Jethro Kloss, Back to Eden p. 47.

Hippocrates 460-377 B.C, is called the father of modern medicine. He is said to be the one to lift medicine out of the realm of superstition and witchcraft and placed it more on a scientific basis, and rescue medicine from religious ideas. Hippocrates believed that there was something in the body that he called Physis, which was a kind of healing power, from which we get the word physician today. Hippocrates had an opponent named Democritus, which believed the human body had no such self-healing properties. This debate started over 2500 years ago and was settled in Western Medicine on the side of Democritus. The goal of modern medicine is to take healing from nature's hand. Let me give you an example; when the body becomes sick and can't kill germs, the doctor will give a patient prescription drugs to kills germs. The goal of the body and the drug are the same. Neither the doctor nor the patient is concerned with discovering the real cause of the illness. They have simply treated a symptom(s).

With the Persians completely absorbed into the Grecian empire, spiritualism, occultism and false healing methods are incorporated in to Greek medicine, as acknowledged by Hippocrates in his oath.

The East-West Connection "Pergamos was for some time the headquarters of this mystery cult. But the King of Pergamos bequeathed his kingdom to the Romans, which has since been the headquarters of this false system... Pergamos thus became the link between ancient Babylon and Rome. It seemed natural for the deification of the emperors to begin in this city."

-Roy A. Anderson Unfolding the Revelation, p. 24, 25.

The Dark Ages – The fourth century A.D., was a very difficult period for the Catholic Church, and the Eastern Orthodox Church. Communication, trade, travel, culture, etc were band between the two. Thus began the long 1260-day prophecy, in <u>which the true Church of God fled into the wilderness, taking her pure manuscripts and God's Health Principles with her</u> (Revelation 12:6, 14, 17).

With the fall of Pagan Rome to the Barbarians, she passed her spiritualism and occultist teachings on to Papal Rome. Papal Rome was established in 538 A.D., after it came to power in 508 A.D. Daniel 7: 7,8 tells us that in order for the papacy to be establish, it had to pluck up three horns by the roots. "These three powers were the Heruli, the Ostrogoths, and the Vandals. The reason they were plucked up and now extinct, was because they were opposed to the teachings and claims of the papal hierarchy, and hence to the supremacy in the church of the bishop of Rome." Daniel and the Revelation, Uriah Smith, page 134. If you take 538 A.D., plus 1260 years, it equals 1798 A.D.

"The early and medieval apostate Christians accepted the doctrine of the power of demons in the lives of men; they saw this power particularly in the demoniac production of disease. They believed in miracles and especially in the miraculous healing of diseases... thus the logical cure of disease consisted in the exorcism of devils. Following Christ example, Christians everywhere became exorcists. ...Nothing has retarded the growth of scientific medicine during the past two thousand years so much as the IRON GRIP of Theology in maintaining practices based on the belief in this supernatural origin of disease."   Devils, Drugs and Doctors, Howard W. Haggard MD, p.297.

"Under the precepts of Jesus the weak and the sick were to be cared for by the strong and healthy. Charity hospitals were founded. For centuries these institutions were simply refuges for the destitute sick. Medical care was not given. It was only in recent times that modern medicine treatment has developed, that hospitals provide proper care. The whole concept of disease, under the early Catholic religion, can be summed up in the words of St. Augustine in the Fifth Century; all diseases of Catholics are to be ascribed to demons, chiefly do they torment the fresh baptized, yea even the guilt-less new born infant." ibid.

"For the medieval Catholics each disease had its patron Saint, just as for the ancient Romans each disease had its god. These saints were thought to have the power of both inflecting and curing the disease.

39

...The association of a saint with a disease was usually determined by how the saint died. St. Agattin was tortured cruelly before she was put to death. Her breasts were cut off. Hence... she was the patron saint of nursing-women. St. Apollonia had her jaw broken and her teeth dashed out. Prayers were directed to her for intercession in toothaches. She was represented in painting as holding a tooth, or a pair of pincers in her hands." lbid.

"The monastic order of St. Anthony was devoted to the care of sufferers from ergotism (ergot fungal growth on rye products causing ergotism in humans). The sufferer is shown here using a crutch to support a withered leg while his raised hand has burst into flames, symbolic of the sensation of the disease. On the left shoulder of St. Anthony's robe is the T representing the order. The hod, which was the inseparable companion of this saint is shown here peering from behind the robe." ibid.

The John Huntsman Cancer Institute in Utah is a very fancy; three wings, six story hospital. It is ultra modern and a very profitable facility. It is a very impressive institute dedicated to fighting cancer. Please notice the symbolism in the sign at the entrance to the John Huntsman Cancer Learning Institute.

This sign inside the Huntsman Cancer Institute, located in Utah bears the Maltese cross on the shield and underneath it the words in Latin, "Under This Sign Conquer". It is very important to remember this sign because it will give us the origin for all cancer research and cancer treatments.

Theophrastus Bombastus von Hohenheim 1493-1541, was a contentious man, and some history book say it is from his name we get the word bombastic, because he was always fighting with people. He was a teacher of medicine, and he burned publicly the works of Galen because he was a rebel in many ways. His father worked in mineral mines, and he saw how they used minerals to purify other minerals and he got the idea that poisonous minerals could purify the human body.

"From 460 BC to AD 1500, a period of over 1900 years, we have no records of anyone giving large doses of poisonous minerals for the treatment of disease until Hohenheim thought of using them after he worked in the mines of Tyrol. During those 1900 years, there had been very little deviation from the beliefs and teachings of Hippocrates that in nature "there is strength" to cure disease.

From 1526-1528 Hohenheim lectured at the University of Basel, but was dismissed because of his refusal to accept time-honored tradition. It is stated that he publicly burned the books of Hippocrates and Galen, threw aside all of their ideas and instead went in for Chemically Purifying the Body by the use of Minerals. Wherever he went, he was met with opposition to his theories." Back to Eden, by Jethro Kloss, p. 52.

"Hohenheim, being egotistical as he was, called himself Paracelsus, after Celsus who was a medical historian. Wherever he went, Paracelsus left a trail of 'Chemical Kitchens.' When his patrons were generous, he built them to suit his alchemical taste; when in poor circumstances, he brewed his drugs on the charcoal beside his hostesses' soup. Experimenting was his exacting pastime, and in exercising it, Paracelsus spared neither himself nor his neighbors. In his experiments and in his medical applications, Paracelsus inaugurated an era of iatrochemistry-the forerunner of twentieth century chemotherapy. It was Paracelsus who introduced... zinc and zinc salts to medicine; used mercury compounds instead of metallic mercury for syphilis ...employed lead, arsenic, copper and iron compounds. His advocacy for the use of pure chemicals for specific diseases was perhaps one of his greater contributions to medicine". George Bender, Robert Thorn, Great Moments in Medicine, p. 82.

"Paracelsus thought and spoke in the language of the people, was popular as no other physician before him... Appointed professor of medicine... at Basel (1527) and imbued with lifelong reverence for Hippocrates... he began his campaign of reform by publicly burning the works of Galen... A year later he was already in violent conflict with the authorities concerning fees and forced to leave the city. Resuming his wandering habits and practicing all over Germany with varying success, he finally met his end from a wound in a tavern brawl in Salzburg (1541)." An Introduction to the History of Medicine, Fielding Garrison, p. 204, 205.

With the revival of poisonous minerals by Paracelus, natural healers were now presented with a choice; those with vision and financial gain as their motivation have propped up allopathic medicine with legal and academic requirements. With the grip of the Church loosening because of the Reformation, and people being taught to regard truth above tradition, science now began to look at new ideas if they were based upon truth. Which in part, lead to the 30 Years War.

Most Natural Healers Remain True to Profession

Earlier, natural healers rejected chemicals and poisons and used God's methods of healing. Some of these earlier healers were:

Arnold Rikli (1823-1906) was well educated as an industrialist but who had no formal medical education, employed the water cure and diet as healing modalities but added the use of air and sunlight baths. He is known for saying, "Water is good; air is better, but light is best of all."

Sebastian Kneipp, Prist (1824-1897) provided the link between the European nature cure and American naturopathy. Kneipp was a priest, and physical healing was as much a part of his ministry as was saving souls. His approach to healing was holistic advocating "the balance between work and leisure, stress and relaxation and the harmony between the mental, emotional, physical, social, and ecological planes". In short, he asked for a different life, not for better pills; he asked for the active patient and rejected the passive one.

Benedict Lust (1872-1945) gave naturopathy its name. Born in Germany, Lust (pronounced Loost) came to the United States in 1892 to seek his fortune. Unfortunately for him, but fortunately for us today, he contracted a severe case of tuberculosis and returned home to die. Instead, he found Father Kneipp and was healed. In 1896 he returned to the United States sanctioned by Kneipp to spread the word about the water cure. Lust's ideas about natural healing were eclectic. While he was a proponent of the Kneipp Water Cure, he combined it with modalities he had learned from many other European doctors. By 1902, Lust had opened a naturopathic sanatorium, established a naturopathic college, began a naturopathic magazine, and opened a store and sold Kneipp products. Benedict Lust was the Father of Traditional Naturopathic Medicine in the United States; the original organization, from which Naturopathic Medicine split off from, upon Dr. Lust death. Persecution from the American Medical Association soon followed, which is partly why Naturopathic Medicine requires licensing.

In 1543 Andreas Vesalius printed his masterpiece on the human anatomy. Prior to this, the Catholic Church said you could not dissect a human body. The books written by Galen were based upon dissecting monkeys and pigs. When Vesalius printed his book, it was not received well as he was going against tradition. Notice who controlled medicine i.e. the Catholic Church! God's true church and health message was still in the wilderness... (Rev. 12:6). The control of medicine and the Catholic Church insistence on the use of unnatural substances was the final issue that brought about the Thirty Years' War, see chapter three.

"...many shall run to and fro, and Knowledge shall be increased." Daniel 12:4.

God refers to the "Time of the End" four times in a short space, Daniel 11:35, 40; 12:4, 9. Beginning with the "Morning Star" of the Protestant Reformation, John Wycliff in the 1300s, to John Huss, Martin Luther, Erasmus, and others, the moral, spiritual, and scientific darkness of the middle Ages was drawing to a close. A new spiritual awakening began. God's true church along with His health and healing message was emerging from the wilderness and it is imperative that Christians understand the significance of the "Time of the End."

At this time, medicine entered into a period of what we call today, "basic discoveries". In 1628, John Harvey discovered the circulation of the blood in the human body. "Perfect health depends upon perfect circulation." Ellen White, Healthful Living, p. 30.

"The limbs, which should have even more covering than any other portion of the body, because farthest from the center of circulation, are often not suitably protected; while over the vital organs, where there is naturally more warmth than in other portions of the body, there is an undue proportion of covering. The heavy draperies often worn upon the back, induce heat and congestion in the sensitive organs which lie beneath. This fashionable attire is one of the greatest causes of disease among women. Perfect health depends upon perfect circulation. If the limbs are properly clothed, fewer skirts are needed."

"These should not be so heavy as to impede the motion of the limbs, nor so long as to gather the dampness and filth of the ground, and their weight should be suspended from the shoulders. The dress should fit easily, obstructing neither the circulation of the blood, nor a free, full, natural respiration. The feet should be suitably protected from cold and damp. Clad in this way, we can take exercise in the open air, even in the dew of morning or evening, or after a fall of snow or rain, without fear of taking cold. Exercise in the invigorating air of heaven is necessary to a healthy circulation of the blood. It is the best safeguard against colds, coughs, and the internal congestions, which lay the foundation of so many diseases. True dress reform regulates every article of clothing. If those ladies who are failing in health would lay off their fashionable robes, clothe themselves suitably for out-door enjoyment, and exercise in the open air, carefully at first, increasing the amount as they can endure it, many of them might recover health, and live to bless the world with their example and the work of their hands." Christian Temperance and Bible Hygiene, Ellen White, p.89.

Vienna physician, Ignas P. Semmelweis (1818-1865) discovered that doctors and nurses were passing on germs to patients because they were not washing hands. He was ridiculed because it was not the tradition of the day. 2500 BC God had already instructed Moses in regards to hygienic principles. So many babies died needlessly because people disregarded the lifesaving principles in scripture. The same results are happening today.

"And whomsoever he toucheth that hath the issue, and hath not rinsed his hands in water, he shall wash his clothes, and bathe himself in water, and be unclean until the evening." Leviticus 15:11.

Chapter Three: *The Lost Chapter in the History of Biology:*
Absolute Power Absolutely Corrupts

Louis Pasteur (1822-1895) & the Babylonian Germ Theory

Today modern medicine is primarily based upon Louis Pasteur's "Germ Theory." Simply put, an invading germ (demon) resides in one of the systems or organs of the body producing symptoms, i.e. cold, fever, fatigue, etc. If you manage the symptoms, you get rid of the germ. However, it appears Pasteur borrowed the concept of the germ theory from the scholar Marcus Terentius Varro (116-28 BC). While not calling it the germ theory, Varro advised caution near swamps-where malarial mosquitoes breed- "because there are bred certain minute creatures which cannot be seen by the eyes, which float through the air and enter the body through the mouth and the nose and there cause serious disease". Ralph Major, A History of Medicine, p. 21.

Traditional Western medicine teaches and practices the doctrine of French chemist Louis Pasteur. His main theory is known as the Germ Theory of Disease. It claims that fixed species of microbes from an external source invade the body and are the first cause of "infectious" disease. The Germ Theory view's the body systemically. That is, different germs affect different bodily systems, i.e., digestive, reproductive, circulatory system, and the sickness is thought to reside in that system. Even the division of specialties in the medical profession shows that illness is viewed systemically. Your gastroenterologist cannot help you with a sinus infection, and no urologist would dare advise an asthma patient. The basic thought is that sickness is localized in one system, and that health will be restored when the microbes are removed from that system. This theory assumes that the rest of the body is healthy and only this one part needs help. The goal of medicine using this theory is to make sure that each system is working properly, independently of each other. This concept is totally foreign to how God created the human body.

"Though Pasteur already had made many important and basic discoveries, the years 1877 to 1886 were filled with new discoveries of greater significance to <u>medicine and to science</u>... during his work on chicken cholera, in 1879, a laboratory 'accident' led Pasteur to discover methods of attenuating bacterial cultures, of decreasing and of increasing their toxic attributes, at will, and of taming dangerous microbes so that they might be changed from killers to benefactor thereby to pave the way for the development of vaccines and antitoxins." George Bender and Robert Thorn, Great Moments in Medicine, p. 264.

"From Christ all truth radiates. Apart from Christ, science is misleading, and philosophy is foolishness. Those who are separated from the Saviour will advance theories that originate with the wily foe. Christ's life stands out as the contrast of all false science, all erroneous theories, all misleading methods."   Ellen White, TDG, p. 324.3.

Antoine Bechamp 1816 – 1908

In her book *Bechamp or Pasteur? A Lost Chapter in the History of Biology*, by Ethel Douglas Hume cites an observation by Florence Nightingale, the famous pioneer of nursing, who worked long hours in the sick wards. As she observed people's symptoms, she noticed them changing spontaneously from one "disease" to another. As a result of her observations, she wrote: "The specific disease doctrine is the grand refuge of weak, uncultured, unstable minds, such as now rule in the medical profession. There are no specific diseases; there are specific disease-conditions." Ms. Nightingale's statement is so logical and explains much. But the specific disease doctrine, like a plague itself, infests the power structure of mainstream Western medicine.

Bechamp earned many degrees and held prestigious positions including: Master of Pharmacy, Doctor of Science, Doctor of Medicine, Professor of Medical Chemistry and Pharmacy, Fellow and Professor of Physics and Toxicology, Professor of Biological Chemistry, Dean of the Faculty of Medicine.

In spite of the historical and scientific importance and many accomplishments of Bechamp, relatively few people are aware of him. His story is a prime example of genius and profound discoveries reaping ignorance. This usually happens when information threatens the status quo or special interest groups. Bechamp attained so many achievements that it took eight pages of a scientific journal to list them when he died. His biological work might then have revolutionized medicine with profound insight into the nature of life. But, in a political world, he found himself up against a skillful politician with wealthy connections - Louis Pasteur.

In Hume's book, Bechamp is said to have stated the following in regard to the germ theory: *"There is no doctrine so false that it does not contain some particle of truth. It is thus with microbian doctrines."* He is later quoted, *"Above all, men of the world are carried away by a specious easy doctrine, all the more applicable to vague generalities and vague explanations in that it is badly based upon proved and tried scientific demonstrations."* *"In other words, although they were drawing the right conclusions from scientific demonstrations, these demonstrations were based upon a false premise. What make the Germ Theory so dangerous is that it seems so obviously true, but it is only true secondarily"*.

You have to understand and mentally grasp the above statement. Your allopathic doctor is treating you for symptoms, i.e. diabetes, heart disease, cancer, etc... The real cause of disease is the changing of the body chemistry, or as Bechamp called it the "inner terrain", or as Ellen White called *"reestablish right conditions in the system"*, or what is known today as "homeostasis" This is further underscored by the following statement: *"If I could live my life over again, I would devote it to proving that germs seek their natural habitat-diseased tissue-rather than being the cause of the disease tissue; e.g., mosquitoes seek the stagnant water, but do not cause the pool to become stagnant"*. --Rudolph Virchow (Founder of Pathology).

So why are Christians taking prescription drugs when C. Everett Koop, the only two term Surgeon General of the United States has documented in his U.S. Surgeon General Report on Nutrition and Health in 1988, that *"**dietary excess and imbalances**" contribute significantly to eight of the leading killer diseases in the United States. As well as, modification of diet can contribute to their prevention and control"*. We have not allowed Jesus Christ to set us free. We are slaves to our taste buds and continue to eat the world's food even though we know it is killing us, then take a pill that is void of life itself and speeding up the process to death, then want to blame God or call upon God to heal us when He has warned us off Satan's enchanted ground.

Pasteur made his theory seem correct by promoting the practice of injecting animals. In fact, Pasteur was responsible in large part for the onslaught of animal experimentation in medical research.
Pasteur used preparations made from the diseased tissues of previously sick animals, thus making the injected one sick. This gave the

appearance that a germ caused a disease, when in fact these preparations were extremely poisonous (vaccinations).

This is not scientific procedure, but simply demonstrates the fact that you can make someone sick by poisoning their blood. The attentive reader will see the errors here: first, Pasteur was confusing disease with its symptoms. Secondly, the method of injection can by no means be said to duplicate a natural "infection." Based on his theory of microzymas, Bechamp warned emphatically against such direct and artificial invasion of the blood. The practice of injecting toxins into the bloodstream was a practice of Pasteur as stated above and condoned to by the AMA, FDA, and other regulatory organizations.

Thirty years prior to the rise of monomorphism, Bechamp brought his attention to tiny "molecular granulations" found in body cells, which other observers had noted before him. They had been scantily defined, and no one had identified their status or function. After 10 years of careful experimentation, Bechamp brought to the world in 1866 the profound revelation that the granules were living elements. He renamed them microzymas, meaning "small ferments." During the next 3 years, Bechamp, with his devoted co-worker, Professor Estor, developed and refined the Theory of Microzymas. The essence of this theory is that the microzyma, an independently living element, exists within all living things, and is both the builder and recycler of organisms. It inhabits cells, the fluid between cells, the blood and the lymph. Bechamp's microzyma is capable of multiplying, and, like Enderlein's protit, it reflects either health or disease. In a state of health, the microzymas act harmoniously and fermentation occurs normally, i.e. beneficially. But in the condition of disease, microzymas become disturbed and change their form and function. They evolve into microscopic forms (germs) that reflect the disease and produce the symptoms, becoming what Bechamp called "morbidly evolved" microzymas. Again, this occurs due to a modification of our terrain by an inverted way of eating and living.

Bechamp observed granules linking together and "lengthening into bacteria." He therefore observed, explored and expressed the concept of pleomorphism as its earliest, and certainly it's most eloquent, spokesman. Thus, being at the foundation of organization in the body, microzymain transformations build up cells and eventually the whole organism in which they exist.

However, as noted, their function is twofold, and they are poised to recycle the physical body upon death. I describe the microzyma as matter which cannot be created or destroyed and is the precursor to all living organized matter. Now we can answer the question: "What comes first, the chicken or the egg?" The answer is neither: it is the microzyma. Our Creator describes the microzyma simply as: "from dust you are and to dust you shall return" (Genesis 3:19). Where illness is concerned, my position is that in an unbalanced terrain (unbalanced body chemistry), fermentative breakdown is not only accelerated, but is taken over by morbid evolutions, including bacteria, yeast, fungus and mold. These are the upper development forms of the microzyma, which feed on vital body substances. This results in degenerative disease symptoms.

"Pasteur denied that bacteria could change their form. Only the unchanging, specific germs of the air were the cause of disease, he said. Bechamp, on the other hand, never denying that the air carried germs, maintained that airborne forms were not necessary for disease. So you see, the well-connected politician wished to establish that we must be invaded (and therefore be protected by profitable vaccination). But the true scientist showed that an independently living element, which could morbidly evolve, already exists in all cells of the body, and showed evidence that it is all that is needed for the appearance of symptogenic organisms (symptom causing)." Sick and Tired, Robert O. Young, p. 26-28.

"Many teach that matter possesses vital power. They hold that certain properties are imparted to matter, and it is then left to act through its own inherent power; and that the operations of nature are carried on in harmony with fixed laws that God Himself cannot interfere with. This is [false science], and is sustained by nothing in the Word of God." {BLJ 241.2}

GERM THEORY (PASTEUR)	CELLULAR THEORY (BÉCHAMP)
1. The body is sterile.	Microbes exist naturally in the body.
2. Disease arises from micro-organisms outside the body.	Disease arises from micro-organisms within the cells of the body.
3. Micro-organisms are generally to be	These intracellular micro-organisms normally function to build and assist in the metabolic

guarded against.	processes of the body.
4. The function of micro-organisms is constant.	The function of these organisms changes to assist in the catabolic (disintegration) processes of the host organism when that organism dies or is injured, which may be chemical as well as mechanical.
5. The shapes and colours of micro-organisms are constant.	Micro-organisms are pleomorphic (having many forms): they change their shapes and colors (shape-shift) to reflect the condition of the host.
6. Every disease is associated with a particular micro-organism.	Every disease is associated with a particular condition.
7. Micro-organisms are primary causal agents.	Disease results when microbes change form, function, and toxicity according to the terrain of the host. Hence, the condition of the host organism is the primary causal agent.
8. Disease can "strike" anybody.	Disease is built by unhealthy conditions.
9. To prevent disease we have to "build defences."	To prevent disease we have to create health.

New information refutes the germ theory:
(a) The body is not sterile: Bacteria and viruses have been found and identified in healthy people.
(b) A particular microbe does not cause a corresponding disease: The same bacteria and viruses that have been associated with disease have also been found in healthy people, where they apparently play a benevolent role.

Gunther Enderlein (1872 – 1968)

Enderlein was a German scientist whose specialties were animals (zoology) and bacteria (bacteriology). Professor Enderlein based his work upon that of a 19th century genius, Antoine Bechamp. It is important that all of the researchers of that day who were opposed to the "Germ Theory" all had at least one important thing in common: they had expressed the understanding that disease is a general condition of one's internal environment. It is not the symptom we see, nor is it an entity that attacks us from somewhere else. If germs are involved, they arise as primary symptoms of that general condition. Though germs don't cause disease, their secondary symptoms commonly called disease are produced in response to their activity. Bechamp and the researchers of that day also adhered to the principle of *pleomorphism* (pleo = many; morph = form). "Many-formism" is the idea that microorganisms ("tiny beings"), such as a specific bacterium, can take on multiple forms. This is a change of function as well as shape. It is more significant than it sounds at first because it crosses certain barriers used to classify different species.

A species is defined as a class unto itself, fixed in its behavior, appearance, internal structure, etc. In pleomorphism, however, a so called species may be just a stage in the growth cycle of a family of beings, with each member functioning differently and look a lot different from the others. Enderlein discovered that certain microorganisms undergo an exact, scientifically verifiable cycle of change in their form. Our inner terrain becomes unbalanced paving the way for unwanted guests. In this unbalanced environment, morbid bacteria can issue from our own cells. As well, these tiny life forms can rapidly change their form and function. Bacteria can change into yeast, yeast to fungus, fungus to mold. He used the term pleomorphism to define this growth cycle, and believed it to be a fundamental aspect of all illness. As profound as the change of a caterpillar into a butterfly, this evolution is even more fantastic, since it can happen quite rapidly, sometimes in a matter of minutes.

During his 60 years of research, Enderlein verified a number of important and remarkable discoveries: (1) One discovery pertains to a basic law of orthodox biology. This law states that the cell is the smallest unit of life. A cell is a capsule of activity in the body, having an outer wall, and having a specific function. Within a cell's wall, all the chemicals and components acting together make up life. Nothing within the cell is said to be alive of itself. Inspired by Bechamp's pioneering work, Enderlein also found evidence for a tiny biological unit of life, which he called a "protit," living within cells. (2) Blood naturally contain tiny life forms capable of provoking disease symptoms if conditions are favorable. This flies in the face of orthodox conviction. (3) He discovered that certain microorganisms undergo an exact, scientifically verifiable cycle of change in their form. Enderlein, Prof. Dr. Gunther. Akmon. Vol. I, Book 2. Hamburg, Germany: Ibica-Verlag, 1957, p. 293.

Because he also took the important step of looking at live blood, Enderlein observed the pleomorphic changes there. He noticed protits remained small in response to healthy conditions, and they built and worked with the body. According to his theory, the life units are contained in the blood clotting and the inflammation response. They are also in the platelets, which are tiny discs in the blood also used for clotting. (This is an area opened up and explored by Bechamp, who wrote a masterwork called The Blood and Its Third Anatomical Element). When the life units (protits) encounter a disturbed inner condition, however, they become enlarged and *symptogenic* (symptom-producing), evolving into more complex forms including bacteria and fungus.

"Dr. Enderlein's most profound discovery was twofold: (1) certain biological laws govern the growth of symptom-genic microorganisms in the human body; (2) there is a healthy (or harmless) and unhealthy form of every germ. Thus, he verified pleomorphism as described by Bechamp, and proved bacterial and fungal changeability. Both Claude Bernard and Bechamp inspired Enderlein to confirm that germs are symptoms. Germs simulate the occurrence of more symptoms as a result of thriving in an unbalanced terrain. "Terrain," a term brought to the fore by Bernard, is the internal environment of the body. A healthy or diseased terrain is determined primarily by four things: its acid/alkaline balance (pH); its electric/magnetic charge (negative or positive); its level of poisoning (toxicity); and its nutritional status". Sick and Tired, by Robert O. Young, p. 20, 21. All four of these conditions can be ascertained by urine and saliva analysis called the Reams Theory of Biologic Ionization, which is termed Body Chemistry. Dr. Lee, N.D. is trained and certified in Body Chemistry Analysis.

Modern Science Validates Band Research of Beachamp, others
Make the connection here Christians and true healthcare advocates. Because you did not know of the past controversy between Pasteur, Bechamp and others, you do not realize that today's medical research scientist have validated much of the earlier pioneers banded discoveries. In the section on Nutrition, I will specifically document how this has been accomplished. I will discuss twice Nobel Prize

winner Linus Pauling, the 74th. U.S. Congress, second session; C. Everett Koop, M.D., Sc.D, former two times Surgeon General of the United States, and the World Health Organization (WHO), all scientifically confirm the correlation between diet and lifestyle and sickness and health. The proof that Dr. Bechamp's microzymas and Dr. Enderlein's Protit's and now Gaston Naessens's Somatid's are scientifically correct has gone virtually unnoticed, until Dr. Dean Ornish and his team proved the existence of poly-morphism (as defined by Bechamp and others, not the AMA) in the human body when they conducted a "Lifestyle Heart Trial." The Lifestyle Heart Trial demonstrated that intensive lifestyle and diet changes lead to regression of coronary arteriosclerosis after one year. The findings were reported in the December 16, 1998 issue of The Journal of the American Medical Association (JAMA), beginning on page 2001 of said journal, we read the following: "Intensive Lifestyle Changes for Reversal of Coronary Heart Disease." See appendix G. As the body chemistry (Inner Terrain) was changed back to normal, the body was able to heal itself. No prescription drugs were used, so how do you account for the success of the group who only had their diet and lifestyle changed?

Remember the quote from Christian health care writer Ellen White: "In the case of disease.... Then, reestablish right conditions in the system, Ministry of Healing, by Ellen White, pg. 127.

Give Us True Unbiased Science:

"...not oppositions of science so falsely called," I Tim 6:20

As a Christian, which system do you believe God would have you follow in order to preserve your body temple so His Spirit can dwell within you? "Whether Bechamp or Pasteur is correct may still be an issue for some people, but the science is on Bechamp's side. Remember Bechamp's statement; in Hume's book, "there is no doctrine so false that it does not contain some particle of truth. It is thus with microbian doctrines." He is later quoted as having said, "Above all, men of the world are carried away by a specious easy doctrine, all the more applicable to vague generalities and vague explanations in that it is badly based upon proved and tried scientific demonstrations. In other words, although they were drawing the right conclusions from scientific demonstrations, these demonstrations were based upon a false premise. What makes the germ theory so dangerous is that it seems so obviously true, but it is only true secondarily."

It does seem unusual, though, that Antoine's name and the controversy itself, has been omitted from history, medical and biology books-even encyclopedias. Given the magnitude and number of Bechamp's discoveries, it is fair to ask if this omission is more than oversight. What is the [AMA, Pharmaceutical industry and Rockefeller's etc], afraid of? [Could it be the loss of prestige, profits, power, control, and the bewitching influence over the masses of humanity]? "It seems that the historical/scientific "assassination" of Antoine Bechamp resulted in medical science drawing conclusions from half-truths. This has meant untold misery for the human race, especially in the West." Robert Young, Ph.D., Sick and Tired 2001, p. 28, 29. Emphasis by Dr. Lee.

A second foundational mistake the medical community made in order to establish its philosophy of drugs, poison and surgery was back in 1764. Albrecht von Haller, a German, first claimed dry mouth as a sign of thirst. In 1918, Walter Bradford Cannon, an English doctor, supported Haller's views; since he was an influential person, his views became fashionable and are reflected in accepted scientific literature to this day; the same way as Louis Pasteur and his "Germ Theory." However, Frenchman Moritz Schiff, had claimed in 1867 that thirst is a general sensation: "It is no more a local sensation than hunger."
The same mistake has been passed on from one generation of medical students to another until present day.

The basic science of medicine believes water is a simple substance that only dissolves and circulates different things. Water is not a simple inert substance. It has two primary properties in the body. The first one is its life-sustaining properties. The other, more important, role of water is its life-giving properties. F. Batmanghelidji, M.D., Water, p. 2. See the information on water in the section on God's Ten Health Laws.

"In the future, truth will be counterfeited by the precepts of men. Deceptive theories will be presented as safe doctrines. <u>False science is one of the agencies that Satan used in the heavenly courts, and it is used by him today</u>. . ." Ellen White, Maranatha, p. 134.5.

The Life of the Flesh is in the Blood, Leviticus 17:14

The true cause of disease is the change in the body's inner terrain, as stated by a renowned Christian health writer Ellen White who wrote, "...no disease can live in a pure bloodstream". She stressed that what we eat and drink, coupled with our lifestyle, determines the condition of the blood. Therefore, the initial and true cause of any disease is because of an impure bloodstream, which is one cause of a changing inner terrain. It becomes the channel and breeding place for all manner of "growing and living bacterial forms" feeding off waste products such as excessive mucus protein, mold, yeast, plaque bacteria growth, and can encourage blood parasites to develop. When the blood becomes overloaded with any of this waste matter, the immune system is suppressed, and white corpuscles cannot consume free radicals sufficiently, and disease results. One of the daily duties allocated to the blood is to supply oxygen to each of some sixty trillion cells. The blood also transports nutrients, carries away wastes and delivers messages via the hormones it carries from the endocrine glands.The American medical establishment does not look at live blood. Since life resides in the blood, it is true then, that the death of the flesh is also resides in the blood. Your medical doctor has not been trained in Darkfield and/or Phase Contrast Microscopy. Medical doctors focus primarily on chemical analysis to make their diagnosis, and in doing so, they are missing the show.

Also, when looking at blood, their practice of "staining" samples disorganizes them. In fact, biological forms and elements have been defined by the artificial convention of this staining, thus throwing their bias on the whole subject. This approach is an engrained technique religiously taught in medical schools and practiced in research. But it is narrow and restricted, virtually blinding those who rely on it. The action of the chemical stain visually enhances certain things, such as the cell wall and nucleus. But this is at the cost of disturbing and organizing all the living, moving, feeding microforms-they become invisible or unidentifiable. Consequently, observers of dead blood refer to these forms as "artifacts," "organelles," "microsomes," etc. Therefore, their role in the development of disease symptoms goes unrecognized.

As Christians, accepting this limited practice of staining, and rejecting or not considering Darkfield, Brightfield, or Phase Contrast live blood cell analysis is to mock God, as the changing of the inner-terrain, i.e., blood, lymphatic fluid, digestive enzymes, colon, etc., sets the stage for friendly bacteria transformation into deadly pathogens which can be seen in live blood cell analysis. Let's see what else Ellen White, the Christian health writer had to say about drugs.

"I was shown that more deaths have been caused by drug-taking than from all other causes combined. If there was in the land one physician

in the place of thousands, a vast amount of premature mortality would be prevented. Multitudes of physicians, and multitudes of drugs, have cursed the inhabitants of the earth, and have carried thousands and tens of thousands to untimely graves." 4 Spiritual Gifts, p. 133.

- Drugs ultimately bring a breakdown of Vital Forces; Med. Min. p. 223.
- Drugs are not the intelligent method. Medical Ministry, p. 40.
- Drugs require less skill. Healthful Living, p. 247.
- Drugs are expensive experiments. Medical Ministry, p. 228.
- Drugs are prescribed instead of telling patient truth. Med. Min. p.225.
- Drugs work by poisoning the current of the blood. CH, p. 303.
- Drugs cause disease to disappear and reappear elsewhere. 4SG, p.135.
- Drugs load the body with poisons it cannot expel. 4SG, p. 135-136.
- Drugs eventually cease to help symptoms. Med. Min., p. 228-229.
- Drugs interfere with Nature's laws. Manuscript 22, 1889.
- Drugs are a poor substitute for simple herbs. Letter 90, 1908.
- Drugs are not responsible for the healing that follow. H.L., p. 224.
- Drugs do not posses curative powers. How to Live, p. 70
- Drugs weaken directly and also by inheritance. How to Live, p. 53.
- "Those who make a practice of taking drugs sin against their intelligence and endanger their whole afterlife…2SM, p. 290-291.
- Drugs are the faithless method. Manuscript 169, 1902.

"Is it not because there is not a God in Israel that ye go to inquire of Baalzebub the god of Ekron"? I Kings 1:3. I ask you today, is there not a God in Heaven that you go to the god of science falsely so called. I Tim 6:20.

    With the increasing number of prescription drugs and the ever increasing dosage taken, it would appear from the above facts that a person is dying a slow and premature death.

List of Murdered Scientists:
"Ye are of your father the devil… John 8:44.

The following are the names and a brief description of lives that were extinguished possibly for doing their job extremely well, www.stevequayle.com/dead_scientist/UpdatedDeadScientist.

Jose Trias died May 9, 1994. Trias and his wife were murdered in their Chevy Chase, Maryland, home. They met with a friend, a journalist, the day before their murder and told him of their plan to expose

Howard Hughes Medical Institute (HHMI) funding of "special ops" research. Grant money that goes to HHMI is actually diverted to special black ops research projects.

Mark Purdey was familiar with the expression "abnormal brain protein." Purdey's house was burned down and his lawyer who was working with him on Mad Cow Disease had been driven off the road by another vehicle and subsequently died. The veterinarian on the case also died in a car crash. Purdey's new lawyer, too, had a car accident, but not fatal. Dr. C. Burton, a CJD specialist, who had just produced a paper on a new strain of Creutzfeldt-Jakob Disease (CJD), was killed in a car crash before his work was announced to the public. Purdey speculates that Burton might have known more than what was revealed in his paper.

On October 4, 2001, four of five unnamed microbiologists on a plane was brought down by a missile near the Black Sea on the Russian border. Traveling from Israel to Russia, their business was not disclosed. Three scientists were experts in medical research on public health. The plane is believed by many in Israel to have had as many as four or five passengers who were microbiologists. Both Israel and Novosibirsk are homes for cutting-edge microbiological research. Novosibirsk is known as the scientific capital of Siberia. There are more than 50 research facilities there, and 13 full universities with a population of only 2.5 million people.

Another plane crash kills three scientists. At about the same time of the Black Sea crash, Israeli journalists had been sounding the alarm that two Israeli microbiologists had been murdered, allegedly by terrorists, including the head of the hematology department at Israel's Ichilov Hospital, as well as the directors of the Tel Aviv Public Health Department and Hebrew University School of Medicine. They were world experts in hematology and blood clotting. Five microbiologists in this list of the first eight people who died mysteriously in airplane crashes worked on cutting-edge microbiology research; and, four of the five were doing virtually identical research, research that had global political and financial significance. Avishai Berkman, age 50; Amiramp Eldor, age 59; and Yaacov Matzner, age 54, died on November 24, 2001.

Dr. Sam Chachoua

For more than seven months, the cancer industry, apparently led by Cedars-Sinai has totally controlled the National Media which had suppressed any mention of Los Angeles US Direct Court Case# CV#97-5595-MMM.

Have you heard or seen it anywhere in the National Media? You have not! That appears to be a clear violation of the peoples' right to know. New cures for cancer and AIDS are being withheld from everyone in the U.S.A. and the world. On August 11, 2000, Dr. Sam Chachoua, a Cancer and AIDS researcher, was awarded $10 million damages by the U.S. District Court from LA's Cedars-Sinai Medical Center for breach of contract by failing to return 36 proprietary vaccines and source cultures to Dr. Chachoua and refusing to publish the results of tests performed by Cedar-Sinai on those vaccines and cultures. Trial records reveal in shocking detail the devious means employed to destroy Dr. Chachoua and steal his Induced Remission Therapy (IRT). Dedicated Explore Medical Magazine was the only media entity to attend and report the trial. Link #1, 19+ pages.

Dr. Sam Chachoua developed an innovative and eminently successful field of medicine called Induced Remission Therapy (IRT). The cancer industry in the fall of 1994, closed ranks and began attempts to destroy Dr. Chachoua and purloin his therapy. Case #CV97-5595-MMM in Los Angeles' U.S. District Court against Cedar-Sinai Medical Center became a necessity. The national media did not report on the trial. MS/NBC TV News in Los Angeles, after the trial, ran a videotape on Dr. Sam and his IRT describing it as a new field of medicine promising to be the most effective therapy against cancer and AIDS in history. That tape had a very short life; it was soon pulled, never to be seen again. Could it possibly have been because several week later, Trial Judge Margaret M. Morrow reversed a unanimous jury verdict and reduced the award from $10 million to a paltry $11,000.00 (a 99.9% reduction) on a technicality. Even though the venerable Los Angeles Times ran 139 articles on Cedars, the year around the trial, the Los Angeles Times did not report on the trial or the technical reason why Judge Morrow reversed the jury's decision.

There are too many accidental deaths of scientists to write about. They may or may not have been killed for their research work, but we do know that since the turn of the 19th. Century a ruthless group of men have put the system in place and they tied it to the U.S. economy, and will do anything and everything to retain control.

Now, Murdered Alternative Doctors: Have they i.e. the government or pharmaceutical companies or some organization connected to the families that profit from health care being tied to the U. S. economy, started murdering Alternative Healthcare Doctors because of their medical advances especially in alternative cancer treatments? Read this story from Health Nut News, 3rd "Alternative" Prominent Doctor from Florida found dead in 2 weeks. Authorities say MD was murdered. First and foremost I'd like to say my heart goes out to the friends, families and patients of all three doctors.

It brings me no joy to report this tragic news, but I feel people need to know. Less than 2 weeks ago the first doctor, a controversial Autism

"Maybe we shouldn't use this form of vaccination to prevent Measles... It's not just 3 kids who had this... they were normal, they got their MMR vaccine, they regressed, and we found Measles virus everywhere... gut, blood, and brain... not brain, spinal fluid to be specific. We have found it in the brain through brain biopsies, by the way."

Dr. Jeff Bradstreet, MD

researcher loved by his patients, <u>Dr. Jeff Bradstreet MD, was found in a river with a gunshot wound to his chest</u>. He leaves behind a beautiful wife and children. His friends and family started a memorial page on June 20th in his honor on Facebook. I waited 3 days after that to report the story out of respect. A few still write that I shouldn't cover these stories, but I am a journalist, and now that 3 doctors have died so quickly from my state (at least one murdered) I feel I need to write about it. I waited until all were covered by mainstream news and or funeral sites. Dr. Bradstreet had lived just 45 minutes from us here in Florida before moving to the neighboring state of Georgia. I also have been with a prominent well known doctor for the last 6 years so this concerns me. Several high profile MD's have contacted me these last 2 weeks who are also concerned and mourn the loss of their colleagues.

The second doctor is <u>Dr. Bruce Hedendal DC PhD</u> of Boca Roton area (E Coast, North of Miami) who died suddenly on Father's day. Sources tell me that he was found in his car, but there was no car accident and it wasn't running. He was just in his car, deceased. He had exercised earlier at an event, but we don't want to speculate. He also leaves behind a beautiful family. As of yet I do not know if it was natural causes or not that took his life. In addition to being a DC, he held a PhD in nutrition from Harvard. A friend who worked with him said he was in great shape and described him as "very healthy". They too didn't know the cause of death and were still in shock. Not sure if anyone knows at this point. Both Dr Hedendal and Dr. Bradstreet had dealt with run-ins with the feds in the past. In fact, Dr. Bradstreet's office was just raided by the FDA days before he died. We know they will both be missed by countless patients, family and friends.

Now we have the inspiring intelligent Teresa Ann Sievers MD, also here in Florida. She was in the Naples area in the South West coast of the sunshine state in Bonita Springs. Her bio on her website describes her many accomplishments and degrees as a medical doctor who believed in a holistic alternative approach. She lived in a safe area where neighbors said they rarely, if ever, had problems. I had actually had just been in that neighborhood last month for a health event and its beautiful and serene. UPDATE: This new video about Dr. Siever's death on CBS News talks about a donation site set up through CBS's official website for those who wish to do so.- See more at: http://www.healthnutnews.com/3rd-alternative-prominent-doctor-from-florida-found-dead-in-2-weeks-authorities-say-md-was murdered/#sthash.G5wU6jtz.dpuf-July 1, 2015 by Erin Elizabeth.

Glenn Thomas, AIDS and Ebola expert and spokesperson for the World Health Organization.
Ebola expert Glenn Thomas was among the 298 people who were killed when Malaysia Airlines flight MH17 was shot down and crashed in Ukraine. It is understood he was one of more than 100 researchers who were aboard the flight on their way to an International Aids Conference in Australia. Among the other delegates

aboard the plane was Joep Lange, a leading AIDS researcher and former president of the International AIDS Society (IAS).

Andrew Moulden MD PhD, 50, Clinical Psychology and Neuropsychology with a master degree in child development, and was also a medical doctor. The death of Andrew Moulden is shrouded in mystery. Some sources say he had a heart attack and others say he committed suicide. A colleague of Dr. Moulden who wishes to remain anonymous reported to Health Impact News that he/she had contact with him two weeks before he died in 2013. Dr. Moulden told our source and a small number of trusted colleagues in October of 2013 that he was about to break his silence and would be releasing new information that would be a major challenge to the vaccine business of big pharma. He was ready to come back. Even though he had been silent, he had never stopped his research. Then, two weeks later, Dr. Moulden suddenly died. Dr. Moulden was about to release a body of research and treatments, which could have destroyed the vaccine model of disease management, destroyed a major source of funding for the pharmaceutical industry, and at the same time seriously damaged the foundation of the germ theory of disease.

Antonio Bechamp warned against vaccinations and they assassinate his life's work.

Melissa Ketunuti, - died January 2013 - Firefighters find charred body of murdered pediatrician who was hog-tied, strangled and set on fire in her basement.

Dr. Kentunuti worked at Children's Hospital of Philadelphia and dedicated her whole life to being a doctor and helping kids with cancer. According to the Philadelphia Inquirer, she earned a doctorate in medicine from Stanford

University and had initially considered working as a surgeon internationally.

She worked on an AIDS research fellowship in Botswana through the National Institutes of Health. She also completed internships at Johns Hopkins Hospital and New York University.

Let's go back to the beginning and see who and how a few took over medicine and has made it corporate medicine. Killing and destroying lives in the name of greed, corporate profits, Global population reduction and in defiance of the word of God.

Story Begins In 1618 A.D. The Beginning of the 30 Years' War
Most of you have not heard this information before because you have been educated in the Rockefeller, American Board of Regents controlled, history of the world. Remember just 75 years earlier, Andreas Vesalius printed his masterpiece on the human anatomy. The Catholic Church was in control of world medicine and opposed Vesalius book. The story begins in the dusty pages of history in 1618, in what has become known as the 30 Years' War. Below is an actual map of Europe from 800 A.D. until 1600 A.D., basically you have the United Kingdom in blue, much the same today. Scandinavia in red is pretty much the same today. To the right, you have Eastern Europe, Russia, and the Balkans. Below the brown, you have Italy and its shape of a boot. In the center, the brown color, which is known today as Germany, Poland, Austria, etc… In 1618 it was called the Holy Roman Empire. In reality, it is the un-Holy Roman Empire. To the far left you have Iberia, which is modern day Spain, and of course France in the green to the right of Spain and left of the Roman Empire.

The Thirty Years' War was fought between 1618 and 1648, and was fought between the Vatican of Italy and Protestant reformers. It was a war of religious ideologies instigated by the Vatican's 'Jesuits' who promoted "pharmacopia" – i.e. "sorcery" and dictatorship. It was a war of Protesters who wanted freedom from the "Papal Yoke". The unholy Roman Empire was a confederation of States, that included Austria, Burgundy, Germany, Lombardy (northern Italy), and parts of France. Its founder was called Charles the Great or Charlemagne. He was crowned Emperor of this unholy Empire by the pope on December 25, 800 A.D.

A major issue for the protesters was the Jesuits insistence of the use of pharmakeia, which helped to bring the hostilities in that part of the world to a climax. According to the *Malleus Maleficarum,* healing is a crime committed by those who must be put to death for their deeds. The *Malleus Maleficarum* called for the eradication of the knowledge of herbal-healing mainly on the grounds that reliance on such measures reduces our dependence on God. The ex-Jesuit Priest Alberto Rivera puts it this way as he answers the question posed to him during an interview with Pastor Jan Marcussen concerning the Catholic church, medicine and Rev. 18:2 "...for by thy sorceries (Pharmakeia or pharmacy) were all nations deceived."

"All medicine and all medical societies are under that spell (Rev. 8:23). The monks, especially the Benedictine and the Dominican monks were the inquisitors. They dealt with Al Chemistry, before any medical society was ever established. The Al Chemistry was ruled and empowered by these monks and even Jews were forced to *wait* scientifically for these monks, to obtain all the scientific research and encyclic of medicines. They were the pioneers of modern medicine. Now you know why modern medicine is going the way it is going."

Ex-Priest Alberto Rivera during an interview with SDA Pastor Jan Marcussen.

Today, Satan, the Pharmaceutical industry and medical doctors still call healing with herbs quackery. However, medical doctors are going back to school to be trained in Naturopathic medicine and become a N.M.D. This education does not make the medical doctor superior to the Naturopathic doctor but elevates the M.D. to the level of an N.D. Healing only comes from God, and He uses herbs and nutrition and His other natural doctors to accomplish it.

> *"Every element, every sickness, and every disease can be traced back to an organic trace mineral deficiency"* Linus Pauling, two time Nobel Prose winner (categorical statement).

To the left you see the original book By Martin Del Rio of "Sorcery" or in Latin – "Pharmacopia". Del Rio's book outlined the Vatican's vision of future world medicine. One of the two best known 16th--century treatises on magic and healing, Disquisitionum magicarum libri sex was first printed in 1599-1600 and is the magnum opus of Martin del Rio (1551-1608), was a Jesuit Priest and Satanist. The book included specific Amulets, incantations, conjuring and controlling spirits, spells, alchemy, prophecy, divination, and many other practices were covertly "practiced" by the Jesuit Order of the Vatican. This is the origin of the medical term: "practice".

The un-Holy Office was established in the thirteenth century to root out heretics, people who did not subscribe to the views of the Catholic Church. By the fifteenth century, control of beliefs extended to all thought, including medicine, which at that time was largely a monastic pursuit, not, as today; a science discipline taught in secular universities and sponsored by large corporations. The extent of church and state in those abysmal times cannot be fully understood until Jesus comes, but the case of Jacoba Felicie most highlights the control and power of the beast at that time. Jacoba Felicie, an educated woman in a Dark Age, was brought to trial by the Faculty of Medicine at the University of Paris in 1322. She was accused of curing her patients of internal illness and wounds and of visiting the sick. Witnesses testified that after university-trained physicians had failed to cure them, they had been healed by Felicie. The issue then, as today, not results but conformity to an authoritarian system that decided what is orthodox and what is not. Under the Auto-Da-Fé (Act of Faith), the first Inquisition execution took place in 1481, in Seville, during the incumbency of the most feared of all Grand Inquisitor, Tomás de Torquemada. The official guidebook for persecution during the Inquisition was the *Malleus Maleficarum* (1486) written by two Dominican monks, Heinrich Kramer and Jakob Sprenger. Though women and homosexuals were the main targets of the *Malleus Maleficarum,* it was midwives who were most severely attacked. *"Midwives cause the greatest damage, either killing children or sacrilegiously offering them to devils...The greatest injury to the faith is done by midwives, and this is made clearer than daylight itself by the confessions of some who were afterwards burned."* Quoted by John Robbins in *Reclaiming Our Health.* During the Inquisition's reign of terror, it is estimated that as many as nine million persons, were burned at the stake, often for such crimes as practicing herbal medicine-because healing interfered with the punishments disease was inflecting on the suffering. According to the *Malleus Maleficarum,* healing is a crime committed by those who must be put to death for their deeds. The *Malleus Maleficarum* called for the eradication of the knowledge of herbal healing-mainly on the grounds that reliance on such measures reduces our dependence on God. However, God says reliance to His health laws, which include the use of herbs and herbal remedies are trusting in Him.

"The only hope of better things is in the education of the people in right principles. Let physicians teach the people that restorative power is not in drugs, but in nature. Disease is an effort of nature to free the system from conditions that result from a violation of the laws of health. In case of sickness, the cause should be ascertained. Unhealthful conditions should be changed, wrong habits corrected. Then nature is to be assisted in her effort to expel impurities and to re-establish right conditions in the system. Pure air, sunlight, abstemiousness, rest, exercise, proper diet, the use of water, trust in divine power--these are the true remedies. Every person should have a knowledge of nature's remedial agencies and how to apply them. It is essential both to understand the principles involved in the treatment of the sick and to have a practical training that will enable one rightly to use this knowledge, White, Ministry of Healing, p. 127.

To further highlight the Catholic Church's control of the sciences, Remember, the true church of God was in the wilderness until 1798 (Rev. 12: 14) when the French under General Napoleon was ordered to take the pope prisoner where he remained until his death. Consider the case of Nostradamus (1503-1566). The pursuit of knowledge encountered obstacles even after the advent of the Renaissance. Nostradamus was a practicing physician during the sixteenth century. He was treating the bubonic plague with little pills containing rose petals. He was accused of possession of books banned by the Church. He was hauled before the Inquisition but rescued by royal intervention as he was a great favorite of Catherine de' Medici, queen of France but daughter of the leading patron of the Italian Renaissance Lorenzo de' Medici, whom Pope Sixtus IV had tried to have assassinated.

Galileo Galilei (1564-16420, was brought before the Inquisition for supporting the revolutionary Copernican view of astronomy; and in 1616, he was ordered not to discuss Copernicnism. When the Cardinal who first brought charges against him died, Galileo published his [heretical] views (as far as the Catholic Church was concern) and in 1633, was sentenced to life imprisonment. Thought the sentence was commuted to house arrest, the trial documents were not published until 1870. Acknowledgment of error by a Papal commission was only accorded in October 1992!

It is truly an offense to God that Protestants have forgotten what their fore fathers fought and died for, including the Textus Receptus (the true word of God). The 30 Years' war ended with the Treaty of Westphalia in 1648, there was nothing left to fight over. Europe was in ruins and France emerged the clear winner. The unholy Empire was greatly weakened when France entered the conflict. To this day, the Vatican holds France responsible for her defeat. The map of Europe that was drawn after the war has still continued unchanged. After the war ended, the new world (America) became the focus of the Jesuit Vatican interest. The Jesuit (Kenite Bloodlines) in Austria and Germany immigrated to America with a bitter enmity towards France. The Jesuit bloodline originated from ancient Babylon through the lineage of the biblical Canaan. In the New Testament these bloodlines became known as Kenite which made up the Scribes and Pharisees of the New Testament. They came to the new world (America) in hopes of starting a new life and the fortunes the new world had to offer. It took them a little over a hundred years but they finally took control of America's education, legal, medical and religious professions. Since the mid 1980's they have had a stranglehold on America, uniting America with their beloved Papacy with the goal of dismantling the American Constitution and Protestantism, which they will accomplish according to Rev. 13:11-18.

On the left you see in the original book of "Sorcery" or in Latin – "Pharmacopia" by the Jesuit, Del Rio, the Jesuit seal on the opening page, the Maltese cross and in Latin the words In His Service (IHS), and under the cross, the words in Latin

under this sign conquer.

You see the same symbolism on the Huntsman Cancer Institute signage to the left. Look closely at the Huntsman signage and you will see, on either side of the letter H is divided into I.H.S., for In His Service. The service of the Black Pope-the Jesuit General. Most Christians to day do not know the origin of this symbol and think it refer's to the service of Jesus Christ. Just in Utah alone, "Research Hospitals" spend billions seeking a "cure" for cancer, and what is the results? Since the 1950's and 60's across this great nation, and one trillion dollars later, the same three options are given to cancer victims: Surgery, Radiation and Chemo-therapy drugs.

Make no mistake about the issue, the medical systen that is in place today is from Satan him self, through the Catholic Church, specifically the Jesuits. John D. Rockerfella himself was the Jesuit that brought pharmakiea or prescription drugs into America, then intrenched it in the U.S. economy; guaranteeing his decendents would benefit financially from the destruction of human lives. The Rockerfellas profited from the Civil War and they continue to profit from the deaths of unsuspecting victums.

What past Presidents had to say about the Jesuits!

To understand the 'deception' (Genesis 3:1), one must understand the playing field, the rules, the strategy, the history, and most importantly the biography of each of the players. In the area of health and wellness, because of the importance to the economy and the financial gain to a few, the general public has unfortunately become mere pawns in the hands of the ruling elite. Who are the 'ruling elite' of the health maintenance arena, and what are their origins and more importantly what are their bloodlines? Who were and are they today?

"Unless we put medical freedom into the Constitution, the time will come when medicine will organize into an undercover dictatorship…To restrict the art of healing to one class of men and deny equal privileges to others will constitute the Bastille of medical science. All such laws are un-American and despotic and have no place in a republic… The Constitution of this republic should make special privilege for medical freedom as well as religious freedom."

-Benjamin Rush, M.D., Signer of the Declaration of Independence, Physician to George Washington, President.

As an American we know that in 1776 the Declaration of Independence was written. Yet not so many of us recall that in that same year 1776, Adam Smith wrote "Wealth of Nations" which was the foundational work for Capitalism and the great Industrial Revolution. Fewer of us still know that in the same year 1776, Adam Weishuapt, a Jesuit organized the Illuminati, which set the goals, aims and methods for the one world government, through what we know today as Communism. Isn't it interesting that almost all history books tell us about the first great event. A number speak of the second. But hardly any even eludes to the last. Let me share an interesting fact with you out of an old Encyclopedia Britannica, 1910 edition. This edition is to old for most of you to recall, but it actually talks about the Illuminati. By the way it is a term that you will have a hard time finding in present day encyclopedias, wonder why?

Anyway the 1910 edition states: "a short term movement of Republican free thought, to who's adherence the name Illuminati was given. Was founded on May Day, 1776, by Adam Weishaupt, professor of cannon law, at Ingolstadt University, an ex-Jesuit." Weishaupt may or may not have divorced him self from the Jesuits. In the book "History of the Freemasonry, by Gould, he remarks, "Weishaupt has unconsciously imbibed that most pernicious doctrine of the Jesuits, that the "end Justifies the means."

Have you heard the story of the scorpion that asked the turtle for a ride on its back across the lake? The turtle said no but the scorpion stated that if I stung you we will both drown. So the turtle agreed and half way across the lake the scorpion stung the turtle. Just before the turtle went under the water, it asked the scorpion why you stung me. The scorpion replied, it's just my nature! While it is true, the Vatican, the United States and its allies will eventually defeat its enemies, the United States will pay a huge price; it will repudiate every principle of its constitution. Read and understand Revelation chapter 13. It is a prophecy almost complete concerning the Papacy, the United States and apostate Protestantism.

 Ex-President John Adams wrote to his successor, Thomas Jefferson: "I do not like the reappearance of the Jesuits. If ever there was a body of men who merit eternal damnation on earth... it is this society..."

"Like you, I disapprove of the restoration of the Jesuits, for it means a step backwards from light into darkness."

-President Thomas Jefferson

"The very moment that popery assumed the right of life and death on a citizen of France, Spain, Germany, England, or the United States, it assumes to be the power, the government of that country. Those states then committed a suicidal act by allowing popery to put a foot on their territory with the privilege of citizenship. The power of life and death is the supreme power, and two supreme powers cannot exist on the same territory without anarchy, riots, bloodshed, and civil wars. When popery will give up the power to life and death which it proclaims as its own divine power in all its theological books and canon laws, then, and then alone, it can be tolerated and can receive the privileges of citizenship in a free country. Is it not an absurdity to give to a man a thing, which he has sworn to hate, curse, and destroy? And does not the Catholic Church of Rome hate, curse, and destroy liberty of conscience whenever she can do it safely? I am for liberty of conscience in its noblest, broadest, highest sense. But I cannot give liberty of conscience to the pope and his followers, the papists so long as they tell me, through all their councils, theologians, and canon laws, that their conscience orders them to burn my wife, strangle my children, and cut my throat when they find their opportunity" Abraham Lincoln as quoted in the book 50 Years in the Church of Rome, by Charles Chiniquy, a Catholic Priest.

However, today few remember that it was the Vatican, the Pope and the papists that were instrumental in the assassination of President Lincoln, which is why congress passed the law in 1868 cutting all ties with the Vatican.

..." there is a power so organized, so subtle, so pervasive, that they had better not speak above their breath in condemnation of it."

-President Woodrow Wilson

However, within months of President Reagan's inaugural in 1981, it became known that he was looking into the challenges of establishing full diplomatic relations with the Vatican. One of the first steps taken

by President Reagan was to obtain the repeal of the 1868 law which prohibited the expenditure of funds for an Embassy to the Vatican. He was successful in obtaining the repeal. There was no real opposition, and this was interpreted as a favorable sign for those who favored full diplomatic relations. On June 7, 1982, a historic meeting took place between President Reagan and Pope John Paul II in Vatican City. Pleased and inspired by the Pope's open and unwavering support for the Solidarity movement in Poland and his open defiance of Communist rule, Reagan sought the counsel of the Pontiff regarding the question of freedom in Eastern Europe. From that point on, the United States and the Vatican began to work ever more closely on their shared objective of defeating the Soviet menace. When that happened, Pope John Paul II made the statement, "They can't stop us now." President Reagan moved quickly and on January 10, 1984, announced that full diplomatic relations between the United States and the Vatican had been established. The President did this over the opposition of the office of the Secretary of State.

Concordant (-kôr′dặt), n. 1. A compact; covenant. 2. An agreement between the Pope and a government for regulation of ecclesiastical matters.

Ecclesiastical (-tĭ-kặl), a. Of or pertaining to the church or its organization or government; not secular.

Have you noticed your churches worship service, baptism and communion resembling the catholic format?

Character and Aims of the Papacy

The defenders of popery declare that she has been maligned; and the Protestant world is inclined to accept the statement. Many urge that it is unjust to judge the Church of to-day by the abominations and absurdities that marked her reign during the centuries of ignorance and darkness. They excuse her horrible cruelty as the result of the barbarism of the times, and plead that civilization has changed her sentiments. Have these persons forgotten the claim of infallibility put forth for eight hundred years by this haughty power? So far from being relinquished, this claim was affirmed in the nineteenth century with greater positiveness than ever before. As Rome asserts that the "church never erred; nor will it, according to the Scriptures, ever err" (John L. von Mosheim, Institutes of Ecclesiastical History, book 3, century II, part 2, chapter 2, section 9, note 17), how can she renounce the principles which governed her course in past ages? The papal church will never relinquish her claim to infallibility. All that she has done in her persecution of those who reject her dogmas she holds to be right; and would she not repeat the same acts, should the opportunity be presented? Let the restraints now imposed by secular governments be removed and Rome be reinstated in her former power, and there would speedily be a revival of her tyranny and persecution, (See Rev. 13:1-9). A recent writer[1 JOSIAH STRONG, D.D., IN "OUR COUNTRY," PP. 46-48.] speaks thus of the attitude of the papal hierarchy as regards freedom of conscience, and of the perils which especially threaten the United States from the success of her policy:--"There are many who are disposed to attribute any fear of Roman Catholicism in the United States to bigotry or childishness. Such see nothing in the character and attitude of Romanism that is hostile to our free institutions, or find nothing portentous in its growth. Let us, then, first compare some of the fundamental principles of our government with those of the Catholic Church."

"The Constitution of the United States guarantees liberty of conscience. Nothing is dearer or more fundamental. Pope Pius IX, in his Encyclical Letter of August 15, 1854, said: the absurd and erroneous doctrines or ravings in defense of liberty of conscience are a most pestilential error--a pest, of all others, most to be dreaded in a state.' The same pope, in his Encyclical Letter of December 8, 1864, anathematized `those who assert the liberty of conscience and of religious worship,' also 'all such as maintain that the church may not employ force.' "The pacific tone of Rome in the United States does not imply a change of heart. She is tolerant where she is helpless. Says

Bishop O'Connor: 'Religious liberty is merely endured until the opposite can be carried into effect without peril to the Catholic world.'. . . The archbishop of St. Louis once said: 'Heresy and unbelief are crimes; and in Christian countries, as in Italy and Spain, for instance, where all the people are Catholics, and where the Catholic religion is an essential part of the law of the land, they are punished as other crimes.'. . .

"Every cardinal, archbishop, and bishop in the Catholic Church takes an oath of allegiance to the pope, in which occur the following words: 'Heretics, schismatics, and rebels to our said lord (the pope), or his aforesaid successors, I will to my utmost persecute and oppose.'"-- Josiah Strong, Our Country, ch. 5, pars. 2-4.

It is true that there are real Christians in the Roman Catholic communion. Thousands in that church are serving God according to the best light they have... They have never seen the contrast between a living heart service and a round of mere forms and ceremonies. God looks with pitying tenderness upon these souls, educated as they are in a faith that is delusive and unsatisfying. He will cause rays of light to penetrate the dense darkness that surrounds them. He will reveal to them the truth as it is in Jesus, and many will yet take their position with His people.

Protestants have tampered with and patronized popery; they have made compromises and concessions which papists themselves are surprised to see and fail to understand. Men are closing their eyes to the real character of Romanism and the dangers to be apprehended from her supremacy. The people need to be aroused to resist the advances of this most dangerous foe to civil and religious liberty. The Great Controversy, 1888, by Ellen White, p. 563-566.

The Catholic Church recently elected a Jesuit as its Pope. Pope Francis is the first Jesuit pope. As this pope has become very popular, like his predecessor John Paul the II. It is clear that his reforms have made him a success with Catholics and Protestants alike. For example, he publically stated he did not want to live in the official housing designated for the popes, riding the bus instead of the pope-mobile, visiting prisons and washing the feet of some of the inmates, visiting hospitals and championing the cause of the poor and those on the margin of society. It seems that Pope Francis is living his life according to the book "The Great Controversy". Concerning the pope's antics, we read:

… At this time the order of the Jesuits was created, the most cruel, unscrupulous, and powerful of all the champions of popery. Cut off from earthly ties and human interests, dead to the claims of natural affection, reason and conscience wholly silenced, they knew no rule, no tie, but that of their order, and no duty but to extend its power… There was no crime too great for them to commit, no deception too base for them to practice, no disguise too difficult for them to assume. Vowed to perpetual poverty and humility, it was their studied aim to secure wealth and power, to be devoted to the overthrow of Protestantism, and the re-establishment of the papal supremacy. Great Controversy, by Ellen White, pg. 234.

When appearing as members of their order, they wore a garb of sanctity, visiting prisons and hospitals, ministering to the sick and the poor, professing to have renounced the world, and bearing the sacred name of Jesus, who went about doing good. But under this blameless exterior the most criminal and deadly purposes were often concealed. It was a fundamental principle of the order that the end justifies the means. By this code, lying, theft, perjury, assassination, were not only pardonable but commendable, when they served the interests of the church. Under various disguises the Jesuits worked their way into offices of state, climbing up to be the counselors of kings, and shaping the policy of nations. They became servants to act as spies upon their masters. They established colleges for the sons of princes and nobles, and schools for the common people; and the children of Protestant parents were drawn into an observance of popish rites. All the outward pomp and display of the Romish worship was brought to bear to confuse the mind and dazzle and captivate the imagination, and thus the liberty for which the fathers had toiled and bled was betrayed by the sons. Great Controversy, by Ellen White, pg. 235.

Now you know that Pope Francis is only doing what Jesuits do, with the motive of overthrowing Protestantism and reestablishment of the papal supremacy. Diplomatic relations had been severed by the U.S. Congress on June 13th, 1867 over Vatican involvement and engineering in the assassination of President Abraham Lincoln. Has anyone ever asked why Reagan reinstated official diplomatic ties with the Vatican? The State Department refuses Freedom of Information Act (FOIA) requests to release the USA - Vatican Treaty. Why? All other U.S. treaties with other countries are available, why is this one top secret? Protestants should be foremost in demanding to see an original copy of this Concordat (treaty)!

The ugly looking character with horns (below, upper left picture) is commonly referred to as the "Goat of Mendes" or "Baphomet". For those in the ccult he's known as the "horned god" or the "god of the witches",   because   that's   what   he   is   to   them: god!

Without a doubt, the "goat headed pentagram" is a powerful symbol to both Satanist and witches, but yet we're starting to see it surface in our "Christian" political system of today. So, why is this? (Note the upside down stars in Hillary's American flag and the Republican Party elephant. See for yourself, Google or Bing Republican and/or Democratic Party Symbols. Wake up Christians, Jesus never interfered or participated in the political affairs of Rome or Jerusalem.

William Avery "Doc" Rockefeller

Soon after the 30 Years' War, one such influential Jesuit/Jewish family moved to America. In 1722, the family of Johann Roggenfeder sold their Austrian mill and came to America. A few decades later, the family changed their surname too "Rockefeller" to sound more American. Here is the birth of an incredible empire with complete loyalties to the Vatican and Kenite bloodlines.

William Avery Rockefeller, also known as "Doc" settled in Rockford, Upstate New York, were son John D. was born in 1839. William Avery "Doc" Rockefeller received the nickname "Devil Bill" from his neighbors because he constantly held séances and was deeply involved in witchcraft. He was merely practicing the craft his Jesuit mentors had taught him. Between 1818 and 1830 in Upstate New York, Rockefeller without any medical education or training, advertised himself as "Doctor William A. Rockefeller, the Celebrated Cancer Specialist", and made a small fortune selling a blend of crude oil and alcohol (whiskey) as a "Medicinal Cure-all Tonic".

William Rockefeller was also a convicted horse thief, rapist, and polygamist, having at least two wives and two separate homes under different names. His poster on his wagon as he went from town to town claimed "All cases of cancer cured, unless too far gone, and they can be greatly benefited. His son John D. learned "Doc's" trade very well. God's Gold, The Story of Rockefeller and His Times, by Flynn, 1932.

To the left you see a Seneca Indian head on one side of the bottle, and a Caduceus symbol of "magical sorcery." Remember, The Caduceus symbol was used in Del Rio book of magical sorcery (pharmakeia), taken from the Chaldeans of the Uruk period well before 3000 B.C. Doc's miracle Seneca oil sold for $25.00 dollars a bottle, and was soon nicknamed "Snake Oil" and the Caduceus became the symbol of the medical profession. Doc Bill's medical cure-all tonic was called Seneca oil because of the symbols on his bottles.

John D. Rockefeller July 8, 1839 – May 23, 1937

John was 22 years old in 1862 when the civil war began and he already had amassed quite a significant fortune selling whiskey in his father's business. He saw a great opportunity to sell his whiskey to the soldiers of both the North and South, and paid a substitute to enlist by proxy in the Union army, serving in his stead. At the close of the war, John D. was one of America's first multi-millionaires, and it all came from selling countless barrels of "medicinal whiskey" to the surgeons of the Civil War. From New York to California, John D. quietly controlled the majority of whiskey distilleries operating in America. In prohibition years the Rockefellers consolidated their cartel and dealt in opium dens across the country. Remember, William Avery "Doc" Rockefeller's original formula was to combine high grade crude oil with alcohol. Doc taught his son, John D. very well and he continued blending crude oil with alcohol to make millions. In 1859, in Clarion, PA, the first U.S. oil field was discovered by Colonel Edwin Drake. John D. quickly formed an alliance with Drake, eventually purchasing his holdings and formed Standard Oil Company in 1870. What happened next established Standard Oil as the undisputed champ of the world, in the oil industry. John D. establishes a secret society with Kenite Jesuit/Jewish brethren. The Southern Improvement Company was the fore runner of the Standard Oil Company. Everybody involved with the company was sworn to the strictest secrecy. Men were warned not to even tell their wives of their activities. J.P. Morgan and the Rothschild Bank already acquired the railroads and they were giving illegal rebates to the S.I. Co. This had the effect of ruining the small, independent oil refiners and forcing them to sell out at a tremendous loss or face financial ruin. The Southern Company was the forerunner of Standard Oil. It was chartered in Cleveland, Ohio, and was a front for the "counter-Reformation" Rothschild Bank, S.I.C.'s sphere of activity was virtually limitless. History of the Standard Oil Company, Vol. 1, by Ida Tarbell, pages 56 and 75.

The Empire Takes Shape

Other oil strikes were made in Ohio, Oklahoma, Texas, Kansas, Arkansas, Colorado, Montana, California, and the last great find was in Alaska. Using his whiskey profits, Rockefeller moved quickly to purchase controlling shares in all proven oil fields. Research began in developing oil based products of every kind and variety. In 1883, Rockefeller moves his empire to New York City and builds a massive Trust or Holding Company at 26 Broadway. John D. Rockefeller was one of the world's first multi-billionaires, as oil was manufactured into kerosene and used to fuel lamps and lanterns.

By 1880, the Rockefeller/Vatican Standard Oil cartel completely dominated the world kerosene market. The only rival to Rockefeller was the Russian market founded by a Swede named Robert Nobel, of the Nobel Prize family. Rapid growth in the Russian oil production had been achieved despite political upheavals that had enveloped the country since the turn of the century, much of which had been centered in the country's oil capital, Baku. Strikes by oil workers had been a regular feature of the protest against the Tsar in 1903 and 1904, and were a major factor in the 1905 revolution, in which the former Josef Dzhugashvilli played a significant, anti Tsarist role. As a result of his revolutionary activity that he fostered in Baku, Dzhugashvilli was exiled to Siberia. Later he would become better known as Josef Stalin. With the invention and eventual globalization of Ford automobiles, Fueled by Rockefeller oil, John D. Rockefeller became the world's second richest man, second only to Armschel Rothschild. Aware that the Rothschilds are an important Jewish family, I looked them up in Encyclopedia Judaica and discovered that they bear the title 'Guardians of the Vatican Treasury'... The appointment of Rothschild gave the black papacy absolute financial privacy and secrecy. Who would ever search a family of orthodox Jews for the key to the wealth of the Roman Catholic Church? –F. Tupper Saussy, Rulers of evil, Harper Collins, page 160, 161.

United States Government Investigates Standard Oil
On May 15, 1911, the Supreme Court of the United States ruled that the Standard Oil Cartel was a "menace to the Republic" and ordered it to be broken up. For the safety of the Republic we (the U.S. Supreme Court) now decree that the dangerous conspiracy must be ended by November 15, 1911. (John D. a Portrait in Oils, page 154). Rockefeller vowed revenge against the U.S. Government and used his vast fortune to buy and control the U.S. government-just as he had the Kremlin.

The breakup of Standard Oil monolith resulted in approximately 37 new companies. Rockefeller still secretly controlled them all by owning a voting majority of stock in the new corporations. Thus Standard Oil would become known as Standard Oil of New Jersey (Exxon), Standard Oil of New York (Mobil), Standard Oil of Indiana (Amoco), Standard Oil of California (Chevron), Atlantic Refining (Arco), etc, etc. It was business as usual at 26 Broadway –the headquarters of the giant. It was at this point in American history that a few wealthy men began to systematically, physically and legally restrict the rights of other healing professions, including Christian natural doctors. There were more natural healing practitioners than medical doctors at this time, but all that was soon to change.

Andrew Carnegie and John D. Rockefeller: John 8:44.

"The concept of specific, unchanging types of bacteria causing specific diseases became officially accepted as the foundation of Western medicine and microbiology in the late 18th century Europe. Also called *monomorphism* (one-formism), it was adopted by America's medical/industrial complex, which began to take shape near the turn of the century (1900).

This cartel became organized around the American Medical Association, formed by drug interests for the purpose of manipulating the legal system to destroy other competing health care disciplines, including God's natural way of healing. Controlled by pharmaceutical companies, the complex has become a trillion-dollar-a-year business. It also includes many insurance companies, the Food and Drug Administration (FDA), the National Institutes of Health (NIH), and the Center for Disease Control (CDC), hospitals, and university research facilities." Sick, Tired 2001, Robert Young, p. 23.

Beginning in 1901, we will see how Rockefeller and Carnegie have shaped modern medicine today. The late John D. Rockefeller set out to take control of American education, primarily medicine, secondly law. The American medical profession at this time was very independent and filled to overflowing with internal and external problems. Many of these problems health writers of that age wrote about, including Christian health educator, Mrs. Ellen White. The Trustees of the

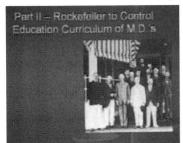

General Education Board, the first Rockefeller foundation pictured at a retreat in Rockland, Maine, in July 1915. Front row, from left: Edward A. Alderman, Frederick T. Gates (former president of Harvard Univ.), Harry Pratt Judson (president of Chicago Univ.), Wallace Buttrick (executive officer of the Board), Second row, from left: Wickliffe Rose (head of the Rockefeller public health programs), Hollis B. Fressil, John D. Rockefeller, Jr. E.C. Sage, Albert Shaw, Abraham Flexner, Third row, from left: George E. Vincent (president of the Rockefeller Foundation), Anson Phelps Stokes, Starr J. Murphy, and Jerome D. Greene on Rockefeller's board, which was separate from the General Education Board, he gathered such politically oriented men as Dr. L.E. Holt; Christian A. Hearder, who later became Secretary of State under President Eisenhower, T.M. Prudent, Herman M. Brigg, William H. Welch, Theobolt Smith, and Simon Flexner. It so happened that Simon Flexner had a brother named Abraham who was on the staff of the Carnegie Foundation for the advancement of teaching. This brought the foundations into a much closer union and enabled them to unite their efforts to take control of the unsuspecting medical professions.

Prior to 1910, the medical professions were in poor condition and had a rather poor public image. Many men wanted to see a change and a better degree of respectability. The American Medical Association (AMA), which had formed in 1847, by namely three men, Dr. George Simmon, Dr. Reed and Dr. J.N. McCormick were also interested in cleaning up its reputation, too. The men organized a council on medical education and tried to make recommendations for improving the profession. By 1908 it had run into committee differences and lacked sufficient funds to continue. It was at this time, in 1908, that Rockefeller and Carnegie combined efforts and moved with brilliant strategy upon the scene. The president of the Carnegie Foundation told the AMA that they would take over the entire project. From the minutes of the meetings of the AMA council held in New York, City in December of 1908, we find that the Carnegie Foundation was to investigate "all the professions; law, medicine, and theology." As a Christian Health Restoration practitioner, I am interested in informing the public concerning the medical aspect of that investigation and findings, and its effect upon the American public today, especially the healthcare consumer. I encourage others in the legal and religious arenas to investigate their professions and share with the public their findings; you will be absolutely amazed at the findings of such research. Mr. Flexner, see appendix C, evidently was the one who wrote the final report which notes the findings of the investigation. This report became known as the Flexner report. It was determined, according to the report, to upgrade the inadequacies of medical education. It also made suggestions for sweeping changes, most of which were sound. This gained the AMA tremendous public support.

However, it should be noted that two of the suggestions later turned out to be hooks and to this day, the American healthcare consumer is paying a hefty price in terms of both outlay of capital and human pain, suffering and death. "Two of these recommendations were to emphatically strengthen the area of pharmacology and bring in the addition of research departments to all medical school. That is all medical school that "qualified." The primary test for the medical school standing or falling was its willingness to accept foundation influence and control. The end result was that all medical schools became heavily oriented toward drugs and drug research, for it was through the increased sales of these drugs that the donors realized a profit on their donations." World Without Cancer, by G. Edwards Griffin, p. 286, 287.

Dr. Simon Flexner

"The Flexner solution was a simple one; to make medical education so elitist and expensive, and drawn out, that most students would be prohibited from even considering a medical career. The Flexner program set up requirements for a four-year undergraduate college, a further four years of medical school. His report also setup complex requirements for their medical schools; they must have expensive laboratories and other equipment. As the requirements of the Flexner report became effective, the number of medical schools was rapidly reduced. By the end of World War I, the number of medical schools had been reduced from 650 to a mere 50 in number. The number of annual graduates had been reduced from 7500 to 2500. The enactment of the Flexner restrictions virtually guaranteed that the medical monopoly in the United States would result in a small group of elitist students from well to do families, and that this small group would be subjected to intense control," Murder by Injection, Eustace Mullins, p. 11,12.

Historian Joseph Golden put it this way, "Flexner had the ideas, Rockefeller and Carnegie had the money and their marriage was spectacular." Now let's look at a couple of little hooks I alluded to earlier. The schools that were to receive the large grants, and as a result, keep their doors open, were required to enter the field of drug medication and also the field of drug research. Remembering that chemicals are the foundation of most drugs and Rockefeller was then the top man of Standard Oil in America, it does not take a lot of imagination to know where he was going. He was not the kind of man who would give away a dollar unless he could get five in return, at least so, history reveals.

David Hopgood, writing in 1969 in the Washington Monthly, said this in reference to where we have come today, or since the Rockefeller, and Carnegie dream. "The medical school curriculum and its entrance requirements are geared to the highly academic student who is headed for research. In the increasingly desperate struggle for admission these academically talented students are crowding out those who want to practice medicine."

According to G.E. Griffin, in his book World without Cancer states "and so it has come to past that the teaching staff of all our medical schools are a very special breed. In the selection and training process, a heavy emphasis has been put on finding individuals who have been attracted by the field of research and especially by research in pharmacology. This has resulted in loading the staffs of our medical schools with men and women who by preference and by training are propagators of the drug oriented science that has come to dominate American medicine."

Rockefeller's Standard Oil Unites with Germany's I.G. Farben

The I.G. Farben Industrial Corporation came into being in 1926 primarily under the auspices of two men, a German industrialist and a Swiss banker. From the beginning the leaders of I.G. Farben have been an integral part of the international banking structure. According to the U.S. Department of Justice, U.S. District Court of New Jersey, on May 14, 1942, the following report was given:

"I. G. Farben is the largest chemical company in the world and part of the most gigantic and powerful Cartel of all history." Now do you see what Mr. John D. Rockefeller Sr. had in mind when in 1928 he interlocked his own financial empire with I.G. Farben. By the way, I.G. Farben is both drug oriented and munitions oriented. Perhaps that explains why during World War II, the massive I.G. Farben complex located in Frankfurt, Germany, was left standing without a scratch.

American and allied air force pilots were ordered not to drop a single bomb on I.G. Farben. Drug medication was the payload, and drug research was the tool needed to promote it. During the Nuremberg trials, it was learned that the business leaders of I.G. Farben actually had controlled the Nazi state. I.G. Farben operated such concentration camps as Auschwitz and Buchenwald.

It is also important to note that during World War II, the Nazis moved their headquarters into I.G. Farben's complex. Could a deal have been struck and the Nazis knew they were safe within I.G. Farben? Medical schools supported by the political AMA which was no more than a figurehead, defended its men in the use and abuse of chemicals. Today, health care in America is a $1.4 trillion industry, or one-seventh of the U.S. economy.

By the early 1930's, Rockefeller chemists had unlocked many "secrets" from the Benzene molecular structure of petroleum. They found a way to create "synthetic rubber" out of oil, and had secured patents on hundreds of unique "drugs" manufactured by the subsidiary pharmaceutical firms of petroleum.

The world was now operating on an oil-based economy, and U.S. Medical Schools were training "physicians" to become peddlers for benzene-derived drugs. This is why Rockefeller funded "education foundations" and "Boards of Regents" and completely controlled the Medical School curriculum by the 1940's. Any school not wishing to follow Rockefeller protocols, were denied funding and ceased to exist. "Snake oil" was now mainstream. One more additional sidelight will help you see how deep the hook went into the unsuspecting medical field when the medical schools took the bait of Rockefeller and Carnegie grants.

Morris A. Beale puts it this way: "Concerning the Rockefellers, "Old Bill" Rockefeller, itinerant pappy of John D. (the first) and a patent medicine showman used to palm off bottled raw petroleum... a cure for cancer... in selling raw petroleum in a pretty bottle, "Old Bill" did nothing new; he merely took a page out of the book of other patent medicine fakirs who were then hawking their wares from the back of wagons. When oil was discovered in Northwest Pennsylvania (1850), the jackals of the oil trade found there was more gold in the jeans of gullible yokels than there was in working for it in the oil fields.

They began to bottle the raw petroleum and palm it off under various names as a cure for everything under the sun... "Old Bill" opened up a new field for himself. He called his bottled petroleum "Nujol" (meaning new oil) and sold it to those who had cancer and those whom he could make fear they would have it. This sounded good to Standard Oil researchers. It sounded better when they found out it cost about $2.00 a barrel to concoct Nujol from crude petroleum, and that one barrel of the raw stuff could make 1,000 six-ounce bottles of the finished Nujol. The druggist... pays about 21 cents for a six-ounce bottle of Nujol which cost Standard Oil 1/5 of a cent.

The breath-taking profits from Nujol made it inevitable that America's largest and most ruthless industrial cartel (The Rockefeller Empire) should soon add the drug traffic to its already vast production and sales domain", The Drug Story, Morris A. Beale, p. 5, 6.

What the average person does not understand is that the world's elite do not have an allegiance to any country, but only wealth, power, and control. Just as the Ford Motor Company sold jeeps to the American and allies during the World Wars, Ford also sold them to the Nazi. "If you are in the oil business, trillions of dollars can be made by supplying armies, navies, and air forces with petroleum products (or with holding them to their defeat or collapse, example Japan WWII). In short, control the petroleum resources driving the war machinery, and you control the eventual outcome of the war, and eventually you control the world.

The second most vital, wealth-creating industry in the world is health and wellness-and this is of course tied directly to war. "Health is mankind's "carrot", while war is the "stick" the overlords use to keep the [sheeple] loyal and in fear. The son of "Doc" Rockefeller created the most powerful and successful "Secret Syndicate" the world has ever known. The Twin Towers in New York City were affectionately named "David and Nelson" [Rockefeller] because David and Nelson were the driving force behind their construction. Immediately after the very public planned demolition of the "Towers" on September 11, 2001, the Rockefeller-Syndicate controlled Pentagon invaded Afghanistan and set up U.S. bases by the Caspian Sea. Caspian Sea and Iraqi oil reserves supplying France were the only solid competition to Standard Oil since 1990 and under the disguise of the "War on Terror" the cartel could now increase prices." The Trial of the Century, by A. True Ott, Ph. D.

"Caspian Sea competition was the topic of many top level conferences at the headquarters of the Trust at 26 Broadway in New York. One of the methods of meeting the threat was price-cutting sweet crude." Rockefeller Billions, page 165.

"The truth is that the "Syndicates" cost of goods sold since 1883 include 75 million war dead from two global wars and "police actions" plus the millions of innocent who die each year from "Cancer" and other "diseases" that could be helped immensely by honest nutrition-based therapies and honest public education on nutrition". The Trial of the Century, A. True Ott, Ph. D.

I would add that nutrition is only one of God's ten laws of health, which will be discussed in part two.

The Word of God Concerning Drugs
"The avoidance of drugs can certainly postpone your date with the undertaker. The drug scene is producing problems no one seems to know how to solve. We all recognize the dangers inherent in the amphetamines, barbiturates, cocaine, morphine, marijuana and others. We all recognize this and are working to this end; but I am thinking now of a problem which may be as bad as or worse than the above. This is the problem of prescription drugs". Raymond L. Knoll, M.D.
How to Live to be 101 and be Able to Enjoy It.
Because of Pharmakeia (see definition below), the Christian world has swallowed the Rockefeller and Carnegie bait hook, line, and sinker.

Because the world holds medicine up based upon science, the Christian church believes it is approved by God. If science is not based upon the word of God, then Paul tells us it is science so falsely called "O Timothy, keep that which is committed to thy trust, avoiding profane [and] vain babblings, and oppositions of science falsely so called: 1 Timothy 6:20. Remember Babylonian medicines, foods, clothing, and sicknesses are for Babylonians. God does not paint a pretty picture of His church. In Revelation 3: 14-22.

God calls His church, in these last days, Laodicea, meaning "Judging of the People." If we do not repent He will spew us out of His mouth, Rev. 3:15. In Matthew 25, just before His second coming, His church is found asleep. All because… "for thy merchants were the great men of the earth; for by thy <u>sorceries</u> were all nations deceived." Revelation 18:23. Let's define the word Pharmakeia from God's perspective.

Pharmakeia

Taken from "Strong's Exhaustive Concordance of the Bible
53231 Rev. 18:23 – Pharmakeia, far-mak-I-ah; medication ("***pharmacy***"), i.e. (by extens.) Magic (lit. or fig.): Sorcery, Witchcraft.
5332 Rev. 18:21 – Pharmakon, (from Pharmakeus) (A ***drug,*** i.e. spell giving potion) a ***druggist, Pharmacist or poisoner***, i.e. (by extens.) A magician; -a sorcerer.
5333 Rev. 22:15 – Pharmakos; the same as 5332 – sorcerer.
3095 Acts 8:11 – Mageia – from 3096 – "magic" – sorcery.
3096 Acts 8:9 – Mageno – from 3097; to practice "magic"; sorcery.
3097 Magos – of for or [7248] a **Magician,** i.e. **Oriental scientist**; by implication a magician: -sorcerer, a wise man. (See Acts 13:6, 8).
7248 Rab-Mag: from 7227 and a for word for a Magician: Chief Magician; Rab-Mag, A Babylonian official; Rab-Mag.
7227 Rab; by contr. From 7231 abundant (in quantity, size, age, number, rank, quality): -(in) abound (-ance, ant, antlyo   captain, elder, enough, exceedingly, full, great. (-ly, man,one), increase, long, (enough, [time]), (do, have) many (-ifold, things, a time, ([ship-] master, mighty, more, (too, very) much, multiply (-tude), officer, often [-times], plenteous, populous, prince, process [of time], suffice 9-ient).
3785 Kesheph; from 3784-magic: sorcery, witchcraft. (See Isaiah 47:9, 12).
3784 Kashaph; a prim. Root; prop: to whisper a Spell, i.e. to Inchant or practice magice: a Sorcerer, (use) witch (-craft. (See Exodus 7:11 and Daniel 2:2).

3786   Kashshaph; from 3784 –a magician: Sorcerer.

6049   'Anan: a prim. Root: to cover; used only a denom from 6051 to cloud over; fig. To act covertly, i.e. practice Magic:-X bring, Enchanter.

2748   Chartom; from the same as 2747; a Horoscopist: (as drawing magical lines or circles): -magician.

2749   Chartom-(Chaldean) same as 2748:-Magician.

Medical Marijuana

Today, most of the world is demanding medical marijuana and the legalizing of recreational marijuana. State Marijuana Laws in 2017 Map - Governing magazine Seven **states** and the District of Columbia have adopted the most expansive laws legalizing marijuana for recreational use. Most recently, California, Massachusetts, Maine and Nevada all passed measures in November legalizing **recreational marijuana**. California's Prop. 64 measure allows adults 21 and older to possess ... www.governing.com/gov-data/state-marijuana-laws-map-medical-recreational.html

Marijuana has now gone from being medical to recreational and it is sad to write but even nominal Christians think that God accepts the use of marijuana in any form, especially since it alters the Frontal Lobe of the brain.

What is marijuana?

Marijuana—also called *weed, herb, pot, grass, bud, ganja, Mary Jane*, and a vast number of other slang terms—is a greenish-gray mixture of the dried flowers of *Cannabis sativa*. Some people smoke marijuana in hand-rolled cigarettes called *joints*; in pipes, water pipes (sometimes called *bongs*), or in *blunts* (marijuana rolled in cigar (wraps).[1]

Marijuana can also be used to brew tea and, particularly when it is sold or consumed for medicinal purposes, is frequently mixed into foods (*edibles*) such as brownies, cookies, or candies. Vaporizers are also increasingly used to consume marijuana. Stronger forms of marijuana include sinsemilla (from specially tended female plants) and concentrated resins containing high doses of marijuana's active ingredients, including honeylike *hash oil*, waxy *budder*, and hard amber like *shatter*. These resins are increasingly popular among those who use them both recreationally and medically. The main *Psycho-active* (mind-altering) chemical in marijuana, responsible for most of the intoxicating effects that people seek, is *delta-9-tetrahydrocannabinol* (THC). The chemical is found in resin produced by the leaves and buds primarily of the female cannabis plant. The plant also contains more than 500 other chemicals, including more than 100 compounds that are chemically related to THC, called *cannabinoids*.[2]

Globally, marijuana (cannabis) is the most commonly used illicit drug. Classified as a Schedule 1 controlled substance, marijuana is a mood-altering (psychoactive) drug that affects almost every organ in the body.

October 20, 2016

New research is providing a more detailed view into the structure of the human cannabinoid (CB_1) receptor. These findings provide key insights into how natural and synthetic cannabinoids including tetrahydrocannabinol (THC)—a primary chemical in marijuana—bind at the CB_1 receptor to produce their effects. The research was funded by the National Institute on Drug Abuse (NIDA), part of the National Institutes of Health. There is considerable interest in the possible therapeutic uses of marijuana and its constituent cannabinoid compounds. Molecules that target CB_1receptors may have promise in treating a variety of conditions such as pain, inflammation, obesity, nerve cell diseases, and substance use disorders. However, some synthetic cannabinoids such as K2 or Spice can produce severe and even deadly reactions, whereas other cannabinoids produce less serious side effects.

Concerning seizures and medical marijuana, when I was in my early 30's and Naturopathy had not entered my mind yet. I was driving down the street when I was startled by strange sounds my 6 or 7 year old son was making in the back seat. As I turned my head and looked over my shoulder, to my amazement, I saw a contorted face and a body violently convulsing. I immediately turned off the road and held my son, calmly talking to him trying to understand what was happening to him. I immediately made an appointment with the Naturopathic doctor who healed my pancreas. He did several tests, including live blood cell analysis (darkfield microscope). The doctor worked on improving his blood quality, changed his diet to vegetarian and placed him on a regiment of supplements. As long as he was on the program, he was seizure free but when he cheated or deviated, he would have a seizure. One night he had a seizure that frightened his mother, ended him up in the emergency room of Emmanuel Hospital and he was diagnosed with Grand Maul seizures. Back then marijuana was not an option and my son controlled his seizures naturally to the point he has not had one in over 25 years.

As with all drug medication, K2 or Spice comes with sever and even deadly reactions. From the word of God we know that on the sixth day of creation God pronounced everything "very good" Genesis 1:31. I other words there were no thorns on roses, no noxious weeds or even weeds, no toxins or mind altering chemicals in plants, etc… it is only after sin that this blights on creation came into existence.

How do I know this? Because God said it "very good" and Isaiah confirms it "They shall not hurt nor destroy in all my holy mountain: for the earth shall be full of the knowledge of the LORD, as the waters cover the sea," Isaiah 11:9. The problem is that nominal Christians think that they have a correct knowledge of God. Secondly, because our example Jesus Christ did not use, not even once in His healing, any noxious, poison, or toxic substance. That takes care of the so-called natural marijuana, but how about the synthetic cannabinoids? The answer is found in Pharmakeia earlier in the chapter. It is called sorcery and it is being legalized at an alarming rate. As marijuana negatively impacts the frontal lobe of the brain, I believe the Devil through false science is going to use it to "deceive all nations" Rev. 18:23.

I have been doing God's natural way of healing science since the late 80's and I have treated everything from Aids to cancer and everything in between, and I will state emphatically that everything that marijuana does, God's herbs do without the negative effect on the frontal lobe of the brain. We have to admit that when we get sick it is because we have violated one or more of God's natural laws of health designed to help and protect the body. Then we want a quick fix and put our trust in man with his false science. Satan steals our usefulness to worship and serve the Lord then we accept our Laodicea condition. As Christians, we have to understand that whatever happens to us is ordained by God. He is either chastising us for our wrong and sometimes wicked ways or He is pruning us, John15. Either way, it is for us to trust God and use His healing methodologies. If you can grasp the significance of the quote below, it will change how you view adversity in your life:

"The Father's presence encircled Christ, and nothing befell Him but that which infinite love permitted for the blessing of the world. Here was His source of comfort, and it is for us. He who is imbued with the Spirit of Christ abides in Christ. The blow that is aimed at him falls upon the Saviour, who surrounds him with His presence. Whatever comes to him comes from Christ. He has no need to resist evil, for Christ is his defense. Nothing can touch him except by our

Lord's permission, and "all things" that are permitted "work together for good to them that love God." Romans 8:28. Mount of Blessings, by Ellen White, pg.71.2.

We know that above all things God wishes that we prosper and be in health. So then, if you become sick... *the curse causeless shall not come,* Prov. 26:2. Then it is because we have violated one or more of God's 10 Commandment moral law and/or His Health Laws. We know that God's divine or permissive will is for the development of your character. Therefore, we violate God's moral or health law then turn to prescription drugs and compound the problem. Consider this warning from the pen of inspiration: *"Those who give themselves up to the sorcery of Satan may boast of great benefit received thereby, but does this prove their course to be wise or safe? What if life should be prolonged? What if temporal gain should be secured? Will it pay in the end to disregard the will of God? All such apparent gain will prove at last an irrecoverable loss. We cannot with impunity break down a single barrier which God has erected to guard His people from Satan's power,"* Testimonies, volume 5, by Ellen White, pg.193-194.

By knowingly and continuing to use prescription drugs after reading this information, for God holds you accountable once you have been blessed to receive light; you are in danger of an *'irrecoverable loss.'* An irrecoverable loss is your soul's salvation and that is how serious it is and how serious God is. Protect the frontal lobe of your brain at all cost, for whom ever controls it (Christ or Satan) or to whom you surrender it to controls your destiny.

An example of how pharmaceutical companies are more concerned with profit than your health was reported by the Wall Street Journal. "Glaxo-SmithKline received a stern warning letter from the FDA over its failure to file regular reports about Avandia trials, B3. As reported by the Wall Street Journal on, Wednesday, April 9, 2008. Avandia is a diabetes drug which is under scrutiny since last year, when a study concluded that patients taking the drug had a higher risk of suffering a heart attack than those taking other oral diabetes medicine or placebo pills." The letter is posted on the FDA's web site.

The New Testament has this to say on the subject of Pharmakeia. "Now the works of the flesh are manifest, which are these, adultery, fornication, uncleanness, lasciviousness, idolatry, witchcraft," etc. Galatians 5:19, 20. So when you take Pharmakeia i.e. witchcraft, you feed the flesh causing it to war against God's spirit, verse 17. It is because Christians feed the flesh that they continue to sin and repent, sin and repent, and don't become over comers as we are told we must do in Revelation 3:21.

God does wink at our ignorance, but now He has caused the light of Truth to shine on our paths. Will we walk in the light? I am not a medical doctor or pharmacist, so I cannot tell you to take drugs or not to take drugs. However, if it is your desire to follow every Word that proceedeth out of the mouth of God, then you have to ask yourself why you are taking prescription drugs when His healing methods are far superior. It is because we have been brainwashed to believe that allopathic medicine is our only and best hope that we put our trust and faith in the religion of medicine and don't trust God?

Quotes from Christian Health Writer, Ellen White:

"Our people should become intelligent in the treatment of sickness without the aid of poisonous drugs." Medical Ministry, Pacific Press Publishing Association 1932, p. 57.

"Special instructions should be given in the art of treating the sick without the use of poisonous drugs and in harmony with the light that God has given. In the treatment of the sick, poisonous drugs need not be used." Testimonies for the Church, Vol. 9, White, Pacific Press Publishing Association 1909, p. 175.

"The dispensing of various drugs have brought their amount of wretchedness, which the day of God alone will fully reveal... These poisonous preparations have destroyed their millions, and have left suffers upon the earth to linger out a miserable existence... Miserable suffers, with disease in almost every form, misshapen by suffering, with dreadful ulcers and pains in the bones, loss of teeth, loss of memory, and impaired sight, are to be almost everywhere. They are victims of poisonous preparations, which have been, in many cases administered to cure some slight indisposition, which after a day or two of fasting would have disappeared without medicine. But poisonous mixtures, administered by physicians, have proved their ruin." Spiritual Gifts, Vol. 4, White, Review & Herald Publishing Association 1958, p. 139.

"Every pernicious drug placed in the human stomach, whether by prescription of physicians or by man himself, is doing violence to the human organism, injures the whole machinery." Selected Messages Book II, White, Pacific Press Publishing Association, p. 280-281.

"The drug science has been exalted, but if every bottle that comes from every such institution were done away with, there would be fewer

invalids in the world today. Drug medication should never have been introduced into our institutions. There was no need of this being so, and for this very reason the Lord would have us establish an institution where He can come in and where His grace and power can be revealed. 'I am the resurrection and the life,' He declares "The true method for healing the sick is to tell them of the herbs that grow for the benefit of man... True education will lead us to teach the sick that they need not call in a doctor any more than they would call a lawyer. They can themselves administer the simple herbs if necessary." Ellen White, Spalding and Megan Collection, p. 137.

"Multitudes of physicians and multitudes of drugs have cursed the inhabitants of the earth and have carried thousands and tens of thousands to untimely graves." Spiritual gifts, Vol. 4, White, Review & Herald Publishing Association, p. 133.

"Drug medication, as it is generally practiced, is a curse. Educate away from drugs. Use them less and less, and depend more upon hygienic agencies; then nature will respond to God's physicians-pure air, pure water, exercise, a clear conscience... Drugs need seldom to be used." Counsels on Health, White, Pacific Press Publishing Association, pp. 261.

Prescription Drugs

More than 10 million Americans take antidepressants and other prescription psychiatric drugs; drugs that are known to cause mental and physical agitation and spark self-destructive, violent behavior. Selective serotonin reuptake inhibitors (SSRIs) are antidepressants that affect serotonin levels in the brain. SSRI antidepressants are so hazardous that the FDA requires that they carry a black box label warning indicating they increase risk of suicidal thoughts and behavior in young people. These drugs can also induce dissocialize reactions, making those who take them insensitive to the consequences of their behavior. We can no longer afford to ignore the growing body of medical literature and clinical observations linking these medications to thousands of suicides, murders, and other brutal acts of violence. The following accounts of bizarre and destructive behavior by individuals using such drugs provide a chilling glimpse into their disastrous consequences, a hint of the damage they can, and do cause. How long can we continue to ignore their obvious dangers? What is it going to take for us to come to our senses?

School Shootings

Blackburg, VA, April 16, 2007: Seung-Hui Cho went on a rampage of violence that ended with 33 dead and more that two dozen injured, making it the most deadly shooting spree in American history. Antidepressants were found among his belongings.

Littleton, CO, April 20, 1999: Eric Harris and Dylan Klebold, armed with knives, guns, and bombs, terrorized Columbine High School, killing 13 and wounding 23 before shooting themselves. Harris was taking Luvox.

Red Lake Indian Reservation, MN, March 21, 2005: Jeffery Weise killed his grandfather and his grandfather's girlfriend, then went to Red Lake High School where he killed seven more people and wounded more than a dozen others before taking his own life. He was taking Prozac.

Springfield, OR, May 21, 1998: Kip Kinkel murdered his parents, and then proceeded to school where he killed two students and wounded more than 20 more. He was taking Prozac.

Bailey, CO, September 27, 2006: Duane Morrison went into Platte Canyon High School and took six teenage girls hostage, sexually assaulting some of them and shooting one in the head before killing himself. Antidepressant medication was found in his jeep.

Violence in the Workplace

Louisville, KY, September 14, 1989: Joseph Wesbecker marched into work with an AK-47 and other guns, killed eight employees, wounded 12, and committed suicide. He was taking Prozac.

Wakefield, MA, December 26, 2000: Michael McDermott gunned down seven of his colleagues at Edgewater Technology. He was taking Prozac.

Meridian, MS, July 8, 2003: Doug Williams opened fire on coworkers at Lockheed Martin with a 12-gauge shotgun, killing five and injuring nine others before taking his own life. He was taking Zoloft and Celexa.

Newington, CT, March 6, 1998: Disgruntled lottery accountant Matthew Beck killed four colleagues before fatally shooting himself. He was taking Luvox.

Royal Oak, MI, November 14, 1991: Ex-postal employee Thomas McIlvane shot nine people, killing three, at his former place of business before shooting himself in the head. He was taking Prozac.

Stoughton, MA, August 5, 1997: Richard Shurman fatally shot two of his business partners. He was taking Zoloft.

Brutal Murders
Huntsville, AL, March 10, 1998: Jeffery Franklin killed both of his parents with a hatchet and attempted to murder three of his younger siblings. He was taking Ritalin, Prozac, and Klonopin.

Purcell, OK, April 12, 2006: Kevin Underwood murdered and sexually assaulted a 10-year-old girl. Authorities said he had plans for cannibalism. He was taking Lexapro.

Augusta, MT, August 26, 2002: Jeanette Swanson shot and killed her two youngest children while they slept. She was taking Paxil.

Bosie, ID, September 2, 2003: Sarah Johnson shot and killed both of her parents, allegedly because they did not approve of the boy she was dating. She was taking Zoloft.

Wakefield, MA, January 10, 2001: Previously mild-mannered 81-year-old Anthony Dalesando repeatedly stabbed his wife of nearly 50 years with a kitchen knife while she slept. He was taking several medications including Prozac.

Alamogordo, NM, July 5, 2004: Fourteen-year-old Cody Posey killed his father, stepmother, and stepsister. He then hid the bodies and broke a window with an ax to suggest an intruder had committed the murders. He was taking Zoloft.

 FDA-approved drugs linked to deaths...this time Botox and Myobloc. Consider this, In America the Food and Drug Administration has approved the practice of injecting toxins under the skin to "relax"

muscles—in the hope that wrinkles will disappear. At the same time, the FDA does not allow a number of naturally sweet herbs—such as Stevia—to be sold as "sweeteners." The toxins   are on record for killing people, as demonstrated by this article, while the herb-sweeteners have health benefit histories, oftentimes dating back hundreds of years.

Y*et it is the use of toxins that is approved!* This only proves that the FDA is guided more by politics and money than it is by an authentic desire for true food safety. Only YOU can truly determine what is good for you—through education and research. US Food And Drug Administration (2008, February 10). Botox Linked To Respiratory Failure And Death, FDA Advises. *ScienceDaily*. 22 March 2008 <http://www.sciencedaily.com/releases/2008/02/080209090530.htm>.

Allopathic Medicine has Lost the "War on Cancer

President Nixon declared war on cancer in 1971. As of January, 2006, more than 30 years later, over 850 Billion has been for cancer research alone. This does not include cancer treatments, cancer hospitals, chemotherapy, cancer drugs, etc. What has been put forth? The same failed, cut, burn and poison therapy, known most commonly as biopsies, mastectomy, tumor removal surgeries, chemotherapy and radiation. These procedures are based on inaccurate scientific conclusions of the germ theory. Society and Christians are programmed to believe that Allopathic Medicine is their only hope for survival, and that every other healing methodology is inferior. Remember the goal is not life but the quality of it and most importantly, eternal life.

Nicholas Gonzalez, M.D.

Thought's on 'winning the war on cancer' from Nicholas Gonzalez, MD. "I guess the people that say we are winning the war on cancer that have a different definition of war and winning, certainly not the definitions I would use. Unless it is the hundred years war that they are talking about from history. We are not really winning the war on cancer, the major cancer killers that I have mentioned, like tumors of the lungs that kill over 200,000 people a year; like tumors of the breast that kill over 45,000 women every year, pancreatic cancer that kill 45,000 people a year, colon and prostate cancer that kills 50,000 people each per year, for these cancers chemotherapy is not effect. The therapies they are using today are really no more effective than therapies used thirty years ago. In fact there are scientist who have studied cancer statistics and they say the majority of patients that are cured today, are the same patients that would have been cured fifty years ago by surgery, when the tumor was found early like in the colon or the breast and they would take it out. But with metastatic disease, the major cancer killers again, and even though today the therapies they have are getting very expensive and sophisticated i.e., targeted therapies you know attacking specific biochemical patterns in the cell, they still do not prolong survival very much. So there really has not been very much improvement in the survival of patients with metastatic, solid tumor cancers. I do not know how you can say we are winning the war on cancer when 600,000 people, in America alone die of cancer each year. The five year survival rates have not improved that much. There are statisticians like Dr. John Bailler who worked at the National Cancer Institute (NCI) for 25 years. Who said that a lot of the so called improvements in cancer are actually fudged statistics, because of the great improvement of diagnostic techniques like CAT scans, M.I.R.'s and P.E.T. scans, cancer is being diagnosed at a earlier stage. But when you actually look at the math, they are actually dying at the same time, it just looks like they have survived longer because they were diagnosed earlier. Fifty years ago, they did not have CAT scans, M.I.R.'s and P.E.T. scans, so he feels like a lot of the so call improvements in cancer survival, when they are claimed are just statistics manipulations. I mean there are some improvements in some cancers like chronic myoacid Leukemia, there is a target therapy called Levac, which does prolong life. But for the major cancer killers with all the billions of dollars invested, all the publicity, the American Cancer Society fund raising programs have not lead to any great advancements, except for the same few cancers like Leukemias', Lymphomas', Myelomas' and testicular cancer that respond to chemo. Those tumors responded to Chemotherapy thirty years ago and they still do today but the majority of other cancers do not." --Nicholas Gonzalez, M.D.

Make no mistake. The Cancer Industry is a well established Global Fraternity of Drug and Pharmaceutical Companies, Research Facilities, Hospitals, Universities, Suppliers, Insurers, and let's not forget the FDA, AMA, ACS, ADA, NCI, NIH and other related alphabet institutions. They all feed on the 1.4 trillion health care trough/portion of the US Economy, and they intend to keep it that way. And they will unless Christians throw off the darkness and superstition and come into God's marvelous light and accept His will concerning sickness and choose His natural remedies, and don't become afraid and panic when faced with the sleep of death. See books; "The Cancer Industry" and "Questioning Chemotherapy" 2nd Edition 10/2000 both by Ralph W. Moss, PhD. Also "Racketeering in

Medicine" by James P. Carter, MD, Dr.PH. Here is real education for everyone who is interested in Cancer and AIDS.

Dedicated local volunteers work hard for the annual cancer drive and are not members of the Global fraternity. They are to be admired for the purpose and compassion of their goal; to help people and save lives. Dr. Sam Chachoua was a driven researcher who went outside the confines of American Cancer Society and National Cancer Institute (ACS/NCI) protocol to discover a new field of medicine, which Cedars-Sinai/UCLA once described as an "Exciting New World of Therapeutic Opportunity." That was before Cedars & UCLA turned on Dr. Sam to declare him, among other things, a charlatan. What is the motivation for all of this? It appears Cedar-Sinai, UCLA and others of the Cancer Industry want Dr. Sam and the trial to go away or be forgotten. Then use his 36 vaccines & cultures to enter the International AIDS Vaccine Initiative (IAVI).

The Cancer Industry has accumulated great wealth, power and influence with the Government agencies and that part of the National Media that supports their wishes. Now we can see what many over the years have suspected and history can now record:

"Everyone should know that most cancer research is largely a fraud and the major cancer research organizations are derelict in their duties to the people who support them." --Linus Pauling, PhD, the only person ever to win 2 solo Nobel Prizes.

A National Cancer Expert Speaks

"My overall assessment is that the national cancer program must be judged a qualified failure" Dr. John Bailer, who spent 20 years on the staff of the U.S. National Cancer Institute and was editor of its journal. I think this would qualify him as an expert and not a "quack".

"The five year survival statistics of the American Cancer Society are very misleading. They now count things that are not cancer, and, because we are able to diagnose at an earlier stage of the disease, patients falsely appear to live longer. Our whole cancer research in the past 20 years has been a total failure. More people over 30 are dying from cancer than ever before... More women with mild or benign diseases are being included in statistics and reported as being "cured". When government officials point to survival figures and say they are winning the war against cancer they are using those survival rates improperly." --Dr. John Bailer, who spent 20 years on the staff of the U.S. National Cancer Institute and was editor of its journal.

"The National Cancer Institute and the American Cancer Society have mislead and confused the public and congress by repeated false claims that we are winning the war against cancer." --Samuel Epstein, M.D.

"Everyone should know that the 'War on Cancer' is largely a fraud, and that the National Cancer Institute and the American Cancer Society are derelict in their duties to the people who support them." --Linus Pauling, Ph.D. Noble Prize Winner.

"The treatment of cancer and degenerative diseases is a national scandal. The sooner you learn this, the better off you will be." --Allen Greenberg, M.D.

For decades, the American people have received nothing but lies concerning the war against cancer, and the only way we know we have been lied to, is by the statements of the people who work for or in the cancer industry. Read the conflicting statements then decide who you believe.

"It's a bunch of sh--." --Dr. James Watson, when asked about the National Cancer Program-1975.

"The American public is being sold a nasty bill of goods." --Dr. James Watson, Nobel Prize Winner, while serving on the National Cancer Advisory Board-1975.

"The next few years will see the emergence of an arsenal of new drugs." --Lucien Isreal, Conquering Cancer-1978.

"... Some 35 years of intense effort focused on improving treatment must be judged as a qualified failure." --John C. Bailar, M.D. The New England Journal of Medicine-1986.

"Cancer deaths can be cut in half by the year 2000." --Peter Greenwald, M.D. The National Cancer Institute-1989.

"For most of today's solid common cancers, the ones that cause 90% of the cancer deaths each year, chemotherapy has never proven to do any good at all." Urich Abel, M.D. University of Heidelberg-1990.

"Overall death rates from many common cancers remain stubbornly – or even higher- than when the war began." --E. Marshall, M.D. Science, 1991.

"Evidence has steadily accrued that [cancer therapy] is essentially a failure." --N.J. Temple, M.D. Journal of the Royal Society of Medicine-1991.

"We have given it our best effort for decades: Billions of dollars in support, the best scientific talent available, it hasn't paid off." --John C. Bailar, M.D. Harvard University-1997.

"... the percentage of Americans dying from cancer is about the same [now] as in 1970... and [even] in 1950..." Fortune Magizine-2004.

"... long term survival for advance cancer has barely budged since the 1970." Fortune Magizine-2004.

"Survival gains for the common forms of cancer are measured in additional months of life, not years..." Fortune Magizine-2004.

"We are going to lick cancer by 2015." --Congressman Benjamin Cardin-2006.

"Surgery, radiation therapy, chemotherapy... seldom produce a cure." American Cancer Society: Cancer Facts & Figures-2007.

Untreated patients live longer than treated patients, Journal of the American Medical Association (JAMA), 1992, 257, p. 2191; Lancet, 1991, August, p. 901; New England Journal of Medicine (NEJM), 1986, May 27, p. 967; NEJM, 1984, March, p. 737; Cancer, 1981, 47, p. 27; JAMA, 1979, February 2, p. 489; A Report on Cancer, 1969, Hardin Jones.

The American Cancer Society's "Good News Campaign"
"As a rule, the good news comes as an announcement that the five-year survival rate for one or another form of cancer has increased." Scientific America-June, 1987.

Center for Disease Control (CDC): More people with cancer surviving. The number of cancer survivors...has more than tripled...because of advancement in detection and treatment...patients diagnosed between 1995 and 2000 have an estimated 64% chance of surviving five years, compared with a 50% rate-a coin toss-three decades ago... The number of cancer survivors...soared from 3 million in 1971 to 9.8 million in 2001... AP June 25, 2004.

Is the "Good News" really that Good?

Overview: The contribution of Cytotoxic Chemotherapy to 5-year survival in adult Malignancies.

Cancer	Percent 5-year Survival:
➢ Kidney	00.0
➢ Melanoma	00.0
➢ Multiple myeloma	00.0
➢ Pancreas	00.0
➢ Prostate	00.0
➢ Soft Tissue Sarcoma	00.0

Creating "Good News" from Bad

The traditional definition of "Cure" is the "elimination of disease." In the case of cancer, a person is cured if they are still breathing in five years. A cancer "cure" does not mean the disease has been cured. If you still have AIDS, heart disease, diabetes, etc., no doctor will pronounce you as "Cured." So why are WE the people allowing the cancer industry to give a false definition to cancer cure?

Early Detection...

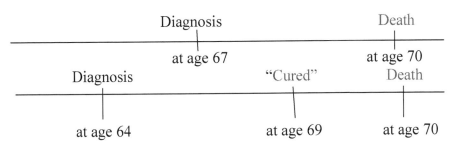

If two people are diagnosis with cancer, one at age 64 and the other at age 67 and they both die at age seventy, the one diagnosed at age 64 is considered cured, even though they died from cancer at age 70. Ridicules, name any other disease that the health care industry considers you cured after five years.

How to Fool Most of the People Most of the Time

Absolute verses Relative Benefit - Let's take a look at a hypothetical: If you take 100 people in a trial study, you would expect two to get cancer. However, if only one person got cancer, that is considered a 50% reduction. Two were expected to get cancer but only one got cancer that is a [Relative Benefit] of 50%. However, remember two people out of 100 were expected to get cancer but only one did. One person out of 100 got cancer that is an [Absolute Benefit] of 1%. You always want to ask your doctor for the [Absolute Benefit]. However,

Few					Some
Benefit					Die
From					From
Treatment					Treatment

Everyone suffers side-effects from treatments

Real World Results:

Lung Cancer Survival: Drug increased survival by 2.3% (relative benefit). Reality: survival increased from 10.2 months to 12. 5 months. The Absolute benefit is only 2.3 months. As well as 5 percent were expected to die from the treatment, this is "within accepted limits."

Now let's take a look at a real life example found in USA Today newspaper, in the Health & Behavior section. The title of the article is called, Study: Liver Cancer Breakthrough Found Chicago Associated Press (AP) –For the first time, doctors say they have found a pill increases survival for people with liver cancer, a notoriously hard to beat disease diagnosed in more than half a million people globally each year… Sorafenib, a pill that zeroes in on malignant cancer cells and cuts off the blood supply feeding the tumor, was found to increase chances for survival by over 44% or about three months, a relative benefit of 44%. Always ask for absolute benefits!

Out of 100 people how many will benefit? What is the absolute benefit in days or months? Remember: *Untreated patients live longer than treated patients*, Journal of the American Medical Association (JAMA), 1992, 257, p. 2191; Lancet, 1991, August, p. 901; New England Journal of Medicine (NEJM), 1986, May 27, p. 967; NEJM, 1984, March, p. 737; Cancer, 1981, 47, p. 27; JAMA, 1979, February 2, p. 489; A Report on Cancer, 1969, Hardin Jones.

"The vast majority of patients with cancer live longer and better if left without the orthodox treatments." --Francisco Contreras, M.D.

"We have a multi-billion dollar industry that is killing people, right and left, just for financial gain." --Glenn Werner, M.D.

"[Chemotherapy is] a marvelous opportunity for rampant deceit. So much money is there to be made..." --George Lundberg, M.D. editor of the Journal of the American Medical Association.

"Bottled Death" --Vice President Hubert Humphrey describing chemotherapy before he died of bladder cancer.

"... an estimated 4,000 to 9,000 women died not from their cancer, but from the treatment." Discover Magazine expose on bone marrow transplant surgery.

"Remember there are worse things than death. One of them is chemotherapy." --Charles Higgins, M.D. Nobel Prize Winner.

Medicine's dilemma is that its own findings undermine its basic principle. If the body's self-acting power is "subject to ordinary physical and chemical laws," medicine has yet to find them, as witnessed by the ease with which the body resists chemotherapy and other drugs. If the body's self-acting power is "not strong enough to withstand the onslaughts of disease," medicine has found nothing stronger, as witnessed by the ease with which bacteria resist antibiotics. Believing in the supremacy of the body's adaptive powers is no longer "unscientific," as shown by this quote from The Skeptical Inquirer, a journal published by Carl Sagan: *"Modern science has taught us that the human body, insofar as it is cured, tends to cure itself. The body is its own greatest protector: the immunological system, which produces antibodies to fight antigens, accounts for almost all recovery from disease... Nothing can save the patient if the internal system (Inner Terrain theory by Claude Bernard) breaks down... This is not to belittle medicine; its discoveries are prodigious and its contributions to health salutary, but the success of modern medicine depends on an understanding of how the healthy body protects itself."* The Skeptical Inquirer, a journal published by Carl Sagan.

"Drugs are not responsible for the healing that may follow" --White, Ellen G, Healthful Living, pg. 224.

"There is no doubt that all these [physicians], in their hunt for popularity by means of some novelty, do not hesitate to buy it with our lives… Hence that gloomy inscription on monuments: 'It was the crowd of physicians that killed me."--Pilney, History of Medicine, p28.

Why is Cancer Research Fraudulent?

Because cancer is scientifically classified as a "chronic metabolic disorder" just like diabetes, scurvy, and heart disease, which means that it does not get better on its own. Also, it occurs inside the body and not externally by a virus, bacteria, or germ, typically. There has never been and never will be in the history of medical research a chemical "cure" for any "chronic metabolic disorder". Chemicals can only work on the symptom of the disease, not eliminate the disease itself. So, despite hundreds of billions of dollars spent for 'research', there will never be a chemical 'cure' for cancer! The 'Cancer Establishment' and the American Medical establishment knows these facts fully well. They are keeping this information from 'We the Sheeple/People' who desperately need this information to bring about change. Chronic, Metabolic, Disorders such as Cancer and Scurvy, are simply due to a vitamin and/or mineral deficiencies within the body. I will discuss Dr. Schimke's and others research findings that prove Chemo is resistance and it provokes the cancer response. Please keep in mind that 'Cancer Research' and 'Treatment' is big business. In terms of Gross Domestic Production (GDP), cancer spending is second only to the Petrochemical Industry. Over 1/3 of American jobs can be traced to the "Cash Cow" of Cancer. With the other 2/3 tied economically to the petrochemical and Financial Service industries. Without these industries, American would have to develop other forms of goods and services to make up the difference. I personally believe that as a nation, we have the ingenuity to develop such commodities that would benefit mankind and not profit a few from diabolic, planned, death and misery. However, the industries are owned and monopolized by a select few individual families.

Number One Killer: The $85-billion Pharmaceutical Industry

According to a recent report from the Commonwealth Fund, the American health care system falls short of what's available in other developed countries. After measuring 37 areas of quality, the study found that the U.S. scored only in the 66th percentile. Though the U.S.

spends the most on healthcare of all the countries studied, it often ranked below Iceland, France, Japan, Italy, Sweden, and several others. What's more, healthcare varied dramatically from state to state and from hospital to hospital. Many practitioners of conventional medicine continue to dispute the health benefits of nutritional supplements, claiming that nature's cures are "unscientific" and potentially dangerous." They usually fail to mention that adverse reactions from prescription drugs kill more than 100,000 Americans each year, according to Stephen Fried's book Bitter Pills: Inside the Hazardous World of Legal Drugs (Bantam Books, 1998).

Fried's book reports that drugs' side effects are the leading cause of death in the United States. To me, that calls into question a suspect allegiance between the American Medical Association (AMA) and the $85-billion pharmaceutical industry.

Wall of Silence: The Untold Story of the Medical Mistakes that Kill Millions of Americans by Rosemary Gibson and Janardan. Wall of Silence takes the readers behind the scenes to expose stories of medical malpractice, careless misdiagnoses and neglect on the part of health care personnel across America. Gibson puts real names and faces to the patients who suffer and die every day because of ineptitude, poor quality and lack of management in a system that's badly broken. Doctors and nurses also provide firsthand accounts of what goes on behind the curtains, describing the mistakes that happen.

Iatrogenic i·at·ro·gen·ic [ī àttrə jénnik]   adj.
1. caused by doctor: describes a symptom or illness brought on
    unintentionally by something that a doctor does or says.

The word iatrogenic in medical terminology means "something a doctor or nurse actually caused to happen." In July 26, 2000, the American Medical Association released the following frightening information.

In the United States:
➢ There are approximately 12,000 deaths per year from unnecessary surgeries.
➢ There are approximately 7,000 deaths per year from medication errors in hospitals.
➢ There are approximately 20,000 deaths per year from various errors in hospitals.
➢ There are approximately 80,000 deaths per year from staph and other various infections in hospitals.

102

- Finally, there are approximately 106,000 deaths per year from non-error related adverse reaction to drug medication.
- That is a staggering 225,000 deaths per year in American hospitals from iatrogenic (physician produced) cause!
- That makes iatrogenic the third leading cause of death in the United States, second only to heart and blood vessel disease and cancer.

[The Journal of American Medical Association, July 26, 2000, 284(4):483-5]. What is absolutely astounding is the rate at which these number have increased and no consumer watch dog group, radio or television talking head, or alternative medicine organization have sounded the alarm to the American people.

In 2003, a group of physicians and researchers calculated that medical treatment is actually the leading cause of death in America. Let's look at those numbers again.

Condition	Deaths per Year	Author(s)
Adverse drug reaction	106,000	Lazaron & Suh
Medical error	98,000	IOM
Bedsores	115,000	Xakellis& Barczak
Infections	88,000	Weinstein MMWR
Malnutrition	108,800	Nurses Coalition
Outpatients	199,000	Stanfield & Weingart
Unnecessary Procedures	37,136	HCUP
Surgery-Related	32,000	AHRQ
Total.....................................783,936		

We could have an even higher death rate by using Dr. Lucien Leape's 1997 medical and drug error rate of 3 million. [14] Multiplied by the fatality rate of 14 percent (that Leape used in 1994 [16] we arrive at an annual death rate of 420,000 for drug errors and medical errors combined. If we put this number in place of Lazorou's 106,000 drug errors and the Institute of Medicine's (IOM) 98,000 medical errors, we could add another 216,000 deaths making a total of 999,936 deaths annually.

ADR/med error	420,000	Leape 1977[14]
Total	999,936	

Annual Unnecessary Medical Events

The enumerating of unnecessary medical events is very important in our analysis. Any medical procedure that is invasive and not necessary must be considered as part of the larger iatrogenic picture. Unfortunately, cause and effect go unmonitored. The figures on unnecessary events represent people ("patients") who are thrust into a dangerous healthcare system. They are helpless victims. Each one of these 16.4 million lives is being affected in a way that could have a fatal consequence. Simply entering a hospital could result in the following (out of 16. 4 million people):

- 2.1 percent chance of a serious adverse drug reaction (186,000) [1]

- 5 percent to 6 percent chance of acquiring a nosocomial [hospital] infection (489,500) [9]

- 4 percent to 36 percent chance of having an iatrogenic injury in hospital (medical error and adverse drug reactions) (1.78 million) [16]

- 17 % chance of a procedure error (1.3 million) [40]

All the statistics above represent a one-year time span. Imagine the numbers over a 10-year period. Working with the most conservative figures from our statistics we project the following 10-year death rates.

Medical Intervention

Projected Ten-Year Death Rates	
Condition	10-Year Deaths
Adverse Drug Reaction	1.06 million
Medical error	0.98 million
Bedsores	1.15 million
Nosocomial Infection	0.88 million
Malnutrition	1.09 million
Outpatients	1.99 million
Unnecessary Procedures	371,360
Surgery-related	320,000
TOTAL	7,841,360 (7.8 million)

Our projected statistic of 7.8 million iatrogenic deaths is more than all the casualties from wars that America has fought in its entire history. Our projected figures for unnecessary medical events occurring over a 10-year period are also dramatic.

Unnecessary Intervention

Projected Ten-Year Statistics		
Unnecessary Events	**10-Year Number**	**Iatrogenic Events**
Hospitalization	89 million	17 million
Procedures	75 million	13 million
TOTAL	**164 million**	**30 million**

These projected figures show that a total of 164 million people, approximately 56 percent of the population of the United States, have been treated unnecessarily by the medical industry—in other words, nearly 50,000 people per day. Source: http://www.ourcivilisation.com/medicine/usamed/deaths.htm.

Iatrogenic Death Spiral Makes the Top Ten Causes of Death in American.

The Top 10 Causes of Death:
1. Heart Disease
2. **Iatrogenic Death Spiral**
3. Cancer
4. Stroke
5. COPD
6. Accidents
7. Diabetes
8. Alzheimer's
9. Pneumonia
10. Kidney Failure

Source: thehappyhospitalist.blogspot.com/2009/.../iatrogenic-**death-spiral**.htm... Sunday, March 29, 2009.

Tragically the American people have bought into the system, to the point that they actually believe that health and life can be perpetuated through the swallowing of a little pill, which is void of life itself. History Documents Medicines Disregard for Human Life.

In the view of the common people, doctors spent much of their time theorizing and arguing among themselves, sometimes killing their patients with promise cures and then asking for payment from relatives. Medicine's bad image was reflected in literature, for example, the historian Pliny wrote: *There is no doubt that all these [physicians], in their hunt for popularity by means of some novelty, do not hesitate to buy it with our lives... Hence too that gloomy inscription on monuments: 'It was the crowd of physicians that killed me.''* Gaius Plinius Secundus, better known as Pliny the Elder.

"Multitudes of Physicians and Multitudes of Drugs have Cursed the Inhabitants of the Earth and have carried Thousands and Tens of Thousands to Untimely Graves", Spiritual Gifts, Vol. 4, 1864, by White, Ellen G, page 133.

Antibiotics: The End of Miracle Drugs?

On March 28, 1994, Newsweek Magazine had the above caption on its front cover. Today, some three million people a year are admitted to hospitals with difficult-to-treat resistant infections, and another two million (5% of hospital patients) become infected while visiting hospitals for routine medical procedures. More and more of the patients are succumbing to disease as the virulence and resistance of bacteria increase. In fact, pathologist and author, Marc Lapp'e of the University of Illinois, College of Medicine, observes, "by conservative estimate, such infections are responsible for at least a hundred thousand deaths a year, and the toll is mounting."

The toll is mounting because the number of people killed by resistant bacteria is increasing, especially in places where the ill, the young or old, or the poor congregate, such as homeless shelters, hospitals, inner cities, prisons, and child care centers. Perhaps the best known and most loved casualty to date is that of Jim Henson, the creator of Kermit the frog, who died in 1990. In the face of enormous inroads that resistant bacteria are making, world-renowned authority on bacteria resistance, Dr. Stuart Levy, comments, "This situation raises the staggering possibility that a time will come when antibiotics as a mode of therapy will be only a fact of historic interest." Drugs cannot solve the problem of the second Law of Thermo-dynamics, so instead of antibiotics winning, the microbe will eventually win, and we trust our lives to this system?

Lapp'e is more blunt, "The period once euphemistically called the Age of Miracle Drugs is dead." Humankind now faces the threat of epidemic diseases more powerful, and less treatable than ever known before. We have let our profligate use of antibiotics reshape the evolution of the microbial world and wrest any hope of safe management from us... resistance to antibiotics has spread to so many different, and such unanticipated types of bacteria, that the only fair appraisal is that we have succeeded in upsetting the balance of nature." Marc Lapp'e, PH.D., author of 'When Antibiotics Fail' 1999, pg. 2, 3.

Many people are now asking themselves how this could have happened. Only a few short years ago, the picture seemed decidedly different. In the late '50s and early '60s, Leroy Burney, then Surgeon General of the United States, and David Cox, President of the Kentucky Medical Association, joined many other physicians in the industrialized nations in declaring that the antibiotic era had come, jointly proclaiming the end for all time epidemic disease.

This 1962 statement by an eminent Nobel Laureate, the Australian physician Sir F. Macfarlane Burnet, is typical. By the end of the twentieth century, he commented, we will see the "virtual elimination of infectious disease as a significant factor in social life." Further study and publication of infectious disease research, he continued, "is almost to write of something that has passed into history." Surgeon General William Stewart, testified to Congress that "it was time to close the book on infectious disease." They could not have been more wrong. Though penicillin was discovered in 1928, only during World War II was it commercially developed, and not until after the war did its use become routine. Those were heady days. It seemed that science could do anything. New antibiotics were being discovered daily; the arsenal of medication seemed overwhelming. In the euphoria of the moment, no one heeded the few small voices raising concerns. Among them, ironically enough was Alexander Fleming, the discoverer of penicillin. Dr. Fleming noted as early as 1929, in the British Journal of Experimental Pathology, that numerous bacteria were already resistant to the drug he had discovered.

By 1945, he warned in a *New York Times* interview that improper use of penicillin would inevitably lead to the development of resistant bacteria. Dr. Fleming's observations were only too true. At the time of his interview, just 14 percent of *Staphylococcus aureus* bacteria were resistant to penicillin. By 1950, an incredible 59 percent were resistant, and by 1995, that figure has jumped to 95 percent. Originally limited to patients in the hospitals (the primary breeding ground of such bacteria), the resistant strains are now common throughout the world's population. Though many factors influence the growth of resistant bacteria, the most important are ecological. Throughout history on this planet, our species has lived in an ecological balance with many other life forms, including the bacterial. Epidemic diseases did flash through the human population from time to time, usually in response to local overpopulation or unsanitary conditions. But epidemics like the bubonic plague that decimated Europe were relatively uncommon. At the end of World War II, this relationship was significantly altered when antibiotics were introduced. For the first time in human history, the microbial world was intentionally being affected on a large scale. In the euphoria of discovery, an ancient human hubris again raised its head when science declared war on bacteria. And like all wars, this one is likely to cause the death of thousands, if not millions, of innocent noncombatants. Marc Lapp'e, PH.D., author of 'When Antibiotics Fail'1999, pg. 3, 4.

Bacteria in Pork Showing Resistance to Antibiotics

By THOMAS M. BURTON
June 16, 2008; Page B6, WSJ

Scientists are beginning to detect antibiotic-resistant bacteria in pork, pigs and some veterinarians, raising the issue of whether these so-called super bugs might find a new route to infect farm workers or even people who eat pork. University of Minnesota veterinary public-health researchers last month reported they found the antibiotic-resistant bugs in 7.1% of 113 swine veterinarians tested. Public-health doctors at the University of Iowa found the same bacterial strains among 147 of 299 pigs tested with nasal swabs. Perhaps of greatest concern, Ontario Veterinary College researcher Scott Weese also detected these bacteria in 10% of 212 samples of ground pork and pork chops collected in four Canadian provinces.

These particular strains of antibiotic-resistant bugs have not so far been shown to sicken patients, at least not in North America. Three patients in Scotland were found to have the same bacterial strain, and there have been serious infections reported in the Netherlands related to these strains. Since an estimated 18,650 deaths a year in the U.S. are estimated to be caused by a range of antibiotic-resistant bacteria, researchers have encouraged U.S. and Canadian authorities to pay attention to the findings."It's potentially relevant to the human population," Dr. Weese said. "The question is whether it can cause problems among humans." He cautions that such bugs in meat and pigs "are not an important source of disease at this point."

In a medical-journal article last year, doctors at the Centers for Disease Control and Prevention estimated that there were 94,360 infections in a recent year in the U.S. from certain strains of antibiotic-resistant bacteria. Most were in patients who had recently been hospitalized or were in long-term care such as nursing homes, but there were also serious infections among people with no such histories. Often, the cases were skin infections, but others are nearly untreatable pneumonia or blood infections.

The concerns over super bugs in pigs and pork take place against a backdrop in which Congress is questioning whether the Bush administration is doing enough about food-borne illnesses. These include the recent cases of salmonella-related illness linked to fresh tomatoes, as well as other outbreaks of E. coli bacterial infections from ground beef. The Agriculture Department acknowledges it isn't testing for the antibiotic-resistant bugs, officially called MRSA, which stands for methicillin-resistant Staphylococcus aureus.

That is understandable, in the view of Lyle Vogel, assistant executive vice president of the American Veterinary Medical Association. "This is something we cannot ignore, but it's a resource issue," he says. Compared with E. coli and salmonella infections, "it does not seem to rise to the top of the priority list." The National Pork Board, an industry trade group, is funding some of the research to evaluate how much of a concern it is for agriculture workers or the public. This includes the University of Minnesota's work.

Eventually, 1 to 2 pounds of our mature body weight will be the billions of bacteria that live in healthy symbiosis in and on our bodies. Many of these bacteria produce essential nutrients that we could not live without. (Friendly and bad bacteria is the theory Claude Bernard, then later Enderling ascribed to, calling it the "Inner Terrain." This theory was opposed to Louis Pasteur's Germ Theory. It is an interesting fact to note, on his death bed Louis Pasteur's supposedly recanted and said "Benard was correct, "the inter terrain is everything and the microbe is nothing". Even more striking, researchers are discovering that many of these friendly bacteria actually fight off more dangerous bacteria in order to keep us healthy. Stephen Harrod Buhner, Herbal Antibiotics, pages 4, 5, Storey Books, Pownal, Vermont.

Last line breached? Deadly gene resisting all forms of antibiotics found in China

Published time: 19 Nov, 2015 12:07

© Stephane Mahe / Reuters

Scientists have identified the first gene helping bacteria resist the only antibiotic group known to be effective when all others fail. Chinese and British experts came to the alarming conclusion that our last line of antibiotic defense has been breached. The conclusion follows a large body of prior research that warns humanity about the dangers of becoming completely resistant to antibiotics. Now, Chinese doctors cooperating with UK specialists from Bristol and Cardiff Universities say we could soon be looking at the spread of uncontrollable superbugs. In the research published in the journal Lancet Infectious Diseases, the researchers predict a return to the Dark Ages, when even common germs like E. Coli put a person in mortal danger.

"These are extremely worryingly results," professor and co-author on the study Liu Jian-Hua, from China's Southern Agricultural University, said in a press release. The research looked closely at Chinese farms, where it's believed this dangerous potential for resistance took its root before spreading to humans. The culprit is the gene MCR-1, which allows common bacteria to develop resistance to polymixins, the antibiotic group considered our safest bet when fighting superbugs. The researchers detected it in the common, yet deadly, E. Coli and K. Pneumoniae, which cause pneumonia and blood disease. What's more, the MCR-1 gene spreads easily from strain to strain, allowing a given bacteria to mutate faster than we can come up with solutions. *"The polymyxins (colistin and polymyxin B) were the last class of antibiotics in which resistance was incapable of spreading from cell to cell,"* the author explained further. *"Until now, colistin resistance resulted from chromosomal mutations, making the resistance mechanism unstable and incapable of spreading to other bacteria."The emergence of MCR-1 heralds the breach of the last group of antibiotics,"* Liu continued.*"Although currently confined to China, mcr-1 is likely to emulate other resistance genes ... and spread worldwide. There is a critical need to re-evaluate the use of polymyxins in animals and for very close international monitoring and surveillance of mcr-1 in human and veterinary medicine."*

The gene was discovered on plasmids – mobile versions of DNA which are more easily copied and transferred between different microbes. This is what worries the scientists, because it means the spread could be much more aggressive and can affect a more diverse range of bacteria.

"This is a worrying report, as polymyxins are often the last resort antibiotic to treat serious infections," Laura Piddock, professor of microbiology at the University of Birmingham, said, according to AFP. *"Equally worrying is that this type of resistance can be easily transferred between bacteria."* And according to Piddock, the spread could mirror other drug resistance mechanisms, such as that of tuberculosis. Colistin is commonly used on Chinese farms, with pigs the prime contenders for hosting bacteria capable with the type of resistance associated with MCR-1. According to the researchers report, the samples containing the gene can be found in pigs, chickens and people in southern China, but that resistance originated in the animals. Drug-resistant typhoid tracked worldwide, public health threat 'critical' - study:

The gene was actually discovered by accident, during routine farm testing on pigs and chickens. The researchers then took the E. Coli and K. Pneumoniae samples collected from the animals and matched them to the lab results they received from patients at two hospitals in the Guangdong and Zhejiang provinces. MCR-1 was found in over 20 percent of tested animals and in 16 of the 1,322 human samples.The researchers say the lower infection rate among humans is proof they weren't the first ones to cultivate the resistance.

"If MRC-1 becomes global, which is a case of when not if, and the gene aligns itself with other antibiotic resistance genes, which is inevitable, then we will have very likely reached the start of the post-antibiotic era," Professor Timothy Walsh of the University of Cardiff, who collaborated on the study, told the BBC News.

"At that point if a patient is seriously ill, say with E. Coli, then

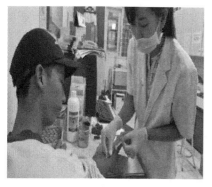 *there is virtually nothing you can do."* Scientists on the research hope the study will serve to ignite the debate on the use of colistin in animal husbandry. *"The finding that this type of resistance can be shared by different bacteria - irrespective of whether from food, an animal or a person - is further evidence that*

the same drugs should not be used in veterinary and human medicine," said Piddock. Further to that, according to Dr. Bruce Hirsch, infectious disease specialist at North Shore University Hospital in Manhasset, NY, doctors and patients should also understand the increasing responsibility to reduce antibiotic intake. *"If you don't need antibiotics, don't take them. You are only giving bacteria extra practice,"* he was cited by HealthDay as saying.

World must act or risk 'post-antibiotic apocalypse' – top doctor
Published time: 13 Oct, 2017 09:58. Harald Theissen, Global Look Press.

England's chief medical officer has warned of a "post-antibiotic apocalypse," calling on world leaders to address the growing threat of drug-resistant infections.

Ahead of a global conference in Berlin organized by the UK government to map out the threat of drug resistance, Professor Dame Sally Davies cautioned against giving patients antibiotics they *"don't need,"* as the drugs will lose their effectiveness and *"spell the end of modern medicine."*

Excessive antibiotic use has made them ineffective on 50% of children – scientists

She warned that the threat of infections posed by antimicrobial resistance (AMR) heightens the risk of carrying out operations such as caesarean sections and hip replacements. *"We really are facing, if we don't take action now, a dreadful post-antibiotic apocalypse,"* she said. *"I don't want to say to my children that I didn't do my best to protect them and their children."* Around 700,000 people around the world die annually due to drug-resistant infections including tuberculosis (TB), HIV and malaria.

If no action is taken, it has been estimated that drug-resistant infections will kill 10 million people per year by 2050. *"This is a serious issue that is with us now, causing deaths." "If it was anything else people would be up in arms about it. But because it is hidden they just let it pass." "It does not really have a 'face' because most people who die of drug resistant infections, their families just think they died of an uncontrolled infection. "It will only get worse unless we take strong action everywhere across the globe. "We need some real work on the ground to make a difference or we risk the end of modern medicine,"* Davies added.

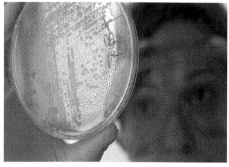

<u>Drug-resistant   gonorrhea spreads in northern England</u>
She also debunked the assumption held by patients that GPs will not prescribe antibiotics because they are *"mean."* They are in fact *"trying to save the drugs, so that they work when they are actually needed."* While in the UK, one in four antibiotic prescriptions is not needed, Davis said *"other countries use vastly more antibiotics in the community and they need to start doing as we are, which is reducing usage,"* she said. *"Our latest data shows that we have reduced human consumption by 4.3 percent in 2014-15 from the year before."* The new project which will map the spread of superbugs is a collaboration between the UK Government, Welcome Trust, Bill and Melinda Gates Foundation, the University of Oxford, and Institute for Health Metrics and Evaluation.

The Living God Created Natures Way of Healing:
On February 7, 1931, the U.S. Congress passed the definition of

Naturopathy without a dissenting vote. There was great opposition by 35 Medical doctors present, by the Board of Commissioners of the healing Arts (allopathic), and by special representatives and attorneys of the American Medical Association and other allopathic forces. The Honorable Katherine G. Langley had this to say: "Naturopathy does not contemplate drugs and surgical operations, nor is it in the scope of their science. To the contrary, they do not use or prescribe drugs as part of their treatment, nor do they advocate or perform surgical operations upon their patients," see appendix D.

Naturopathy simple means "Natures way of healing pathological conditions - Nature-o-pathy. There is a fundamental difference between Naturopathy and its counterfeit, Naturopathic Medicine. Naturopathic Medicine has bought into the allopathic model and now, in sixteen States of the United States they can prescribe four out of the five psychotropic drugs available, along with other prescription drugs and minor surgery. Naturopathic Medicine It does not fit the definition of Naturopathy as defined by the U.S. Congress. Today, this federal law, which defines Naturopathy, is still on the books of every state at the federal level. The Honorable Katherine G. Langley went on to say that Naturopathy is not a threat to society and Naturopathy comes under Public Health Laws. The real issue of licensing requirements is control, financial gain and replacing God as the head of the health work.

For example, teachers are required to receive their teaching certificate then are required to be licensed. Then they are qualified to teach at a reputable school or organization that has received accreditation from a governmental organization. As of this writing, only sixteen states in the United States require Naturopaths to be licensed, because the list changes, Google or Bing Naturopathic Licensed States. The problem with Naturopathic Medicine is that, as the newer N.M.D.s are allowed to prescribe more and more prescription drugs, because of greed, materialism, capitalism, it will be a temptation to simply listen to patients and their symptoms and write a prescription. God's way of healing is based upon hygienic agencies then nature will respond to God's physicians-the ten laws of health. Naturopathy as a profession was born out of God's methodology of health restoration, which does not include spiritualism or pagan practices.

Pagan and Spiritualistic naturopathic practitioners have perverted God original healing methods given in the scriptures; the first three chapters of Genesis. The licensing of Naturopathic Medicine Physicians should not legally exclude Naturopaths from society, whose main focus is educating its clients in health preservation and health restoration. Naturopathic Medicine is a hybrid and because of the definition of Naturopathy and the Congressional definition of Naturopathy, Naturopathic Medicine should be legally made to remove the word Naturopathy from its name.

A Place for Allopathic Medicine and Prescription Drugs?
Is there a place for allopathic medicine and prescription drugs? I answer yes. Today the bulk of scientific evidence now suggests that

allopathic medicine is great for acute conditions. For example, if I have an acute infection, I should have access and care from a M.D. If I have an acute allergic reaction with anaphylactic shock, I need the protection and intervention of a drug. If you need a life saving surgery because of an accident or injury, then allopathic medicine is the answer. However, for chronic conditions such as, arthritis, cancer, heart disease, diabetes, etc, which today we know are caused by poor diet and lifestyle choices, to use the conventional medical approach long term will always have the effect of worsening the condition. So, in very limited circumstances and after one has faithfully tried God's natural healing methods and for whatever reason(s), i.e. lack of faith, not following the protocol 100%, etc., they were not successful in healing the condition, then I suggest and recommend prescription drugs. Remember, I am referring to God's natural way of healing as found in His ten natural laws of health and only a Christian Health Restoration Practitioner can help you with a protocol to apply these ten laws to anatomy and physiology.

Chapter Summary

1. The Catholic church has a global vision for world medicine as outlined in the book "The Original Book of Sorcery or in Latin-"Pharmacopia" written by the Jesuit Martin Del Rio.

2. Satan's plan to deceive the whole world is through prescription drugs-sorcery, Rev.18:23.

2a. Satan through prescription drugs is capturing the minds, i.e. Frontal lobe of the brain (see the section on the frontal lobe), which causes especially Christians and individuals not to be able to discern spiritual things. Satan is attempting to destroy as many non-Christians as possible before they can make an intelligent decision concerning eternity by keeping their minds medicated until they die.

2b. While causing Christians to lose their salvation through defiling their God given new-birth body temple, 1 Cor. 3:16, 17: "Know ye not that ye are the temple of God, and *that* the Spirit of God dwelleth in you? If any man defile the temple of God, him shall God destroy; for the temple of God is holy, which *temple* ye are".

3. William Avery "Doc" Rockefeller was a practicing Jesuit and brought him the Babylonian Caduceus to the United States. He was also a convicted horse thief and a polygamist.

3a. John D. Rockefeller and Andrew Carnegie through their wealth took over the AMA and greatly influenced it shortly after the turn of the 19th century. It was John D. Rockefeller who help to establish the Babylonian Caduceus as the symbol of the American Medical Association and The documentation more than suggests that the medical establishment assassinated the life work of Antoine Bechamp to establish the current modern medicine model that America and most of the western world worships today.

Chapter Four: *Spiritualistic Medicine Section*

Three Unclean Spirits like Frogs: Rev. 16:13, 14

As noted in chapter two, The Island of Cos, is the birthplace of Hippocrates. He developed the Hippocratic Tradition of Medicine that spread from Greece to Egypt, to Persia in the east, and then on to Italy in the west. The Yellow River of China is the home of Chinese Medicine, the third of the three is found in the Indus Valley of India, which is the seat of Ayuvedic Medicine. Some of the belief systems shared by these three systems were the Separable Soul, which was the forerunner of Vital Essence, which later became known as Out of Body Experiences. Elements are as personal forces in nature, which is pantheism (Religious belief) of today; that the colon as a route of disease; diagnostic of the part from the whole, which is modern medicine's diagnostic approach of today.

"The heathen oracles have their counterpart in the spiritualistic mediums, the clairvoyants, and fortunetellers of today. The mystic voices that spoke at Ekron and Endor are still by their lying words misleading the children of men. The prince of darkness has but appeared under a new guise..." The Mainstreaming of New Age, Pacific Press Publishing Association, Manuel Vasquez,

While we in the 21st Century, with all of our intellectual and scientific advancements, speak with scorn of the magicians of old, the great deceiver laughs in triumph as we yield to his arts under a different form. His agents still claim to cure disease. They attribute their power to electricity, magnetism, or the so-called 'sympathetic remedies.' *In truth, they are but channels for Satan's electric currents. By this means he casts his spell over the bodies and souls of men."* Shall We Consult Spiritualist Physicians, Counsels on Health, Pacific Press Publishing Association, Ellen White, page 454.

Chinese Medicine

"Chinese Medicine is the balance of "Universal Energy" as god. It is the child of Chinese religion," and at their core lies the same fundamental belief in the dual universal energy of chi and the five elements. The concept of yin and yang is at the base of all Chinese medicine. It serves to explain the organic structure, physiological functions and pathological changes of the human body, and in addition guides clinical diagnosis and treatment. The Mainstreaming of New Age, Pacific Press Publishing Association, Manuel Vasquez, page 131.

"Applied kinesiology is a unique blend of ancient Chinese medicine and American chiropractic theory that tests the muscles for organ dysfunction. It is not to be confused with formal or standard kinesiology (biomechanics), a legitimate science, which is the study of bodily movements and the muscles that control them. Applied kinesiology and behavioral kinesiology operate on the same principle of innate energy imbalance in the organs related to the muscle via the appropriate acupuncture meridians."

The Mainstreaming of New Age, Pacific Press Publishing Association, Manuel Vasquez, page 142.

"Homeopathy, one of the most "apparently innocent" forms of New Age alternative medicine is based on the "Law of Similar" that "like cures like." The word itself comes from two Greek words, *homoiois*, meaning "like", and *pathos* meaning "pain" or "suffering." Homeopathy, like acupuncture, is based on the Chinese theory of universal energy, chi. Homeopathy remedies are prepared by using minerals, botanical substances, zoological substances, and other sources, weakened by multiple dilutions. Homeopathic Dr. Vithoulkas states "clearly this phenomenon cannot be explained by ordinary chemical mechanisms. The dilutions are so astronomical that not even one molecule of the original medicine is left!" The Mainstreaming of New Age, Pacific Press Publishing Association, Manuel Vasquez, page 155.

Homeopathy: one of the most "apparently innocent" forms of New Age alternative medicine is homeopathy,

• Based on the "Law of Similar" that "like cures like".

• The word itself comes from two Greek words, *homoiois*, meaning "like", and *pathos* meaning "pain" or "suffering."

• Homeopathy, like acupuncture, is based on the Chinese theory of universal energy, Chi.

• Homeopathy remedies are prepared by using minerals, botanical substances, zoological substances, and other sources, weakened by multiple dilutions.

• Homeopathic Dr. Vithoulkas states "clearly this phenomenon cannot be explained by ordinary chemical mechanisms. The dilutions are so astronomical that not even one molecule of the original medicine is left!"

- Samuel Hahnemann (1755-1843), a German Doctor. In 1910 he published his "Organon of Medicine," this is the manual for the homeopath as the Bible is for the Christian.

- As a young man he joined the Free Masons, in actual fact on the title page of his "Organon" appears their motto "Aude Sapere" which means "dare to be wise;" which also obviously explains his reference to Jesus Christ as an "arch-enthusiast". In other words he does not acknowledge Him to be God or the Savior of the world.

- To quote Hahnemann, "the man of sorrow who took the darkness of the world on himself was an offense to the love of etheric wisdom" (ether means: (archaic) the fifth and highest element after air, fire, water and earth; was believed to be the substance composing all heavenly bodies).

- He was a definite professed non-Christian.

- Attracted to eastern Religions and a strong admirer of Confucius, clearly indicating the "vital force" theories.

- Ask yourself: if the solution in its diluted form is invaluable, yet has some effect, what causes it? And if its origins are not Biblical, then guess who is behind it? –the devil!!

- The counterfeit is camouflaged convincingly under the disguise of "natural medicine" known as homeopathy.

Massage Therapies: Acupressure, Shiatsu and Reflexology
"Another Traditional Chinese Medicine (TCM) method of healing using the accupoints in massage. In India and other countries of the Orient, touch is highly valued as a method of healing. Through touch, life energy is thought to be transmitted from one person to another. This is the basis for various types of massage therapy such as acupressure, shiatsu, and reflexology. Acupressure is Chinese, shiatsu is Japanese, and reflexology is a Western variety of energy-balancing techniques. Though the massage techniques in the various therapies may vary, the idea that the therapy manipulates the flow of energy comes from the same source." The Mainstreaming of New Age, Pacific Press Publishing Association, Manuel Vasquez, page 138.

Massage: In both western and oriental medicine, massage has long been used as a method of natural healing.
- It is also one of the best relaxation techniques.
- In scripture, the laying on of hands is part of the divine process.

- Today, new age techniques are incorporated into this highly effective healing art form.
- One of these techniques is Jade or hot rocks.
- One way Jade or hot rocks are used is to help circulate Chi inside our bodies.
- Chi in oriental medicine is the power, the life force, the essence of everything. In western religious terms, we call this pantheism.

Therapeutic Touch: "is an energy manipulation therapy that is now widely practiced and promoted by the nursing profession. Dolores Krieger, R.N., a Buddhist, the founder and one of the chief promoters of therapeutic touch, was greatly influenced by the healing theories and practices of Ayurvedic, Tibetan, Chinese, and Native American medicine and yoga, in resurrecting the ancient healing art of the therapeutic use of hands. Therapeutic touch is considered to be America's equivalent of Reiki, the energy healing system based onancient Tibetan medicine. The main principle of Therapeutic Touch is that the body is nurtured and maintained by prana, a vital energy force. Essentially, the treatment consists of a therapist's extending his or her hands slightly above the patient's body, locating excess energy fields and moving energy to deficient areas in the body where it is needed. At no time is there physical contact between the patient and therapist". The Mainstreaming of New Age, Pacific Press Publishing Association, Manuel Vasquez, page 157.

Iridology: Like other New Age holistic health therapies, iridology is based on the perception of mystical universal energy fields in the body.
- The diagnostic method, examining the iris of the human eye for indications of illness, can be traced back to the ancient Chinese and Japanese.
- The Babylonian, Chaldeans and the Egyptians suggested that the human eye played a significant role in medicine.
- Dr. Bernard Jensen, is considered the father of American Iridology. Jensen further developed Dr. von Peczely's chart on iridology to what it is today.
- Dr. Jensen's chart, which resembles Hindu teachings, outline ninety-six zones or divisions of the eye just as Hindu divided the "third-eye chakra."

- This inner-eye chakra, which is supposedly located on the forehead between the eyes, has a corresponding foot massage point located in "the area of the sinus at the tip of the big toe."

In fact, all seven Hindu chakras are said to be affected by massaging their corresponding massage point on the foot, just as in reflexology. The Mainstreaming of New Age, Pacific Press Publishing Association, Manuel Vasquez, page 159.

Reflexology: also known as hand reflexology, foot reflexology, and zone therapy, is a form of massage on the sole of the foot or the palm of the hand. Reflexologists believe that the bottom of the foot and the inside of the hand contain nerve endings connecting the vital organs with other specific parts of the body. They believe that by pressure massaging and stroking specific areas of the hands and feet, they can affect these areas in the body. Reflexology is related to the New Age holistic health energy-manipulating therapies, such as acupuncture, acupressure, applied kinesiology, Reiki, and therapeutic touch. Reflexology is considered a novel form of acupressure because, like acupuncture, it manipulates and attempts to balance the life energy force of chi. Ankerberg and Weldron, The Facts on Holistic Health and the New Medicine, p. 41.

Dr. William Fitzgerald is the physician credited with rediscovering reflexology, which has its roots in ancient Chinese acupressure. In 1913, Dr. Fitzgerald introduced and developed the reflexology of modern times. He divided the area on the bottom of each foot into five zones corresponding to ten areas in the body. The ten zones ran from the tip of the ten fingers up to the arm and the neck, to the top of the skull, and then downward through the body to the legs, finally culminating in the ten toes. The zones originating in the left hand covered the left side of the body and those in the right hand covered the right side. Melton, Clark, and Kelly, *New Age Almanac,* p. 242

"The roots of reflexology are traceable back to ancient forms of pressure therapy known in Egypt as early as 3000 B.C." Williams, *New Age Healing,* p. 22. It also has elements of the universal energy forces basic to Traditional Chinese Medicine and Ayurvedic Medicine, which makes it yet another entryway into the subtle New Age movement.

Pendulum Divination: The use of a pendulum for divination purposes is a modern form of the ancient practice of divination, or divining.
- Basically, pendulums work on the premise of either placing the pendulum over an object or simply asking the pendulum questions that require a "yes" or "no" answer.

- If the pendulum rotates or swings clockwise, the answer signifies a positive yes, male quality.
- If it swings counter-clockwise, in a circular fashion, it indicates a negative, no, or female quality answer.
- Read Exodus 28: 29, 30.
- At the right and left of the breastplate were two large stones of great brilliancy. These were known as the Urim and Thummim.
By them the will of God was made known through the high priest.
- When questions were brought for decision before the Lord, a halo of light encircling the precious stone at the right was a token of the divine consent or approval,
- While a cloud shadowing the stone at the left was an evidence of denial or disapprobation.
- In matters of diagnosing and proscribing remedies and therapies, the pendulum is suspended over the patient's organ or other area affected by disease.
- The practitioner, called a pendulumist, ask questions of the pendulum, such as: "Is this organ malfunctioning?" "Is this organ hyperactive?" "Is this organ inflamed?"
- Based on the pendulum's motion response, the machine is able to diagnose and recommend a therapy or remedy. Even though the pendulum is used by some Christians, it should be pointed out that God specifically mentions "divination" in Deuteronomy 18:9-14 as an abomination. The Mainstreaming of New Age, Pacific Press Publishing Association, Manuel Vasquez, pp. 162.

Integrative Medicine: Based upon the documentation previously provided, it should not be necessary to comment on the A.M.A. controlled Integrative Medicine system in America. Your primary care physician (allopathic) has to approve you to see an alternative health care practitioner. Now a day, you can find clinics of M.D.s, massage therapist, acupuncturist, etc… under the same roof. Cancer Treatment Center of America has a Naturopathic department in its center, as does hospitals. A name means much, when you have a child you buy a book of names and look up their meanings. God has many names, Jehovah, Jesus, etc… So the name Integrative Medicine should warn you that Western allopathic medicine has joined forces with Eastern medicine to perpetrate a false system of healing upon the unsuspecting public. Integrative Medicine does not have a single definition: The term alternative medicine, as used in the modern Western world, encompasses any healing practice "that does not fall within the realm of conventional medicine". From Wikipedia, the free encyclopedia. Integrative medicine is healing-oriented medicine that takes account of the whole person (body, mind, and spirit), including all aspects of lifestyle. It emphasizes the therapeutic relationship and makes use of all appropriate therapies, both conventional and alternative," -Andrew Weil.

"This is the practice of combining alternative, complementary and conventional therapies to take advantage of the strengths of each system and to offset their weaknesses," Heartland Naturopathic Clinic. What the true Christian must understand is that Satan has supernatural powers and can give the appearance of health and healing for a time, while all the time these counterfeit healing philosophies are leading Christians away from the Creator and the Word of God. It is this counterfeit healing that gains your trust and you begin to practice the religion associated with the healing philosophy. This is the same principle Jesus and the disciples used to win converts to Christianity, albeit true healing in their instance. Nither complimentary medicine, alternative medicine, allopathic medicine, and integrated medicine is from God or it is not. If it is not, then why as Christians do we trust our health and life to an inferior system of healing? Job 14:4, Romans 8:7. While many are in pain and suffering, we have to be honest and admit that it is because of our disobedience to God's word, the Ten Natural Laws of Health primarily, as to why we are in the condition we are in. Then instead of confessing our sins to God and accepting His will for our lives, we inquire as did King Ahaziah, of Baal-Zebub the god of Ekron, jeopardizing your salvation. II Kings 1:2, 3.

Yoga is in all reality an introduction to Eastern Mysticism. The majority of the stretches are actually poses to their gods. You say that you are not bowing to their god just stretching. However as human flesh, we do not have control over spirits; good spirits (angels) or evil spirits (evil angels). I have nothing against stretching as I do myself, but just understand as you open up your conscience to eastern mysticism philosophy because in the process of time, you will wake up to the fact that you are worshiping false deities.

Chapter V: The Case against Allopathic Medicine

"Very few know that the birth hour of the pharmaceutical industry is actually a deliberate decision by a handful of people on this side (Europe) and the other side (America) of the Atlantic Ocean to define disease as a marketplace, and build what has now become the largest investment industry upon that simple thought; so cancer is just one element of this unspeakable business of defining disease as a marketplace. Everything else, if you see today around the pharmaceutical industry: the tremendous profits, the inability to eliminate disease are the propaganda war from that side [pharmaceutical industry] that they are actually making progress in any disease. All that comes from the fact that it is a business model in the investment industry that thrives on the continuation of existing diseases and the launching of new diseases," –Dr. Matthias Rath, M.D.

Allopathic medicine has set itself in direct opposition against the great and mighty God of the universe by stating as one of its regulations: "Only a drug can cure, prevent or treat a disease." This regulation was no doubt developed by a drug company. The FDA further states, Natural substances cannot cure disease. Put another way, "only unnatural substances can cure disease. Man and his toxic chemicals never can and never will cure, heal or treat disease.

The Word of God clearly and plainly teaches that: …"*for I am the Lord that healeth thee*", Exodus 15:26. *"Pure air, sunlight, abstemiousness (temperance), rest, exercise, proper diet, the use of water (internally & externally), and trust in divine power,-these are the true remedies,"* Ministry of Healing, Pacific Press Publishing Association, Ellen White, p. 127.

Finally, God has commissioned his disciples to teach the people His healing remedies: *"Every person should have a knowledge of nature's remedial agencies and how to apply them.* Ministry of Healing, Pacific Press Publishing Association, Ellen White, p. 127, 1909.

In I Corinthians 12:9, the Word of God tells us that God has given "to another the gifts of healing by the same Spirit… As disciples of Christ, we have the same decision to make today, as did Peter and the other apostles in their day… "We ought to obey God rather than men", Acts 5:29.

Remember, I am specifically referring to chronic diseases like cancer, diabetes, arthritis, heart disease, etc. God has said all these false systems, discussed in this section, have "No Healing Medicines", Jeremiah 30:13, 46:11.

After more than 100 years of control by the Rockefellers and Carnegies, through the American Medical Association, FDA, and other institutions, are we as Americans any healthier today? Let's examine the facts: Do you really believe research is designed to find a cure? Jonas Edward Salk discovered the first effective vaccine used as a preventative against poliomyelitis. It was developed in 1952.

Dr. Salk's earlier work on an anti-influenza vaccine during the 1940s led to his discovery.

By the mid-1950s the vaccine had been widely distributed in the United States, greatly reducing the domestic incidence of polio. Question: what was used as a treatment protocol for polio prior to Dr. Salks discovery? Answer: the Iron Lung machine.

Question: what happened to the iron lung machine after the discovery of the vaccine? Answer: the $100,000.00 plus (a lot of money in those days) machine became obsolete putting a lot of people out of work and a loss of profits for certain companies.

Question: what would happen if the American Cancer Society or American Diabetes Association found cures for their respective diseases? Answer: there would be no more need for expensive surgeries, or debilitating chemotherapy, or poisonous drugs. Once again, expensive five-color argyle lasers, etc…would become obsolete. If enough of these cures were found in a reasonable time frame it could potentially and seriously affect the American economy.

Question: since 1952, when Dr. Salk discovered the polio vaccination, can you name a single cure for a disease that has been discovered? Answer: you guessed it, No! In the introduction, I shared with you my testimony concerning hypoglycemia and how I am totally cured. As long as the Diabetes Association continues to advocate and teach managing blood sugar levels, and not focus on teaching the public how to heal the pancreas, they will never go out of business and you will not overcome your blood sugar issues. In many respects, the guardians of our health are actually perpetuating the system and even causing sickness.

The American Cancer Society

The American Cancer Society was officially formed in May, 1913 at the Harvard Club in New York. I would like to show how it has been instrumental in taking millions of dollars from the unsuspecting American public with very little to show for a return except a wake of heartache and death. Just the names behind the organization should tell us something; General Motors, AT&T, Standard Oil, etc…

Let me put it another way. The American Medical Association owns half of the patent rights to 5 FU. This is the chemical name given to a popular toxic drug which has been used as an acceptable medicine for the treatment of cancer. When you realize that the drug is manufactured by the Hoffman-LaRouch Laboratory, which is directly related to the I.G. Farben/Rockefeller Cartel then you can begin to see the tie into this money-making machine. What we the American sheeple (people) fail to realize or understand is that in order for this vast sick care system to work, it depends on one thing and one thing only—that you, the people become sick. The health (sick) care system in America is a $1.4 trillion industry, or 1/7 of our capitalistic economy. Who would loan the money for multi-billion dollar hospitals, or the million dollar pieces of equipment like C-Scans, five color argyle lasers, etc, or the hundreds of thousands of dollars in hospital administrator salaries, or hundreds of thousands of dollars in surgeon and physician fees, or tens of thousands of dollars in hospital fee, if you were not getting sick? It is called the Law of Large Numbers, and the insurance industry is the master of this game. It is in their best interest to get you and keep you sick. It keeps the economy healthy. Please understand that by law, drug companies have a fiduciary responsibility to their shareholders and not to you the sick. Has it ever dawned on you that perhaps it would not be in the best interest of a multi-billion dollar industry to find a cure that would put them out of business? Not to mention the closing of many hospitals and research centers, and the shutting down of scores of useless machines that cost millions of dollars to produce.

No, business is too good to close. Remember, if you can really get the people thinking you are searching for a cure for cancer or any other disease, while all the time you are building an empire behind their backs, then the dying will give you their last dollar, hoping against hope that one day soon that you will be able to cure them.

The Truth about Chemotherapy: By Nicholas Gonzales, MD

This is a story that most Oncologist do not know. During World War II the department of Defense had stockpiles of nerve gas from world war one and they were not using them in world war two. Someone at the Department of Defense had this brilliant idea to try and convert these nerve gases into useful therapeutic modalities. Serendipitously at the same time, it turned out that a group of American soldiers were inadvertently exposed to some nerve gas at an experimental research center. The death of the soldiers was followed up with autopsy and what they noticed was that their white blood cell count had gone down and their bone marrow had been suppressed. So one of the Department of Defense doctors got this brilliant idea, this was about 1945, that perhaps you could use nerve gas, in this case it was nitrogen mustard, to treat leukemia and lymphoma by knocking out the bone marrow.

Leukemia and lymphomas are diseases of the while cell line and the nerve gas seemed to wipe it out. So the Department of Defense actually contracted with doctor Gillman of Yale University, one of the preeminent pharmacologists of the day and gave him a huge amount of money to test it in animal models. So in 1946, doctor Gillman up at Yale tested it in animal model of Lymphoma and low and behold the tumors regressed, but of course all the animals died. But it was very impressive; it was the first time in history that anyone had seen cancerous tumors regress from a drug treatment. So then they decided to try it on a patient, they had a patient with advanced Lymphoma and there were no treatment for Lymphoma in 1946; so they gave him this nitrogen mustard derivative and low and behold all his tumors regressed, which they thought was a miracle, of course six weeks later he was dead. But it was an extraordinary event because it was the first time in medical history that doctors had witnessed and documented the regression of tumors in a patient with advanced disease. So they started to tweak it and over the next ten, fifteen years they gradually developed a variety of drugs, beginning at Yale but then it went to other medical centers, where they are using these toxic chemicals. Ironically, from nerve gas, the original derivative was nerve gas used to kill people as therapeutic modality chemotherapy.

Few people realize the whole generation of chemotherapeutic drugs that are being used today, and there are over a hundred of them, really developed from poisonous nerve gas developed for warfare. That is how it all began, it did not develop from anything good, its origins are pretty unpleasant but that is how it all began with the Department of Defense contracting doctors to use their nitrogen mustard stores to see if they could use it to treat any kind of disease. Even though at that time, there were promising alternative treatments to cancer but the medical community became enthralled with the research of chemotherapy. After the initial enthusiasm in the mid 1940's, chemotherapy becoming a standard protocol for cancer treatment was a really slow process. The initial enthusiasm was tainted by the fact that most patients were not responding, indeed tumors would shrink, and patients would die. It was not until the late 1960's that the idea that chemotherapy had this magical effect on cancer was accepted.

Again, it was a single incident; it was really the development of the MOPP treatment for Hodgkin's disease. This was developed by Doctor Vincent Deveto who at that time was working at the National Cancer Institute and he was studying Hodgkin disease. He put together a variety of chemotherapy drugs that had already been developed in the 1960's, a four drug regiment and started treating advanced Hodgkin's disease. Low and behold it was like 1946 all over again, all these tumors magically disappeared. Now the interesting thing is that with some of these Hodgkin's patients, the results were long standing and they seemed to be cured and this was the first time that there was a significant long term effect from synthetic toxic chemicals. The treatment worked for a lot of these Hodgkin patients, fifty percent of the advance cases seemed to respond beautifully for long periods of time. Yea, there were side effects, yea there was toxicity, but Doctor Devito's work with Hodgkin really prompted a new enthusiasm for chemo. By the mid 1960's, a lot of the enthusiasm from the 1940's had kind of waned because they were not getting the results that they thought they would, and Doctor Devito really revived this whole new interest in the use of toxic synthetic medications in the treatment of cancer. Of course it was like 1946 all over again because Hodgkin's is a very unique disease, it is one of the few of the hundred cancers that actually respond to chemotherapy. It just happened to be the disease he was working on and it happened to be one of the few cancers that respond to toxic chemotherapy drugs, but again, as they did in 1946, the oncology establishment generalized, they assumed that if chemotherapy could work so effectively for Hodgkin's disease, which in those days was a deadly illness, it must work for all the other cancers. That was an assumption that was not warranted and turned out to be erroneous, but because of Doctor Devito work and his work specifically with Hodgkin's disease and specifically with the MOPP-Chemotherapy regiment, there was a burst of new enthusiasm.

Question: why is chemotherapy so ineffective for most cancers, especially at the stage four levels? Answer: There are over a hundred different types of cancers depending on which text book you consult. The great majority of them do not respond to chemotherapy. As it turns out, the cancers that respond to chemo are generally the blood related cancers like Leukemia and Lymphoma. They are not that common compared to the major cancer killers like lung, colon, prostate, pancreatic, and breast cancer do not respond to chemotherapy. Typical solid tumors, tumors of the breast, lungs, stomach, colon, pancreas, liver, uterus, ovaries, and prostate do not respond generally to chemotherapy. It's the rare cancer like Hodgkin, Hodgkin's is a very rare cancer, Lymphomas are not that common, and Leukemia's are rare cancers. They tend to respond to chemotherapy very nicely and there is a interesting reason why, there are all kinds of theories as to why chemo works when it does work and why it does not work, when it does not, but actually chemotherapy, as the 1946 study showed kind of wipes out the bone marrow.

Leukemia's, Lymphomas and multiple Myelomas, are the cancers that do respond to chemotherapy and they are diseases of the bone marrow, so with toxic chemo you are actually knocking out the bone marrow. So of course these diseases will regress but the other solid tumors, the major cancer killers, like tumors of the breast, lungs, etc., there not bone marrow cancers. So you can wipe out the bone marrow and the cancer is still going to grow because they do not derive from bone marrow stem cells. So for the great majority of major cancer killers, chemotherapy is ineffective.

Simple Modern Chest X-ray

For example, a simple X-ray treatment is dangerous and can cause disease. However, some would say X-rays today are different. If you would care to do an independent study, you will be quick to find that X-ray treatments, even as given today are causing no end of trouble. Dr. Ernest Sternglass, Professor of Radiation Physics at the University of Pittsburgh, did a study on the live births that were affected by the gases and emissions from the Three Mile Island accident.

Four-hundred thirty infant deaths were the results. These are hospital statistics, and the U.S. government wishes to remain silent to these findings neither admitting nor denying them. Enough radioactive iodine was emitted, within the first two days before the pregnant mothers and small children could be evacuated that within the first three months, the death rate had skyrocketed. These were premature, underweight and died of respiratory distress, at least that is what the present record states. Now, let's look at radiation levels and the simple chest X-ray, and I am not even including the radiation emitted from your microwave, radar range, color TV, digital watch, radio and TV towers that numbers in the hundreds, etc... As far as safe levels of radiation are concerned, apparently no medical textbook in the world says there is a safe level of radiation. Even low levels of radiation we know today can kill. In fact, if the truth were allowed to surface, we would be told it is one of the known causes of genetic defects and a contributing factor in the cause of cancer. We would also be told that low-level radiation exposure actually weakens, if not destroys, the immunity of man to resist disease.

Could this be why the incident of measles increased 45 times during the year following the Three Mile Island episode? Consider the simple modern chest X-ray, and yet many doctors think nothing of giving a whole series to a patient. They come in handy for dentists too. Depending on the equipment and duration of a full chest X-ray you would be exposed to between 30 to 50 millirems. G.I.s, during the atomic bomb test in the U.S., were exposed on an average to a little less than one thousandths millirems. As a result, their leukemia rate doubled that of the national average. Today, the established rate of radiation exposure is 1.25 millirems per quarter.

Dr. Alice Stewart

Another example of how information is kept from the public concerns Dr. Alice Stewart, a British Epidemiologist, who fought for ten years to have her studies recognized in the medical field, in the area of X-ray and its effect upon the human body. Today, she has been accepted into the medical field, even though much of her material has not been made available to the general public. She has proven that a single abdominal X-ray to a pregnant woman would increase the likelihood of leukemia in the child by 40 percent. With a grant of £1,000, she launched her landmark study of the causes of childhood cancer. Beginning from a hunch that mothers might remember something that the doctors had forgotten, she devised a questionnaire for women whose children had died of any form of cancer between 1953 and 1955. By the time a mere 35 questionnaires had been returned, the answer was clear: a single diagnostic X-ray, well within the exposure considered safe, was enough almost to double the risk of early cancer. This news was a surprise to Stewart and was not welcome in the scientific community. Enthusiasm for nuclear technology was at a high point in the 1950s, and radiography was being used for everything from treating acne and menstrual disorders to ascertaining shoe fit. X-rays, as Stewart said. "Were the favorite toy of the medical profession. The British and American governments were investing heavily in the arms race and promoting nuclear energy, and there was little willingness to recognize that radiation was as dangerous as Stewart claimed. What was the reward she received for making the world a safer place to live? She never again received a major grant in England. For the next two decades, however, she and her statistician, George Kneale, extended, elaborated and refined their database at what became the Oxford Survey of Childhood Cancer.

In the 1970s, major medical bodies recommended that pregnant women should not be X-rayed, and the practice ceased. The Oxford survey had collected information on hundreds of thousands of children across Britain in a 30-year period. Stewart and Kneale had demonstrated that children incubating cancer have greatly increased susceptibility to infections. The study turned up a connection between inoculations and resistance to cancer which suggests links between cancer and the immune system. They also had theories about ultrasound and sudden infant death syndrome that they would have liked to test – but such funding was cut off.

For more than 40 years, the epidemiologist Alice Stewart challenged official estimates of the risks of radiation. Her research in 1956 and 1958 alerted the medical profession to the link between fetal X-rays and childhood cancer. Two decades later, in her seventies, she again called for a change in working practices when she published a study showing that workers at nuclear weapons plants are at greater health risk than international safety standards admit. In 1974, having officially retired and moved from Oxford to Birmingham, where she had accepted a research appointment, the 68-year-old Stewart received an unexpected phone call from America. Dr Thomas Mancuso, who had been at work on a government study of the health of nuclear workers at Hanford, the weapons complex that produced plutonium for the Manhattan Project, wanted her to "take a closer look" at his data. Mancuso's study had been going on for more than a decade, and was not expected to turn up anything troubling, since workers' exposure at Hanford, the oldest and largest nuclear weapons facility in the world, was well within the safety limits set by international guidelines. But Stewart and Kneale, her statistician found that the cancer risk to the workers was about 20 times higher than was being claimed, a discovery that put them at odds with the multimillion-dollar Hiroshima and Nagasaki studies on which international safety guidelines are based.

The American Department of Energy dismissed Mancuso and attempted to seize the data. But Stewart and Kneale took their work back to England, and, together with Mancuso, published a series of studies which continued to corroborate a cancer effect considerably higher than the Hiroshima studies indicated. The Energy Department denied the scientists further access to the workers' records and kept research under strict government control. In 1986, when she was 80, she received the Right Livelihood Award, the "alternative Nobel" as it is called, which is awarded in the Swedish Parliament the day before the Nobel Prize to honor those who have made contributions to the betterment of society. She published more than 400 papers in scientific journals. However, although she could deliver her findings in person with exceptional clarity, her publications were often very hard to decipher.

Also in 1986, Stewart received a $1.4 million grant to study the effects of low-dose radiation. This came not from a government agency or academic institute, but from activists, and derived from a fine imposed upon the Three Mile Island facility.

To undertake the study, Stewart needed access to the nuclear workers' records, but the American government refused to release them. It took several years and several Freedom of Information suits to get at them. When in 1992 Stewart was finally granted access to the records of one third of all workers in nuclear weapons facilities in the US, the front page of The New York Times called it a blow for scientific freedom. See appendix E.

Tri-State Leukemia Study

I think one simple, yet classic, case should help convince some of you as to the validity of what I just wrote. The largest study that has ever been conducted anywhere in the world, at the time, was the Tri-State Leukemia study conducted by Dr. Bertel and Dr. Bross of the Roswell Park Memorial Institute. This study involved 30 million people. Such a huge study had never before been undertaken. The study produced overwhelming evidence that leukemia does increase when the use of such treatments as X-ray and radiation are used. In other words, the so-called cure for cancer is actually a contributing factor in its cause. What was the reward for this scientific discovery? The National Cancer Institute "stopped all grants to that particular research body.

Just another case in point that health care in America is money-motivated, not cure-driven. See appendix F.

Dr. Robert T. Schimke

Finally, not all the scientific evidence and information is available. However, if the previous information does not cause you to stop and rethink and research for yourself, then no further information will. Congress declared war on cancer in 1971 when it passed the National Cancer Act under President Nixon. Since then more than $30 billion has been spent on cancer research alone. In 1985, a prominent cancer researcher, Robert T. Schimke, made a startling admission about the progress in that war. Chemotherapy, he declared, tends to make cancer worse. The problem, he explained, is that cancer cells resist chemotherapy, and that resistance mimics the very processes of cancer itself. Dr. Schimke drew his conclusion from research sponsored by the American Cancer Society. He reported his findings in the Journal of Cancer and gave a lecture at the National Institutes of Health (NIH) in Bethesda, Maryland. The NIH is as high as you can go in America, as far as traditional allopathic medicine is concerned. Dr. Schimke was being honored for receiving the Alfred P. Sloan Jr. award for his research in cancer.

His talk was about "Gene Amplification" from which we now know that chemotherapy provokes resistance in tumor cells. The resistance and the cancer are the same, chemotherapy literally provokes the process we call cancer, and this is resistance to chemotherapy. Journal of Cancer, [Cancer Research 44, p.1735-1742, May 1984]. In Dr. Schimke's concluding comments he writes: "In this "Perspectives" article, the phenomenon of gene amplification in somatic (non-reproductive cells or tissue) has been reviewed briefly. It would appear to be a relatively common process in cells in cultures and, perhaps, in tumors as well. Current available studies indicate that amplification occurs by over-replication of portions of the genome in a single cell cycle, i.e. disproportionate replication, and this process can be enhanced by the very agents in cancer chemotherapy as well as by known carcinogenic agents. I have speculated that such over-replication may have a role in not only the generation of drug resistance clinically, but also the progression from a normal to malignant cell. Clearly, it is more than a platitude to state that far more research is needed to understand the underlying mechanism(s) of gene amplification and processes of drug resistance, as well as the possible role of genome over-replication-recombination in overcoming normal growth constraints"

What is absolutely amazing is that science calls it resistance but God calls it [vital force]. You can not destroy resistance, i.e. vital force and expect a patient to live. When you overcome the resistance, or waste away the vital force a person dies. This is why chemotherapy, radiation and surgery will never be a successful treatment for cancer or any other symptom that man calls disease. *"God endowed man with so great vital force that he has withstood the accumulation of disease brought upon the race in consequence of perverted habits, and has continued for six thousand years. This fact of itself is enough to evidence to us the strength and electrical energy that God gave to man at his creation. It took more than two thousand years of crime and indulgence of base passions to bring bodily disease upon the race to any great extent. If Adam, at his creation, had not been endowed with twenty times as much vital force as men now have, the race, with their present habits of living in violation of natural law, would have become extinct...* Ellen White, Testimonies for the Church, vol. 3, p. 138.2.

Notice this statement from a researcher at *University of Michigan*: **Breakthrough new science conducted at the *University of Michigan*:** A clinical study gave mice lethal injections of chemotherapy that would, pound for pound, kill most adult human beings, too. The study authors openly admit: "All tumors from different tissues and organs can be killed by high doses of chemotherapy and radiation, but the <u>current challenge for treating the later-staged metastasized cancer is that you actually kill the [patient] before you kill the tumor</u>." Chemotherapy is deadly. It is the No. 1 cause of death for cancer patients in America, and the No. 1 side effect of chemo is more cancer. Jian-Guo Geng, associate professor at the University of Michigan.

After reviewing and researching the scientific literature available on cancer and traditional cancer treatments, individuals, especially Christians still go the conventional medical route of surgery (cut), radiation (burn) and chemotherapy (poison), mainly out of fear. "If any man defiles the temple of God, him shall God destroy; for the temple of God is holy, which *temple* ye are". 1 Cor. 3:17. "What? know ye not that your body is the temple of the Holy Ghost *which is* in you, which ye have of God, and ye are not your own"? 1Cor. 6:19. We continue to take prescription drugs for symptoms which are termed disease like diabetes, heart disease, etc… increasing the number and increasing the dosages the longer we stay on them, poisoning our blood stream which is the current of life. It only shows how much the American people have been brainwashed to believe that if modern medicine cannot cure cancer or disease then no one can, then pass laws making it illegal for natural remedies to treat cancer and disease.

"What I propose is that the buzzards have shown us that principle. Nature has its own laws and may not allow intrusion without revenge. Intrusion creates resistance, and it is resistance that transforms our noblest intentions into the opposite. The things we seek for ourselves— health, wisdom, prosperity, and peace—are all expressions of freedom, and freedom is the one thing we can't achieve through the principle of control. And if control can't give us freedom, neither can it give us anything else. If that is true, our only choice is to seek a way of getting along with nature that doesn't pit us against her, that instead allies us with her, capturing her strength for our own. Does such a way exist? I believe it does. Our great challenge, in health and every other area of life, is to find it" Black, Dean; Health at the Crossroads, Tapestry Press, *p. 9-11.*
What is of interest to note, is that Dr. Black refers to God. The answer that he is looking for is God, the creator of nature. God established nature's laws, just as mankind's health laws were created and given by God. We can never capture nature's strength, but rather work with nature in her efforts to restore health.

"The Savior in His miracles revealed the power that is continually at work in man's behalf, to sustain and to heal him. Through the agencies of nature, God is working, day by day, hour by hour, moment by moment, to keep us alive, to build up and restore us. When any part of the body sustains injury, a healing process is at once begun; nature's agencies are set at work to restore soundness. But the power working through these agencies is the power of God. All life-giving power is from Him. When one recovers from disease, it is God who restores him." White, Ellen; The Ministry of Healing, Pacific Press Publishing Association, p.112. Freedom is only to be found in the Son of Righteous, and when He sets you free, you are free indeed. John 8:36.

True Vital Force Based Upon Christian Principles

As I stated earlier, reserve energy or vital force is essential to the preservation of life and health. When the reserve energy drops below a certain level it will never come back, the individual grows weaker, preferring death to life, eventually the individual dies, usually sooner than later.

"God has endowed us with a certain amount of vital force. He has also formed us with organs suited to maintain the various functions of life, and He designs that these organs shall work together in harmony. If we carefully preserve the life force, and keep the delicate mechanism of the body in order, the result is health; but if the vital force is to rapidly exhausted, the nervous system borrows power for present use from its resources of strength, and when one organ is injured, all are affected. Nature bears much abuse without apparent resistance; she then arouses and makes a determined effort to remove the effects of the ill-treatment she has suffered. Her effort to correct these conditions is often manifest in fever and various other forms of sickness." White, Ellen; Ministry of Healing, Pacific Press Publishing Association, p. 234.

"Those who make great exertions to accomplish just so much work in a given time, and continue to labor when their judgment tells them they should rest, are never gainers. They are living on borrowed capital. They are expending the vital force which they will need at a future time. And when the energy they have so recklessly used is demanded, they fail for want of it. The physical strength is gone, the mental powers fail. They realize that they have met with a loss, but do not know what it is. Their time of need has come, but their physical resources are exhausted. Everyone who violates the laws of health must sometime be a sufferer to a greater or less degree. God has provided us with constitutional force, which we need at different periods of our lives. If we recklessly exhaust this force by continual

over taxation, we shall at sometime be the losers." White, Ellen; Child Guidance, p. 397.

"*Children are generally untaught in regard to the importance of when, how, and what they should eat. They are permitted to indulge their tastes freely, to eat at all hours, and to help themselves to fruit when it tempts their eyes; and this, with the pie, cake, bread and butter, and sweetmeats eaten almost constantly, makes them gourmands and dyspeptics. The digestive organs, like a mill which is continually kept running, become enfeebled, vital force is called from the brain to aid the stomach in its overwork, and thus the mental powers are weakened. The unnatural stimulation and wear of the vital forces make them nervous, impatient of restraint, self-willed, and irritable. They can scarcely be trusted out of their parents' sight. In many cases the moral powers seem deadened, and it is difficult to arouse them to a sense of the shame and grievous nature of sin; they slip easily into habits of prevarication, deceit, and often open lying*." Child Guidance, Ellen White, p. 388.

"At least part of the body's resistance to drugs comes from the operation of the Second Law of thermodynamics. This law says that natural process in closed systems move from order to chaos. (Closed systems are ones that don't receive energy from the outside).

To reverse that—to transform chaos into order—we've got to add energy, and all systems end up consuming more energy than they produce. Every now and then someone claims to have invented a perpetual motion machine. Christians scoff because a perpetual motion machine would be the creation of a god, the one and true God is the great I AM. I suggest that medicine faces the same barrier, that the law that reverses our well intentioned medical intrusions is the Law of Vital Force. If that is true, then the hope of overcoming the body's resistance to drugs is as doomed as the myth of perpetual motion. To see why, let's look at our genes and what they do.

Genes are protein makers, and as they make their proteins, we come to exist. What make proteins useful are their bumpy surfaces. They have nooks and crannies that let them grab hold of other molecules. In chemical terms, this grabbing is known as binding, they lay, so to speak, the bricks that make us. We are, in a very real sense, stuck together proteins. Other proteins are much more dynamic and active. They attract and bind, not copies of themselves, but other molecules, many of which aren't proteins at all. These dynamic and active proteins may be antibodies of the immune system that binds to invaders. Or the hemoglobin in blood that binds to oxygen. Or chemical signals like hormones and neurotransmitters that bind to "receptors" on the surface of other cells, and so let the parts of us talk to one another. Perhaps the most intriguing of these dynamic proteins are enzymes. Enzymes not only bind to molecules they transform them. An enzyme may grab a single molecule, for example, and slice it in two. Or it may grab a molecule and rearrange it into another molecule. Or it may grab two or more molecules and stick them together to form a more complex molecule. All of our chemical processes are brokered in this fashion by enzymes. When the body needs a chemical reaction, it creates, through the genes, an enzyme to handle it… All proteins, whether enzymes or otherwise, are made from tiny building-block molecules called amino acids. To form a protein molecule, our genes first hook amino acids together in a string, attaching the head of one amino acid to the tail of another. Then the string gets folded and tucked in upon itself, and with this folding and tucking we arrive at a point in our physiology where the Law of Vital force come into play. This folding and tucking is perhaps the most critical step in the protein-making process. It rounds the amino-acid string into a globe-like molecule, and, in the process, gives it those bumpy nooks and crannies that are just the right size and shape for binding molecules. If the folding goes wrong, the protein ends up with the wrong nooks and crannies and doesn't work.

While Mr. Black and other secular doctors and scientists call this process "entropy," which is nature's process of randomization, this process speaks clearly of "Intelligent Design," as much as a budding flower or the chirp of a bird. It is God who has ordained this process, and if you talk with any Christian doctor, they will tell you it is not by random chance but an intelligent God who has designed this process. When we give our bodies wholesome, nutrient dense foods, we maintain order or homeostasis. When we eat the "Sad American Diet" (SAD) of processed foods, fast foods and enriched/refined foods, we set the stage for chaos or dis-ease with in our bodies; the end result is disease, sickness, and death. Let me give you a scriptural example. In the Garden of Eden, Adam and Eve were created to live forever. However, to do so they had to eat from the Tree of Life, Genesis 3:22. In Genesis 2:16 God gave permission for them too freely eat from every tree in the garden. This command must have included the Tree of Life with its wholesome, nutrient dense food which the body turns in to energy for fuel. Now, understand verse 17, "But of the tree of the knowledge of Good and Evil, thou shalt not eat of it: for in the day that thou eatest thereof thou shalt surely die."

All around Adam and Eve was food, but only food from the Tree of Life could sustain everlasting life. Today, we have the same choices and decisions to make as our first parents. There are foods (fruit, grains, nuts and vegetables) designed to keep us healthy and restore health, and there are foods that will deplete the body of nutrients causing sickness and death. Did Adam and Eve die the day they ate from the tree of the knowledge of good and evil? Yes, they died spiritually! That is why we must be born again. The day they ate from the Tree of Good and Evil, began the process of physically dying. Verse 24 of Genesis Chapter 3 tells us that man was driven out of the garden and a guard was stationed at the east of the garden to "keep the way of the Tree of Life."

In Revelation 22:2, we read once again about the Tree of Life and those who have the right to eat from it. God could have created man without the necessity of eating from the Tree of Life to sustain life; but He chose not to. God is the only perpetual motion for we know that He never slumbers or sleeps. He existed from the beginning, and nothing was made that was not made by Him. So, what did He eat before he created food? Prescription medication and chemotherapy is a failed man-made system that was doomed to fail from the beginning. It is a system built upon capitalism at the expense of human and potentially, eternal life. "Be sober, be vigilant, because your adversary the devil, as a roaring lion, walketh about, seeking whom he may devour" I Peter 5:8. It is this point that Christians must understand, as we continue to look at the Law of Vital Force.

How Allopathic Medicine Opposes the Law of Vital Force

"As allopathic medicine has developed, it has come more and more to explain health and disease in terms of the level of those active chemicals that our enzymes make for us. The power of this point of view is that it immediately suggests logical therapies. When the cause is too little of a molecule (as in the case of diabetes), we therapeutically add it from the outside (insulin). When the cause is too much of a molecule (as in the case of hay fever with its histamine overload), we therapeutically block it from the outside. Drugs add to our supply of an active chemical, or they block it. In this fashion, the doctor adjusts our molecule levels up or down, depending upon what he or she perceives to be the problem. Now, consider what goes on in the body. Even though the doctor doesn't like the molecule levels the body has chosen for itself, they are nonetheless the ones the body has chosen" Dean Black, Health at the Crossroads, Tapestry Press, p. 29.

Because of Intelligent Design, when the human body chooses a level that is either too little or too much, it is because your body is trying to communicate with you that it does not have the necessary nutrition (minerals) in order to sustain health. Our job as Christian Health Restoration Practitioners is to help and assist nature in this delicate balancing act. Let's take a fever, for example. Fever is not a disease but a symptom that may indicate the presence of disease. Normal body temperature ranges from 98° F to 99° F degrees. One should not have undue concern unless the body temperature rises above 102 degrees in adults and 103 degrees in children. This defense mechanism of the body acts to destroy harmful microbes. When destructive microbes or tumor cells overpower the body, the immune cells rush to fight them, releasing proteins that tell the hypothalamus to raise the temperature. This is one of nature's ways of fighting disease, yet a fever can also cause problems for people with cardiac problems and for women in the first trimester of their pregnancy, a fever higher than 105° F, especially for prolonged periods, can cause dehydration and brain injury. This is why it is important to work with a Christian Natural Health Restoration Practitioner who knows how to apply God's Eight Natural Laws of Health to anatomy and physiology, to assist nature in restoring health.

Preserving one's immune system, while fighting cancer is crucial for survival and health restoration. There are alternative God-centered, natural treatment methodologies to the allopathic cut, burn and poison treatments. Just research the lack of the quality of life and the death rate of cancer patients after five years of so called remission. Remember, as a Christian, to worship, praise, and glorify God are our main reasons for being created. We praise and glorify Him with our life as well as in our death, if it is done according to His will. Optimal health is maintained through proper understanding of God's Eight Natural Laws of Health and their role in dis-ease prevention and restoration, especially during the early stage of dis-ease before it becomes disease.

Dis-ease is the stage between health and sickness. You know, when you go to the doctor(s) and they cannot diagnose anything wrong with you and they tell you it's all in your head, you're depressed. But you know something is wrong, that something is not right but you just do not know what. You are in the state of DIS-EASE! You are probably experiencing nutritional deficiency, as it is a scientific fact that a nutritional deficiency must exist first before most disease can develop.

Example: Possible effects of nutritional deficiency:

▪ Vitamin A (beta carotene): eye disorders, lung disorders, dry, scaly skin, night blindness, frequent infections, sterility, cancer, nerve deterioration, stunted growth, glandular malfunctions, premature aging, over-active mucus membranes, and inhibited healing process.

▪ Vitamin D: bone disease, rickets, cataract, calcium mal-absorption, gun disease, hair loss, muscle weakness, tooth decay, retarded growth, and osteoporosis.

▪ Vitamin C: scurvy, bruising easily, mouth and gum disease, fragile bones and joints, ulcers (gastric), frequent colds and flu, cancer, adrenal malfunction, stiff joints, anemia, low resistance to infection, deficient lactation, poor circulation, lung disorders, asthma, and bronchitis.

▪ Vitamin F: heart disorders, high cholesterol, female disorders, yeast infections, all skin disorders, low fertility, intestinal disorders, hypertension, cystic fibrosis, liver disorders, celiac disease, and malformation of tissue.

▪ Vitamin K: hemorrhoids and bruising, hemorrhaging, delayed blood clotting, colon disorders, multiple sclerosis, liver disorders, leg ulcers, diverticulitis and colitis, intestinal disorders, and hemophilia.

▪ Vitamin B: pernicious anemia, pellagra, beriberi, digestive disorders, poor appetite, tongue (cracks, shiny, or purple), memory loss and confusion, cardiovascular disorders, weight loss, dull and loss of hair, skin disorders, depression, fatigue, canker sores, itchy and burning eyes, and eczema (especially around genitalia area).

▪ Vitamin E; cardiovascular and circulatory, premature aging, hot flashes and female problems, fertility, impotence, nervous system, heart disorders, and weakened immune system.

If we added diseases associated with mineral deficiencies to this list you can now begin to see why a nutritional deficiency is the root cause of all diseases.

➤ It is a fact, 99% of Americans are deficient in organic minerals because *"inorganic, i.e. (toxic, synthetic, dead and inert) chemicals, pesticides, and herbicides have destroyed nearly all the critical organic complexes, elements, and minerals in our soils."* 74th. Congress, second session regarding organic minerals, (categorical statement).

➤ *"Every element, every sickness, and every disease can be traced back to an organic trace mineral deficiency"* Linus Pauling, (categorical statement).

139

Medical doctors are only required to take minimal hours of nutritional studies while in medical school. The human body requires approximately 88 nutrients to be healthy and function properly. Most modern-day scientific medical equipment is not designed to diagnose the dis-ease stage, but can only tell you that you have a disease after the disease has manifested itself. The Bio-Equilibrium analysis (body chemistry analysis) identifies missing nutriments in the human body.

Two hundred years ago, Dr. Benjamin Rush declared, in essence, *"Although a certain self-acting power does exist in the organism, it is subject to ordinary physical and chemical laws, and in any case, it is not strong enough to withstand the onslaught of disease."* Physicians, therefore, *"are the masters of nature,"* and should *"take the business [of healing] out of nature's hands."* Modern medicine, from that time until now, has been constructed on that basic principle.

Today, Carl Sagan has a different opinion based upon scientific fact. *"Medicine's dilemma is that its own findings undermine its basic principle. If the body's self-acting power is "subject to ordinary physical and chemical laws," medicine has yet to find them, as witnessed by the ease with which the body resists chemotherapy and other drugs. If the body's self-acting power is "not strong enough to withstand the onslaughts of disease," medicine has found nothing stronger, as witnessed by the ease with which bacteria resist antibiotics."* Believing in the supremacy of the body's adaptive powers is no longer "unscientific," as shown by this quote by Carl Sagan. *"Modern science has taught us that the human body, insofar as it is cured, tends to cure itself. The body is its own greatest protector: the immunological system, which produces antibodies to fight antigens, accounts for almost all recovery from disease... Nothing can save the patient if the internal system (Inner Terrain theory by Claude Bernard) breaks down... This is not to belittle medicine; its discoveries are prodigious and its contributions to health salutary, but the success of modern medicine depends on an understanding of how the healthy body protects itself."* The Skeptical Inquirer, a journal published by Carl Sagan. Do you grasp the meaning of the statement by Dr. Sagan and others, and the message I am trying to communicate to you in this book? We have to understand who and what allopathic medicine is for. The allopathic, prescription-drug model was invented by Babylonians for Babylonians who want to eat, drink, and live like Babylonians. As Christians, we are instructed to live by every word that comes from the mouth of God, Matthew 4:4. It is time to understand that allopathic medicine is starting to admit that they have no answer to cancer.

140

Study: We'll Never Cure Cancer

RESEARCHERS SAY IT'S AS OLD AS LIFE ITSELF

By John Johnson, Newser Staff, Posted Jun 26, 2014 12:54 PM CDT

(NEWSER) – When it comes to the war on cancer, it's time to lower our expectations, a new study suggests. Or as the lead author of the study in *Nature* puts it, "Cancer is as old as multi-cellular life on earth and will probably never be eradicated." German researchers discovered that an ancient organism similar to coral already carried cancer genes that could develop into tumors, explains the website Laboratory Equipment. In fact, one of those ancient tumors is similar to ovarian cancer in humans. Cell mistakes that result in cancer seem to be inevitable as organisms evolve, which makes the idea of "curing cancer" misguided, the study asserts. "The logic behind it was pretty naive," researcher Thomas Bosch of Kiel University tells the *Washington Post*. "'We can send people to the moon, we can eradicate cancer.'" He and his team suggest we focus more on understanding how the disease occurs and treating it rather than hoping for a simple fix. "Our study also makes it unlikely that the 'War on Cancer' proclaimed in the 1970s can ever be won," says Bosch. "However, knowing your enemy from its origins is the best way to fight it, and win many battles."

Chapter Summary:

1. For any created entity to have order, it needs the correct nutrients to function properly and orderly. In the case of the human physiology, to function properly and orderly, approximately 88 nutrients are required. When the body does not receive its daily supply, over time the system develops a nutritional deficiency leading to organ and/or system weakness. Then internal chaos ensues because the brain starts robbing organs and tissue of minerals to give to other more important organs. This weakened state leads to disease, sickness and death.

2. Resistance is a process God put within every one of our approximately 300 trillion cells. Resistance or vital force, i.e. Your will to live, has to be overcome by medicine before prescription drugs or chemotherapy could even be considered an acceptable form of treatment. We know this is impossible, because resistance is life!

3. Rockefeller and others are profiting from the perverted appetites and unhealthy lifestyles of Christians and non-Christians alike. As Christians, we are living in the anti-typical Day-of-Atonement. This place's a responsibility of utmost important upon us

to live above sin and sickness so we can live and proclaim the two Great Commissions of Matthew 28:19, 20 and Psalms 67:2.

4. Antoine Bechamp, Gunther Enderlein and others have scientifically proven that before one can become sick, the internal terrain or homeostasis must change first. Therefore, Louis Pasteur's "Germ Theory" is only correct secondarily as to disease symptoms. God's Ten Natural Laws of Health, especially a correct understanding and application of minerals to human nutrition is what keeps the system in the correct condition. "In the case of sickness... re-establish right conditions in the system." Ministry of Healing, Ellen White, p. 127.

5. Study: We'll Never Cure Cancer: When it comes to the war on cancer, it's time to lower our expectations, a new study suggests. Or as the lead author of the study in *Nature* puts it, "Cancer is as old as multi-cellular life on earth and will probably never be eradicated."

6. *"Ye cannot drink from the cup of the Lord, and the cup of devils: ye cannot be partakers of the Lord's table, and of the table of devils,"* I Corinthians. 10:21. So true to God's word, He has made us free moral agents. Free to choose to worship him or to reject him. Free to choose health or free to choose sickness. There is another principle in scripture "The curse causeless shall not come." Proverbs 26:2. In other words, every disease has a cause, and it is our responsibility to reason from cause to effect.

Chapter VI: Personal Responsibility

God Dwells in you, His Living Temple: The Lord has graciously revealed to His children how important an understanding of the Sanctuary and its services are to our salvation. It is so important that God gives us a clue of how to know Him in Psalms 77:13.

Sanctuary, Throne Room of God

"Thy way, O God, *is* in the sanctuary: who *is so* great a God as *our* God? Hebrews 8:2 tells us that our elder brother Jesus Christ is a Minister of the sanctuary and of the true tabernacle, in heaven that the Lord pitched and not man. We are also told in verse 5, that Moses was admonished to make the tabernacle on earth "according to the pattern shewed to thee in the mount". You can read about the earthly sanctuary and its services in the book of Leviticus, especially chapter 26.

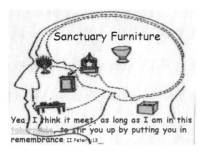

Sanctuary Furniture

Yea, I think it meet, as long as I am in this tabernacle, to stir you up by putting you in remembrance: II Peter 1:13

In I Corinthians 6:19, God makes a statement of almost disbelief, that you His professed child do not know that He dwells in you. "WHAT? KNOW YE NOT THAT YOUR BODY IS THE TEMPLE OF THE HOLY GHOST WHICH IS IN YOU. WHICH YE HAVE OF GOD, AND YE ARE NOT YOUR OWN? FOR YE ARE BOUGHT WITH A PRICE: THEREFORE GLORIFY GOD IN YOUR BODY, AND IN YOUR SPIRIT, WHICH ARE GOD'S". 1 COR. 6:19. Not just God but every piece of furniture in the heavenly sanctuary dwells in you as well. He is God, therefore He has to have a throne room in you. Remember, He admonished Moses to make it according to the pattern. Greek Dictionary of the New Testament #4636: skenos: a hut or temporary residence , i.e. the human body (as the abode of the spirit);-tabernacle. No wonder David exclaimed "I will praise thee; for I am fearfully *and* wonderfully made: marvellous *are* thy works; and *that* my soul knoweth right well," Psalms 139:14.

As we study human anatomy and the earthly sanctuary, we see God, His way and His original plan to dwell in humanity. The apostle Peter said "Yea, I think it meet, as long as I am in this tabernacle, to stir you up by putting you in remembrance; II Peter 1:13. Let us study to see how God has placed the furniture of His sanctuary in the human habitation. The sanctuary is a miniature representation of God's throne room, read Revelation chapters 4 and 5 in your study time.

The structure of the sanctuary consisted of 48 boards in the building, read: Exodus 26:18, 20, 22, 23

1. 20 boards on the south side southwards: Exodus 26:18
2. 20 boards on the north side: Exodus 26:20.
3. 6 boards westward: Exodus 26:22.
4. 2 boards for the corners of the Tabernacle in the two sides. Exodus 26:23-25.

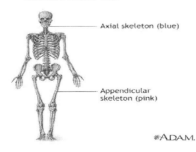

Axial skeleton (blue)

Appendicular skeleton (pink)

*ADAM.

The supporting structure of the human anatomy consists of 24 Vertebrae's, & 24 Ribs coupled together in the central part of the axial skeleton. God used 48 items in the frame of both the sanctuary and human tabernacle to support the structure.

The Sanctuary Veil

The Sanctuary Veil: And thou shalt make a veil of blue, and purple, and scarlet (red), and fine twined linen of cunning work: with cherubim shall it be made.... Exodus 26:31.

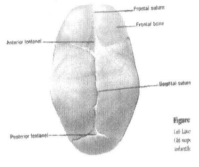

The structure of the sanctuary was coupled in the middle. The five outer lobes of the brain are coupled in the middle. This layer has three parts representing the 3 colors of the veil. Exodus 26:33. The sanctuary had 3 parts: the court yard, the holy place, and most holy place, representing the different parts of the head.

The Sanctuary had Three coverings: "And thou shalt make curtains of goats hair... Exodus 26:7 (white), And thou shalt make a covering for the tent of rams' skins dyed red ... Exodus 26:14, And a covering above of badgers' skin (black)... Exodus 26:14.

The body temple has the same 3 coverings as the sanctuary;

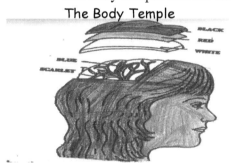
The Body Temple

1). the first layer is white bone, protecting the brain with the frontal bone doubled at birth.
2). Next is a solid piece of scalp with no couplings, which contains many blood vessels. 3). the hair is the outside covering. God was very particular about the number so that it would truly represent the covering on the head.

5 Pillars represent the 5 senses

There were 5 pillars holding the entrance curtain to the sanctuary. They represent the 5 senses of hearing, sight, taste, touch and smell; by which information is reported to the brain to be processed and become part of the character.

144

The 5 Avenues to the Soul

"Those who would not fall a prey to Satan's devices, must guard well the avenues of the soul; they must avoid reading, seeing, or hearing that which will suggest impure thoughts. The mind must not be left to dwell at random upon every subject that the enemy of souls may suggest. The heart must be faithfully sentineled, or evils without will awaken evils within, and the soul will wander in darkness. The body is the only medium through which the mind and the soul are developed for the up building of character. Hence it is that the adversary of souls directs his temptations to the enfeebling and degrading of the physical powers. His success here means the surrender to evil of the whole being. The tendencies of our physical nature, unless under the dominion of a higher power, will surely work ruin and death." E.G. White, Counsel on Diets and Foods, p.73.

Shofar; Trumpet or Ram's Horn

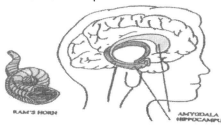

The trumpet that was used to call the people to the sanctuary was called the Shofar, a rams horn. It was used to bring to remembrance the instructions – a call to worship, to war, to march, a warning, etc. This part of the brain is involved in memory and emotions. You had to remember the different signals, imagine the emotion when Jesus comes and we hear the trump of God – 1 Thess. 4:13-17.

Divinity & Humanity in the Plan of Salvation

It is ordained by God, according to the Plan of Salvation, divinity and humanity must work together. As soon as we consent to give up sin, to acknowledge our guilt, the barrier is removed between the soul and the savior. Selected Messages, bk 1, p. 325.

If we confess our sins, he is faithful and just to forgive us [our] sins, and to cleanse us from all unrighteousness, I John 1:9. "Whosoever is born of God doth not commit sin; for his seed remaineth in him: and he cannot sin, because he is born of God" 1 John 3:9.

Alter of Sacrifice

Grate

The alter of sacrifice was the first thing seen when entering the courtyard. It represents the sacrifice of the lamb of God upon the cross. "...behold the lamb of God which taketh away the sins of the world" (John 1:29). The grate on the alter and the table of showbread were the same height, as are the mouth and the medulla. When you slice the medulla, it looks like a grate. This part of the brain is involved in involuntary functions, such as respiration, heart rate, etc., that occur without conscious thought. Ever since the fall of mankind,

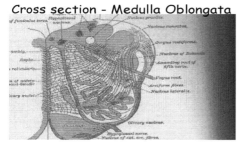
Cross section - Medulla Oblongata

sin is practiced naturally, without conscious thought. The sacrifice of Christ was to change that process and make us a new creature, if we choose.

The LAVER

And he set the laver between the tent of the congregation and the altar, and put water there, to wash *withal*.
And Moses and Aaron and his sons washed their hands When they went into the tent of the congregation, and

when they came near unto the altar, they washed; as the LORD commanded Moses, Ex. 40: 30-32.

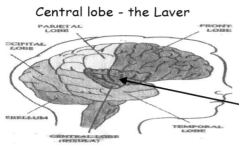
Central lobe - the Laver

Buried under all the other lobes of the brain is the insula, which is especially protected. It lies deep within the folds of the lateral sulcus. Science has not fully discovered all the functions of this part of the brain, but it is shaped like a bowl laver).

Foramen Magnum

The priests and high priest went in and out of the curtain (foramen magnum) of the sanctuary receiving instructions from the Lord.

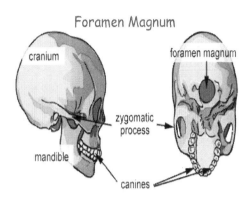
Foramen Magnum

cranium

foramen magnum

zygomatic process

mandible

canines

In the picture on the left, you can see the opening in the Occipital Bone through which the spinal cord passes from the brain. The first structure upon entering the foramen magnum is the brainstem. This part of the brain is involved in involuntary functions such as heart rate, respiration, that occur without conscious thought.

And thou shalt set upon the table shewbread before me always, Exodus 25:30.

And Jesus said unto them, "I am the bread of life..." John 6:35.

The table of showbread had a shelf with a crown, and a border of a hand's breadth with another crown. God was very specific in this instruction.

Eating the word of God

TABLE OF SHEWBREAD

The Bread is ingested through the mouth, where we have 2 sets of crowns, one on a wide bone, the other one on a narrow bone.

147

7 Golden Candle Stick

The candlestick was to give light in the sanctuary. It was never to go out, Lev. 24:4.
Read Zechariah 4 and note the similarity of the trees and pipes.

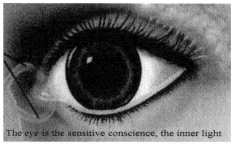

The eye is the sensitive conscience, the inner light

The eye is the sensitive conscience, the inner light, of the mind. Upon its correct view of things, the spiritual healthfulness of the whole soul and being depends. The "eye-salve," the Word of God, makes the conscience smart under its application, for it convicts of sin. But the smarting is necessary that the healing may follow, and the eye be single to the glory of God. . . . Says Christ, by renouncing your own self-sufficiency, giving up all things, however dear to you, you may buy the gold, the raiment, and the eye-salve that you may see. Ellen White, Our High Calling, p. 350.

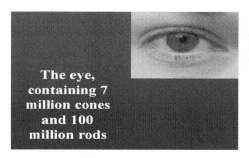

The eye, containing 7 million cones and 100 million rods

The eye, contains seven million cones and one hundred million rods.

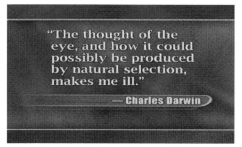

"The thought of the eye, and how it could possibly be produced by natural selection, makes me ill."
— Charles Darwin

"The thought of the eye, and how it could possibly be produced by natural selection, makes me ill."

-Charles Darwin

Remember, we are discussing God's throne room in the human habitation. Showing each article of furniture in the earthly sanctuary as it corresponds with the same article of furniture in the human tabernacle, the abode of God the Holy Spirit. Both tabernacles are an exact pattern of the heavenly sanctuary.

Alter of incense - Prayer

The Alter of Incense was the place of prayer. The incense had four spices plus salt, making five ingredients in all. Five is the number of grace and redemption and the smoke from the incense represented the merits of Jesus, which went up with the prayers of the saints. In order to make the incense, it had to be "beaten". In order to make the Shewbread it was kneaded, the candle stick and the incense were beaten, Ex. 25:31 and Lev. 16:12. This beating represented the beating Christ would subject Himself too.

HE WAS WOUNDED FOR OUR TRANSGRESSIONS

"But he *was* wounded for our transgressions, *he was* bruised for our iniquities: the chastisement of our peace *was* upon him; and with his stripes we are healed." Isaiah 53:5.

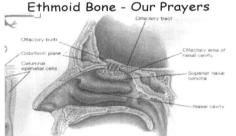
Ethmoid Bone - Our Prayers

The nerves of the sense of smell travel through the Ethmoid Bone to the Olfactory Bulbs. This is the only one of the five senses that is not routed through the Thalamus; it represents our prayers.

Thus your prayers are accepted, becoming unto God a sweet-smelling savor in the beloved. Thus you enter into his rights, and become an heir with God and joint heir with Jesus Christ. You will enter into His

149

victories, and the reward of eternal life will be given you. "But as many as received him, to them gave he power to become the sons of God, *even* to them that believe on his name: Which were born, not of blood, nor of the will of the flesh, nor of the will of man, but of God." Jn. 1:12.

Ark of the Covenant

The Ark of the Covenant is located in the Most Holy place of the heavenly, earthly and human Sanctuary, it contains Manna (grain), Ex. 16:33, Almonds (nuts), Num. 17:8, pomegranates (fruit) Ex. 39:24, and God's 10 Commandment Law, the Mercy-Seat and His Holy Shekina.

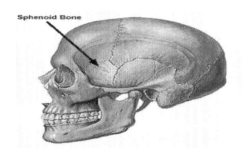

The Sphenoid bone in the head represents the Ark of the Covenant. Because of its location and how it protects the content with in.

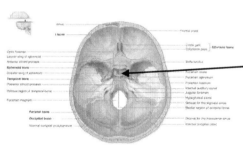

The Sphenoid bone touches all the bones of the head. Notice the wings, notice the box called the Sella Tursica. This is the space were the Pituitary gland sits. Over it is a membrane that represents the mercy seat.

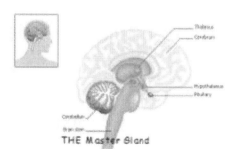
THE Master Gland

The Pituitary is the master gland; it has two working parts, —the anterior lobe, or adenohypophysis, and the posterior lobe, or neurohypophysis, which represents the two tables of the 10 Commandments.

In the sanctuary the glory of God was manifested above the Ark

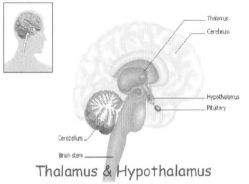

Thalamus & Hypothalamus

of the Covenant in the most holy place. There are 8 nuclei in the hypothalamus; 8 is the special number of the Holy Spirit, the number of regeneration. There is 1 thalamus on each side. ..."behold I see the heavens opened, and the Son of man standing on the right hand of God (acts 7:56).

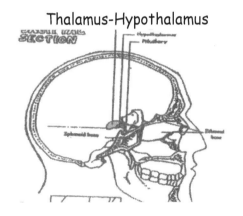

Thalamus-Hypothalamus

The three persons of the Godhead are represented here in the throne room of the brain. The thalamus (Jesus Christ) interprets and defines messages and passes instruction to the hypothalamus (Holy Spirit), John 16:13-15. Satan wanted to sit on this throne (Isa. 14:12-14).

Angels around the throne of God

"And I beheld, and I heard the voice of many angels round about the throne and beasts and the elders; and the number of them was ten thousand times ten thousand, and thousand of thousands;" Rev. 5:11. There were angels embroidered on the first covering of the sanctuary to impress the fact that angels are ever present to help us, Hebrews 1:14. You can read the description of the throne room of God in Revelation chapters 4 & 5.

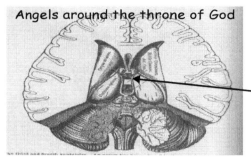

Angels around the throne of God

In this coronal view of the brain from Gray's Anatomy, the form of an angel wing is apparent. In the middle of the form of an angel is where the throne room of God is located in the brain.

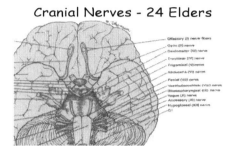

Cranial Nerves - 24 Elders

There are 12 cranial nerves on each side of your brain that help the brain to govern the body. They represent the 24 elders in Rev. 4 & 5. These people went with Jesus from the earth at the time of His ascension, Matt. 27:52, 53 and are helping in the Judgment in heaven. Those who came forth from the grave at Christ's resurrection were raised to everlasting life. They were the multitude of captives who ascended with Him as trophies of His victory over death and the grave. . . . Christ Triumphant, p. 286.2.

Pure river of water of life

"And he showed me a pure river of water of life, clear as crystal, proceeding out of the throne of God and of the Lamb. In the mist of the street of it, and on either side of the river, was there the tree of life, which bare 12 manner of fruits, and yielded her fruit every month: and the leaves of the tree were for the healing of the nations" Rev. 22; 1, 2. There was a tree on either side of the river but it came together as one tree at the top, just as the cerebellum contains 2 parts, but is joined in the middle. The spinal fluid runs between the two trees.

Cerebellum - Tree of Life

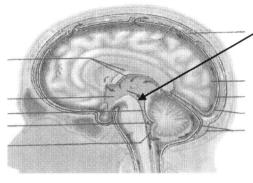

The spinal fluid originates in the ventricles in the throne room area of the brain, just as the river of life proceeds out of the throne of God, Rev. 22:1, 2. The spinal fluid must be pure or there will be major health problems, usually death.

Circulation of Cerebrospinal Fluid (CSF)

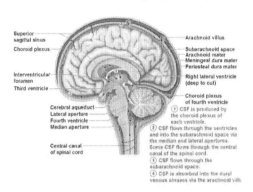

The spinal fluid runs down between the arbor vitae (medical term in Latin meaning tree of life) in the cerebellum, just as the river of life has the tree of life on either side.

"And they shall see His face; and his name shall be in their foreheads."

Revelation 22:4

Their minds were given to God in this world; they served Him with their heart and intellect, and now He can put His name in their foreheads. He takes them as His children, saying, Enter ye into the joy of your Lord. The crown of immortality is placed on the brow of the over comers. They take their crowns and cast them at the feet of Jesus, and touching their golden harps, they fill all heaven with rich music in songs of praise to the Lamb. Then "they shall see his face; and his name shall be in their foreheads." Ellen White, Our Father Cares, p. 142.2.

"Know ye not that ye are the temple of God, and that the spirit of God dwelleth in you? If any man defiles the temple of God, him shall God destroy; for the temple of God is holy, which temple ye are." 1 COR.

3:16, 17. As Christians, we had better earnestly seek God's council before we allow any doctor to cut (surgery), burn (chemo and radiation therapies), or poison (prescription drugs) His body temple.

God's Plan: is to "Be In Health" 3 John II

At the beginning of the "Time of the End" (Daniel 1:35, 40 & 12:4, 9), God's true church was emerging from the wilderness (Rev. 12:13) with its pure scriptures and God's true methods of healing (Psalms 67:2). In 1863, God gave to the Seventh-day Adventist Church, His healing methods as a gift to the world. On June 6, 1863, Ellen White gave her first comprehensive vision on health. It was written in June of 1864. A copy of this foundational health message can be found in the book Spiritual Gifts, Vol. 4, Review & Herald Publishing Association, p. 120-151; the article is simply entitled "Health. The importance of this gift is directly related to your salvation, for God wants to write His name in your forehead (Frontal Lobe, Rev. 22:4).

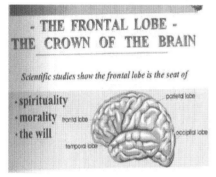

The Frontal Lobe, both right and left lobes are the largest lobes of the brain. It is the crown of the brain. Scientific studies show that the frontal lobe is the seat of spirituality, morality, the will, reasoning, and intellect. It is the control center of our entire being. Most people are unaware that our daily lifestyle practices can indeed affect our temperament, our emotions, and our behavior. The front part of our brain can either be enhanced or compromised by our diet and/or lifestyle. As Christians, let us be sure we understand the importance of protecting our frontal lobes. This is the location were God is going to write His name; Rev. 22:4 and Satan is attempting to capture. Spirituality, character, morality, and our will are the characteristics that give us our unique individuality. Therefore, a person with a damaged frontal lobe may look the same as they always did, but if you interact with them, it is usually apparent that they are "just not the same." This is why there is so much sinning and repenting.

Drugs that damage our Frontal Lobes: Illicit drugs, certain prescription drugs, other legal social drugs, i.e. alcohol, caffeine, nicotine, the "ine" cousins, i.e. cocaine, lidocaine, etc.

Drugs that commonly affect the mind: Asthma medications—Beta agonists; blood pressure medication — Beta blockers, calcium channel blockers, centrally acting agents (Clonidine, Methyldopa, etc.); Tranquilizers and sleeping pills—benzodiazepines antidepressants (Note: tricyclic antidepressants are also used for headaches, insomnia, etc.); anti-ulcer pills — H2-blockers (Tagamet, Zantac); anti-inflammatory drugs — NSAIDS; pain relievers, narcotics; cold and allergy medications —antihistamines (also used for insomnia, etc.), decongestants (especially in children; e.g., pseudoephedrine as in Actifed).

Effects of Compromised Frontal Lobes: Impairment of moral principle, social impairment (loss of love for family), lack of foresight, incapable of abstract reasoning, cannot interpret proverbs, diminished ability for mathematical understanding, loss of empathy, and lack of restraint (boasting, hostility, and aggressiveness).

Frontal Lobe Diseases: Mania, obsessive compulsive disorder, increase appetite, attention deficit/ hyperactivity disorder, and depression. Proof Positive, Neil Nedley, M.D., p. 260.

What Did Jesus Our Example Do!

 Let us look to the author and finisher of our faith and see what He did when faced with the agonies of death upon the cross, and was given a narcotic to drink. Mark 15:23, puts it this way: And they gave Him to drink wine mingled with myrrh; but He received it not.

Myrrrh=to tincture with myrrh, i.e. embitter (as a **narcotic**):-mingle **with myrrh. Greek Dictionary of the N.T. p. 66, No. 4669.**

"To those who suffered death by the cross, it was permitted to give a stupefying potion, to deaden the sense of pain. This was offered to Jesus; but when he had tasted, He refused it. He would receive nothing that could becloud His mind. His faith must keep fast hold upon God. This was His only strength. To becloud His senses would give Satan an advantage"! Desire of Ages, Pacific Press Publishing Association, White, p. 746.

So, what did the Romans attempt to give Jesus Christ to drink when He cried out "I thirst" while dying on the cross? They gave him vinegar to drink mingled with gall: and when he had tasted thereof, he would not drink, Matthew 27:34. Greek Dictionary of the New Testament p. 5521"Gall" poison or an anodyne (wormwood, poppy, etc): -gall. Webster's Dictionary, p. 54. An-o-dyne adj. A medicine that relieves pain. Chaldee and Hebrew Dictionary 7219. Same as

7218; a poisonous plant, prob. The poppy (from its conspicuous head); gen. Poison:-gall, hemlock. As I discussed earlier, Strong's Exhaustive Concordance of the Bible, Greek Dictionary of the N.T pg. 75. 5332 Rev. 21:8 *Sorcerers; Pharmakon,* (from Pharmakeus) (A drug, i.e. spell giving potion) a druggist, pharmacist or poisoner, (by extends) A magician–sorcerer.

You see, the Romans attempted to give Jesus a narcotic to deaden His pain, but he refused because He had to keep His mind clear; the battle had not yet been won. As a believer, with your life in the balance, Peter advises: *"Be sober, be vigilant; because your adversary the devil, as a roaring lion, walketh about, seeking whom he may devour,* 1Peter 5:8. If he can cause you to doubt, then he has gained the advantaged. When Christians consent to take strong narcotics such as morphine during hospice care, we possibly give the adversary of souls the advantage. I am not a medical doctor, nor am I a pharmacist so I cannot advise you to take or not to take prescription medication.

However, as a Christian Health Restoration Practitioner and Naturopathic Doctor, trained in God's Ten Laws of Health, I help my patients to build up their bodies naturally so that their medical doctor can begin to reduce the dosage until the patient is off their prescription medication.

Also, I can point you to our example Jesus Christ and the agony He suffered on the cross at Calvary. With your conflict with your enemy (Satan and Self), I share with you this comforting thought: Strength for Every Trial: *Our heavenly Father measures and weighs every trial before He permits it to come upon the believer. He considers the circumstances and the strength of the one who is to stand under the proving and test of God, and He never permits the temptations to be greater than the capacity of resistance. If the soul is overborne, the person overpowered, this can never be charged to God, as failing to give strength in grace, but the one tempted was not vigilant and prayerful and did not appropriate by faith the provisions God had abundantly in store for him. Christ never failed a believer in his hour of combat. The believer must claim the promise and meet the foe in the name of the Lord, and he will not know anything like failure.*--MS 6, 1889, Our High Calling, Ellen White, p. 323.

When God see's that your gold has been purified by fire your pain and suffering will cease. When He sees that you are safe to bring into the society of holy beings, as your body is ravaged by cancer or any other degenerate disease, God will begin to shut down the systems of your body and you will slip into a comma and rest in the Lord until He comes; prayerfully the second time.

 Let us consider the origin of Morphine, A 20 year old German pharmacy assistant named Friedrich Serturner surmised that there was a specific component of opium that gave pain relief, but only if sufficiently concentrated. Using ammonia, he separated the various constitutes of the drug, and called the narcotic substance he discovered 'morphine' after Morpheus the god of sleep.

With Christ as our example, believers must fulfill all righteousness. Righteousness: The greatest gift that God has for you next to your salvation is health: *"Beloved, I wish above all things that thou mayest prosper and be in health, even as thy soul prospereth,"* III John 2. As Christians, we must understand that health is righteousness, and it is our responsibility to *fulfill all righteousness* (Matt. 3:15). Health is part of our reasonable service: *"I beseech you therefore, brethren, by the mercies of God, that ye present your bodies a living sacrifice, holy, acceptable unto God, [which is] your reasonable service.* Romans 12:1.

God is preparing for Himself a people *"That he might present it to himself a glorious church, not having spot, or wrinkle, or any such thing; but that it should be holy and without blemish,"* Ephesians 5:27. Today, Christians think God accepts whatever they have left to give. However, Malachi 1:8 says, *"And if ye offer the blind for sacrifice, is it not evil? And if ye offer the lamb and sick, is it not evil? Offer it now unto thy governor; will he be pleased with thee, or accept thy person saith the Lord of host."* If a human being will not accept your evil, how much more is God offended, yet has empathy and compassion for His sick, deceived children. Remember we are talking about fulfilling Righteousness.

Please follow me closely: *"The secret of the LORD [is] with them that fear him; and he will show them his covenant."* Psalms 25:14. *"All scripture [is] given by inspiration of God, and [is] profitable for doctrine, for reproof, for correction, for instruction in righteousness:"* II Tim 3:16.

In Rev. 12:1 we read, *"And there appeared a great wonder in heaven; a woman clothed with the sun and the moon under her feet and upon her head a crown of twelve stars:"* If you study scripture, you will find the word Sun in this verse represents the gospel. Mal. 4:2 tells us, *"But unto you that fear my name shall the Sun of*

157

righteousness arise with *healing* in his wings; ..." Here is the link between the gospel and health, the word temperance. Gal. 5:22 *"Fruits of the spirit are...TEMPERANCE."* Eph. 5:9: *"For the Fruit of the Spirit, is in all goodness and righteousness and truth."* Paul tells us the *"Every man that striveth for the mastery is temperate in all things..."* I Corinthians 10:25.

I John 5:17: *"All Unrighteousness is sin"* Now, please follow me closely, now that we understand health is righteousness and disease and sickness is unrighteousness. God wants to make known to the world His way of healing: *"That thy way may be known upon earth, thy saving health among all nations."* Ps 67:2. *"Thy way, O God, [is] in the sanctuary: who [is so] great a God as [our] God?"* Ps. 77:13.

How can we, as ambassadors of Christ, make known God's saving health among all nations, when we are just as sick as the Babylonians and use the Babylonians doctors of today? While continuing using pharmaceutical drugs that defile God living temple, especially now that you know that the Catholic Church invented pharmakea and are using it to deceive all the nations. Also, knowing that a group of men and Cartels made disease a part of the investment market place with no intentions of healing people. Now that you understand the issue, if you continue to use them on a regular bases, you very well can be "weighted in the balances and found wanting."

"And if it seem evil unto you to serve the LORD, choose you this day whom ye will serve; whether the gods which your fathers served that [were] on the other side of the flood, or the gods of the Amorites, in whose land ye dwell: but as for me and my house, we will serve the LORD", Joshua 24:15.

Let us pray for strength to understand, trust, and obey God's simple, yet powerful, health restoration program. We have been deceived into believing that man's way is superior. The issue of life is not living or dying, but eternal life. The problem is that so many believers are afraid to die, so we try anything and everything under the sun and end up losing our soul salvation. Make peace with God and trust to His healing way, and if you live, praise God; if you sleep the sleep of death, your hope is in the resurrection of the righteous. This is the peace you must make with God before you hear the dreaded, "You Got Cancer," and they scare and intimidate you into chemotherapy that Dr. Schimke has already proven provokes the cancer response.

God's Design

"All the members of the body unite to form the human body and each performs its office in obedience to the intelligence that governs the whole. The relation that exists between the mind and the body is very intimate; when one is affected the other sympathizes. The condition of the mind affects health to a far greater degree that many realize.

Many of the diseases that man-kind suffer from are due to mental depression, grief, anxiety, remorse, anger, guilt, distrust, etc... all tend to break down life forces (vital force) and invite decay and death" Counsel on Health, Ellen White, p. 344.

In order to restore health we must first understand what disease is. *"Impurities of the body, if not allowed to escape, are taken back into the blood and forced upon the internal organs. Nature, to relieve herself of poisonous impurities, makes an effort to free the system. This effort produces fevers and what is termed disease."* Council on Health, Ellen White, p. 61.

OPTIMAL HEALTH AND HOW TO ACHIEVE IT

Remember the Reader's Digest November 1968 article referred to in the introduction of this book. It described a fascinating discovery by the researchers at NASA's Ames Research Center which confirmed the Bible's account that every single element found in the human body exists within the soil. The scientists concluded, *"The biblical scenario for the creation of life turns out to be not far off the mark."*

With that statement from a very credible source, then you have to look to nutrition as the foundation of optimal health, and not allopathic medicine. Since researchers at the Ames Research Center validates creation by intelligent design, then we have to go to the Creator's owner's manual for instruction on how to properly care for our bodies. The first half of this book documented how health care in America is money driven [U.S. Economy] not cure motivated, in order to help your mind, grasp these simple, yet affordable concepts that anyone can use to improve their health.

The following are God's eight natural laws of health instituted in the Garden of Eden, which a person has to know and implement in his lifestyle to achieve optimal health. So, if your doctor, Christian or not, does not share with you, or does not know how these health laws correlate with the human body and optimal health, then it is my recommendation that you hire a health care practitioner who does. Because without applying the eight natural laws of health to one's life and making it a lifestyle, then it is impossible to achieve optimal health.

The Creator's Ten Natural Laws of Health:
"You Seventh-day Adventists have had the truth and have not shared it, shame on you." Rev. George Malkamus, Hallelujah Acres.

In the November 2005 issue of National Geographic, the front cover read "The Secrets of Living Longer." The article entitled 'What if I said you could add up to ten years to your life?' States researchers studied a group of Seventh-day Adventists who rank among America's longevity all-stars. Two other groups, one in Sardinia, Italy and Okinawa, Japan, were also studied. "Residents of these three places produce a high rate of centenarians, suffer a fraction of the diseases that commonly kill people in other parts of the developed world, and enjoy more healthy years of life." What all three groups have in common are, "they all don't smoke, put family first, are active every day, keep socially engaged, and eat fruits, vegetables, and whole grains.

Let me give you an example of how important these eight laws are and their relationship to optimal health. The liver, which I will discuss later in the book, will not uptake nutrients out of the blood unless there is the proper amount of water and oxygen at the same time and at the right time.

Water is the main transport vehicle of the body and exercise (circulation) moves the nutrients i.e., vitamins, minerals, herbs, prescription drugs, etc., throughout your body.

The following 8 Health Laws, God instituted in the Garden of Eden before the creation of mankind. It is obedience to these Laws that protect from sickness and restores back to health without side effects when one or more of these laws are violated. It is crucial that you know and understand how these laws apply to the physiology of the human body, or you go to a Christian Healthcare Practitioner who.

1. Trust In Divine Power
Genesis 2:7, 16, 17 [A Psalm] of David. "Bless the LORD, O my soul: and all that is within me, [bless] his holy name. Bless the LORD, O my soul, and forget not all His benefits: Who forgiveth all thine iniquities; who healeth all thy diseases;" Psalms 103:1-3.

Christian meditation and prayer have their greatest benefits when they provide a respite from stressful thoughts and feelings, and an opportunity to find solutions for dealing with life's most pressing stressors. For such processes to occur, the reasoning powers of the brain must be active during the meditative process. Our high intellectual powers, including spiritual reasoning, reside in the part of the brain called the frontal lobe. When this brain region is intimately involved in our thinking, a type of brain wave called the beta wave predominates. If you were to measure brain activity with an electroencephalogram (EEG) and it shows the beta wave, it would indicate that healthy thinking is occurring, characterized by dynamic frontal lobe activity.

Studies show that Christian meditation involves the frontal lobe and beta activity. This is what one would expect. After all, prayer from the Bible perspective is an extremely active process. Whether we are reflecting on God's goodness, thanking Him for helping us in specific ways, seeking to know His will in a perplexing situation, or praying for individuals who have specific needs, Christian meditation and prayer involve an active frontal lobe.

"The great Physician in Chief is at the side of every true, earnest, God-fearing practitioner who works with his acquired knowledge to relieve the sufferings of the human body. He, the chief of physicians, is ready to dispense the balm of Gilead. He will hear the prayers offered by the physician and the missionary, if His name will be glorified thereby; and the life of the suffering patient will be prolonged. God is over all.

He is the true Head of the Missionary Health Restoration profession, and blessed indeed shall be that physician who has connected himself with the chief physician, who has learned from Him not only to treat the suffering bodies, but to watch for souls, to understand how to apply the prescription, and as an under shepherd use the balm of Gilead to heal the bruises that sin has made upon the souls as well as upon the bodies of suffering humanity under the serpent's sting. Oh, how essential that the physician be one divested of selfishness, one who has a correct knowledge of the atonement made by Jesus Christ, so that he can uplift Jesus to the despairing soul, one who holds communion with God! What a treasure he possesses in his knowledge of the treatment of the diseases of the body, and also the knowledge of the plan of salvation. Resting in Jesus as his personal Savior, he can lead others to hopefulness, to saving faith, to rest and peace, and a new life in Jesus Christ..." Council on Health, White, Pacific Press Publishing Association, p. 356.

"The Lord is to be the efficiency of every physician. If in the operating room the physician feels that he is working only as the Lord's visible helping hand, the Great Physician is present to hold with His invisible hand the hand of the human agent and to guide in the movements made. The Lord knows with what trembling and terror many patients come to the point of undergoing an operation as the only chance for saving life.

He knows that they are in greater peril than they ever have been in before. They feel as if their life were in the hands of one whom they believe to be a skillful physician. But when they see their physician on his knees, asking God to make the critical operations a success, the prayer inspires them, as well as the physician, with strong hope and confidence. This confidence, even in the most critical cases, is a means of making operations successful. Impressions are made upon minds that God designed should be made". . . Medical Ministry, Ellen White, p. 34.

In the medical literature, there are indications those individuals who trust God live longer. For example, Dr. Jeremy Kark and colleagues recently compared two ethnically Jewish groups that seemed to be very similar except for religious observance.
Among members of a secular community, the risk of death at any age was nearly doubled that of those members of a religious community, that is, those who were religiously observant.
(Kark JD, Shemi G, et al. Does religious observance promote health? Mortality in secular vs religious kibbutzim in Israel. *Am J Public Health* 1996 Mar; 86(3):341-346.

In a similar study, recent stressful life events increased the risk of health problems in a secular community. Members of a comparative religious community seemed to be protected from the negative effects of stress. Dr. Kark's team proposed some reasons why the members of the religious community experienced stress-buffering and improved longevity:

➢ Emotional well−being fostered by a sense of belonging to a religious community.
➢ Belief in God.
➢ A relaxation response induced by frequent prayer.
➢ Highly stable marital and family bonding.
➢ Social support providing a buffer against stressful life events.

One fascinating study looked at the religious experience of those Americans who reached the golden age of 100. Among the centenarians, the researchers found that religiosity significantly enhanced physical health. Although there are still many unanswered questions, the benefits of trust in God are due to more than simply attending religious services. (Levin JS, Vanderpool HY. Is frequent religious attendance really conducive to better health? Towards an epidemiology of religion. Soc Sci Med 1987;24(7):589-600.

Furthermore, the far-reaching benefits of faith seem to transcend age and racial boundaries. A study of African-Americans found that those who engage in organized religious activities had improved health and life satisfaction. Levin JS, Chatters LM, Taylor RJ. Religious effects on health status and life satisfaction among Black Americans. J Gerontol B Psychol Sci Soc 1995 May;50(3):S154-163.

Even those who engage in religious pursuits outside of organizational structure experienced this boost in satisfaction. Indeed, one of the most consistent findings-across racial groups-is that spirituality profoundly improves quality of life. The profound benefits in the quality of life brought about by exercising faith are described by a Duke University researcher who stated:

➤ Religious attendance and private devotion strengthen a person's religious belief system.

➤ Strong religious belief systems, in turn, when accompanied by a high level of religious certainty, have a substantial positive influence on well-being.

➤ Individual with strong religious faith report:
  ✓ Higher levels of life satisfaction
  ✓ Greater personal happiness
  ✓ Fewer negative psychosocial consequences of traumatic life events.

Ellison CG. Religious involvement and subjective well-being. J Health Soc Behav 1991 Mar;32(1):80-99. Proof Positive, Neil Nedly, M.D. p. 506.

Where do you turn for renewal? What is at your core, your center of being? Take some time to step back and think about what is truly important to you. Look beyond the clamor of daily activity to the universal themes of life. Choose an inspiring book, listen to some uplifting music, and give thanks for the marvelous gift of life and health. Every breath you take is a miracle. Every morning is the beginning of the rest of your life; a gift from God, that is why it is called [present]. Religion then, is not a piece of information for the mind. It is a way of life, which includes all that we are, all that we do all our hope and aspirations, all the moments of our lives.

2. Fresh Air

Genesis 1:6, 7 "The lungs are constantly throwing off impurities, and they need to be constantly supplied with fresh air." The Ministry of Healing, Pacific Press Publishing Association, Ellen White, p. 274.

Throughout most of recorded history, it seems that people have taken fresh air for granted. However, with the advent of the industrial revolution, followed by current concerns for indoor and outdoor air pollution, fresh air has become a more valued commodity. Air is composed of about 20 percent oxygen. It takes approximately 9 percent to sustain human life, presently there are major U.S. cities whose oxygen content is down to 12 percent. Fresh air is chemically different than the re-circulated indoor air that most people breathe. High quality fresh air is actually electrified. The life-giving oxygen molecule is negatively charged or "negatively ionized." This negatively charged oxygen gives rise to a number of benefits; improved sense of well-being, increased rate and quality of growth in plants and animals, improved function of the lung's protective cilia, tranquilization and relaxation (decreased anxiety), lowered body temperature, lowered resting heart rate, decreased survival of bacteria and viruses in the air, improved learning in mammals, and decreased severity of stomach ulcers.

Polluted air is usually full of positive ions. It's commonly found in Laundromats, freeways, at airports, and in closed, poorly ventilated areas, like homes and work offices, etc. Without air, man dies. Air is the most frequently needed of the vital elements for man and animals. One may live for days without water, and for weeks without food, but deprived of air a person will perish within minutes. More and more, we are discovering that the quantum leap in U.S. industry has led not only to positive outcomes—such as a higher standard of living-but also severely negative ones-such as the pollution of our environment. Air pollution is especially insidious. Millions of people suffer from a wide variety of ailments that are partly caused by an insufficient supply of oxygen. The problem is that most people do not breathe correctly, and this continually weakens their health. "In order to have good blood, we must breathe well. Full, deep inspirations of pure air, which fill the lungs with oxygen, and purify the blood is crucial. They impart to it a bright color and send it-a life-giving current-to every part of the body. A good respiration soothes the nerves; it stimulates the appetite and renders digestion more perfect; and it induces sound, refreshing sleep. If an insufficient supply of oxygen is received, the blood moves sluggishly. The waste, poisonous matter, which should be thrown off in the exhalations from the lungs, is retained, and the blood becomes impure. Not only the lungs, but the stomach, liver, and brain are affected. The skin becomes sallow, digestion is retarded; the heart is depressed; the brain clouded; the thoughts are confused; gloom settles upon the spirits; the whole system becomes depressed and inactive, and peculiarly susceptible to disease." The Ministry of Healing, Pacific Press Publishing Association, Ellen White, p. 272-273.

Along with improper breathing techniques, "many health professionals also believe the current rise in breathing problems is linked to pollution. We tend to think of breathing as simply taking in air. But that's just the first step. Your lungs also need to be able to absorb the oxygen out of the air you inhale. Then you must be able to expel the carbon dioxide from your lungs to make way for the next batch of air. When any of these steps break down, breathing troubles begin. You will cough, choke, wheeze and gasp; develop asthma, bronchitis and emphysema; and eventually die.

When your lungs are not functioning at their peak capacity and it's hard to breathe, you can neither expel carbon dioxide nor deliver the optimal amount of oxygen to your body. This can cause your body to shut down." Journal of Longevity, vol. 9/No 7, p. 3, 5. Every cell of your body must receive a constant supply of oxygen or they will weaken and die.

But that air must be fresh in order to help you the most. When you breathe stale or polluted air, the supply of oxygen is insufficient to keep the cells strong and healthy. Apart from oxygen from the air you breathe, they die within a few minutes. "Air is the free blessing of Heaven, calculated to electrify the whole system. Without it the system will be filled with disease, and become dormant, languid, feeble." Testimonies for the Church, Vol. 1, Pacific Press Publishing Association, Ellen White, p. 701.

"Fresh air will prove far more beneficial to sick persons than medicine, and is far more essential to them than their food... Thousands have died for want of pure water and pure air, who might have lived." Counsels on Health, Pacific Press Publishing Association, White, p. 55.

The human body operates on oxygen. Make sure your get enough by exercising, keeping your house well ventilated even in winter, and pausing frequently to take slow deep breaths. Place one hand on your chest and the other on your stomach. Breathe normally for a few moments, noting the movement of each hand as you inhale. Which hand rises more dramatically? If it is the one on your belly, take it off and pat yourself on the back. You have excellent respiration technique. But if it's the hand on your chest, you'd better take a deep breath—though you probably can't. You're breathing wrong. To breathe properly try this simple breathing exercise.

It will energize and refresh you. Stand or sit with your back straight. Exhale deeply through your mouth. Now, draw the air back into your lungs. As you do, imagine it going right down into your belly, filling it. Feel your stomach expand as you inhale. When your lungs are full, slowly begin to exhale. It should take you a little bit longer to exhale than it does to inhale. Tighten the muscles of your stomach as you gently push the last bit of air out. Repeat the process, slowly, five or six times, several times a day. The fresh morning air is best, if possible step outdoors into the fresh air.

You can also flush your body with oxygen by exercising. Activity opens up blood vessels and speeds those oxygen-laden red blood cells on their rounds. And remember the house plants. Placing at least one plant for every 100 square feet of indoor space is recommended.

Live plants not only eat many toxic pollutants and freshen the air with oxygen; they probably slip in some extra negative ions as well. Remember a meal eaten of high-fat reduces your blood's ability to carry oxygen. I highly recommend you read the book entitled Why is Fresh Air Fresh? By Dr. Bernell Baldwin.

3. Pure Water

Genesis 2:10 "And a river went out of Eden to water the garden; and from thence it was parted, and became into four heads."

"In health and in sickness, pure water is one of Heaven's choicest blessings. Its proper use promotes health. It is the beverage that God provided to quench the thirst of animals and man. Drunk freely, it helps to supply the necessities of the system, and assists nature to resist disease." Counsels on Diet and Foods, Review & Herald Publishing Association, Ellen White, p. 419.

The human body is about 80 percent water. So why is this colorless, tasteless, calorie-and-salt-free substance so absolutely necessary? The answer lies in the physiology of the body. It is the lubricant that makes everything else work. It is the water that transports the prescription drug, herb, vitamin, etc. throughout the body to be were it is needed. A drink of water is exactly what the body needs to carry out all its life processes. Water is an essential nutrient that is involved in every function of the body. It helps transport nutrients and waste products in and out of cells. It is necessary for all digestive, absorption, circulatory, and excretory functions, as well as for the utilization of the water-soluble vitamins.

It is also needed for the maintenance of proper body temperature. By drinking an adequate amount of water each day-50% of your body weight in ounces, minimum-you can ensure that your body has all it needs to maintain good health.

Drink enough water a day to keep the urine pale. Our kidneys alone process approximately 50 gallons of fluid in a day. In a 24-hour period, more than 8 quarts of digestive juices flow into the digestive tract. Much of this water is recycled over and over again by your kidneys. But about 4 to 6 cups of water a day are lost through the urine, lungs, skin, feces, and perspiration. For this reason, if you do not keep drinking water, your kidneys cannot perform their function well, and kidney disease will result.

If you have a choice, when drinking water from pipes, it is better to drink hard water than soft water. The hard water, which mainly has calcium and magnesium in it, will lower your chances of acquiring cardiovascular and kidney disease.

The Journal of American Medical Association for October 7, 1974, reported on Monroe County, Florida, where, by changing its source, the hardness of the drinking water was dramatically increased from 0.5 ppm to 200 ppm. "The death rate from cardiovascular disease dropped from a range of 500 to 700 to a range of 200 to 300 only four years after the increase in water hardness." Oddly enough, you can purchase water-softening equipment and supplies-but no one sells anything to artificially harden it. Hard water results primarily from the presence of calcium and magnesium salts in the water, while softness is due to the absence of these salts. These two minerals help protect the water from absorbing dangerous minerals from the ground-or from pipes.

"When we come to the individual need for water, it is readily realized that water is certainly our most precious mineral. It is the most essential of all minerals for our bodies. An animal can lose all its fat, about half its protein,-but if it loses as much as one-tenth of its water, it will die."-Jonathan Forman, M.D., in "Water and Man.

The countless millions of cells inside of you are constantly being bathed in water. And this is not merely a soaking process, but a re-washing activity done by your blood stream. Water in the blood brings nutrition and oxygen to your tissues, and carries off wastes.

"Rest, freedom from care, light, pure air, pure water, and a good

diet, are all they need to make them well" 2 Selected Messages, Review & Herald Publishing Association, Ellen White, p. 458.

"In health and in sickness, pure water is one of heaven's choicest blessings. Its proper use promotes health. It is the beverage, which God provided to quench the thirst of animals and man.

Drunk freely, it helps to supply the necessities of the system, and assist nature to resist disease.

The external application of water is one of the easiest and most satisfactory ways of regulating the circulation of the blood. A cool or cold bath is an excellent tonic. Warm baths open the pores, and thus aid in the elimination of impurities, which is essential in keeping body toxicity levels low. Both warm and neutral baths soothe the nerves and equalize the circulation.

But many have never learned by experience the beneficial effects of the proper use of water, and they are afraid of it. Water treatments are not appreciated as they should be, and to apply them skillfully requires work that many are unwilling to perform. But none should feel excused for ignorance or indifference on this subject. There are many ways in which water can be applied to relieve pain and check disease.

All should become intelligent in its use in simple home treatments. Mothers, especially, should know how to care for their families in both health and sickness" Ministry of Healing, Pacific Press Publishing Association, White, p. 237.

"Taken with meals, water diminishes the flow of the salivary glands; and the colder the water, the greater the injury to the stomach. Ice water or iced lemonade, drunk with meals, will arrest digestion until the system has imparted sufficient warmth to the stomach to enable it to take up its work again" Review & Herald, White, July 29, 1884.

"Food should not be washed down; no drink is needed with meals. Eat slowly, and allow the saliva to mingle with the food. The more liquid there is taken into the stomach with the meal, the more difficult it is for the food to digest; for the liquid must be first absorbed... Hot drinks are debilitating; and besides, those who indulge in their use becomes slaves to the habit...Do not eat largely of salt; give up bottled pickles; keep fiery spiced food out of your stomach; eat fruit with your meals, and the irritation which calls for so much drink will cease to exist. But if anything is needed to quench thirst, pure water, drunk some little time before or after a meal, is all that nature requires... Water is the best liquid possible to cleanse the tissue' Review & Herald, White, July 29, 1884.

All told, a wealth of information has been published on the subject of blood flow characteristics and its impact on a variety of disease states. The research often is published under the title of "hemorheology." This term comes from "hemo" which refers to blood and "rheology" which refers to the study of the flow properties of complex materials. Among the implications of this research is that adequate water drinking combined with other aspects of a healthful lifestyle may help postpone or prevent a variety of diseases and their complications. A few of the benefits that may accrue from improvement in the blood flow caused by a more liberal intake of water are: diabetic complications, stroke, high blood pressure, heart disease, and symptoms of intermittent claudication (leg pain due to blockage in leg blood vessels).

Many times, people are suffering from lower back pain when most of the time it is their kidneys screaming for more water. The next time you have mild lower back pain try drinking more water and see what happens. Remember there are times when your body requires more water than usual. For example on hot days, during physical exercise, if you have diarrhea or a fever, etc. Toxicity is a major cause of immune system weakening leading to hundreds of diseases, which could be simply eliminated by drinking water. Get into the habit of drinking water liberally. To systematically hydrate the body, one should drink four ounces of water every waking hour. Drink on arising, having one to two glasses of water before breakfast, in midmorning and mid-afternoon. Start the day off right. Give the early morning drink some zest by adding a twist of lemon. Real natural lemon and your liver were made for each other.

Try replacing the coffee stimulation with a glass of water and quality vitamins; also avoid the nervous system disorders caused by caffeine. When tempted to snack between meals weakening your digestive system, reach for a glass of water and drink liberally, habitual hunger pangs will soon go away. I highly recommend the book "Your Body's Many Cries For Water" by F. Batmanghelidg, M.D. or go to www.watercure.com.

4. Nutrition

Genesis 1:29 "And God said, behold I have given you every herb bearing seed, which is upon the face of all the earth, and every tree, in which is the fruit of a tree yielding seed; to you it shall be for meat." At creation God gave to mankind the best possible diet to stay fit and strong. His staple was fruits, nuts and grains, while vegetables were added to the diet after sin intruded. "...Thou shall eat the herb of the field." Genesis 3:18.

"Those foods should be chosen that best supply the elements needed for building up the body. In this choice, appetite is not a safe guide. Through wrong habits of eating, the appetite has become perverted. Often it demands food that impairs health and causes weakness instead of strength.

We cannot safely be guided by the customs of society. The disease and suffering that everywhere prevail are largely due to popular errors in regard to diet" The Ministry of Healing, Pacific Press Publishing Association, White, p. 295.

Good nutrition is the foundation of good health. Everyone needs the four basic nutrients-water, carbohydrates, proteins, and fats—as well as vitamins, minerals, and other micronutrients. By choosing the

169

healthiest forms of each of these nutrients and eating them in the proper balance, you enable your body to function at its optimal level.

It is plain and simple; the human body needs approximately 88 different nutrients to be healthy. The quality of food you eat determines the quality of blood the body produces. In the first ever  U.S. Surgeon General Report in 1984, titled "Nutrition and Health," C. Everett Koop, M.D. stated unequivocally that the Western diet (Sad American Diet) was the major contributor to these diseases. These diseases are heart disease, cancer, and stroke, and seven out of 10 Americans are suffering and die prematurely from them annually. He confirmed that saturated fat and cholesterol, eaten in disproportionate amounts, were the main culprits. He reminded us that animal products are the largest source of saturated fat as well as the only source of cholesterol. To compound the problem, Dr. Koop pointed out that these foods are usually eaten at the expense of complex-carbohydrate-rich foods such as grains, legumes and vegetables. The average risk of heart disease for a man eating meat, eggs and dairy is 45 percent. The risk for a man who doesn't eat meat is 15 percent.

However, the coronary risk of a vegetarian who doesn't eat meat, eggs, and dairy products drops to only 4 percent. An editorial in the Journal of the American Medical Association commented on these advantages. It said, "A total vegetarian diet can prevent up to 90 percent of our strokes and 97 percent of our heart attacks."

Going beyond prevention, in the December 16, 1998, issue of The Journal of the American Medical Association (JAMA), beginning on page 2001 we read the following: "Intensive Lifestyle Changes for Reversal of Coronary Heart Disease." The article states "The Lifestyle Heart Trial was the first randomized clinical trial to investigate whether ambulatory patients could be motivated to make and sustain comprehensive lifestyle changes, and, if so, whether the progression of coronary atherosclerosis could be stopped or reversed without using lipid-lowering drugs." The results were amazing and should be a wake up call to all who are serious about optimal health. The experimental group (change of diet and lifestyle) patients (20 of 28 or 71%) patients completed a 5-year follow-up) made and maintained comprehensive lifestyle changes for 5 years, whereas usual-care control group (15 of 20 patients or 75% completed 5-year follow up) made more moderate changes. In the experimental group, the average percent diameter stenosis at baseline decreased 1.75 percentage points after 1 year (a 4.5% relative improvement) and by 3.1 absolute percentage points after 5 years (a 7.9% relative improvement).

In contrast, the average percent diameter stenosis in the control group increased by 2.3 percentage points after 1 year (a 5.4% relative worsening) and by 11.8 percentage points after 5 years (a 27.7 relative worsening). Twenty-five cardiac events occurred in 28 experimental group patients vs. 45 events in 20 control-group patients during the five-year follow-up.

Conclusions: More regression of coronary atherosclerosis occurred after 5 years than after one year in the experimental group. In contrast, in the control group, coronary atherosclerosis continued to progress and more than twice as many cardiac events occurred. The intervention that was used during the Lifestyle Heart Trail was a 10% fat, whole foods, vegetarian diet; aerobic exercise; stress management training; smoking cessation; and group psychosocial support for 5 years. Has your medical doctor shared this report with you? Probably not because most medical doctors are not vegetarian and until recently were only required to take minimum hours of nutrition while in medical school. See appendix G.

The World Health Organization (WHO) has confirmed Dr. Koops research. The WHO commissioned a panel of nutrition experts from around the world. The result, a 200 page technical paper entitled, "Diet, Nutrition and the Prevention of Chronic Diseases," was published in 1990. In addition, an executive summary was published in 1991. They concluded: Medical and scientific research has established clear links between dietary factors and the risk of developing coronary artery disease, hypertension stroke, several cancers, osteoporosis, diabetes, and other chronic diseases. These are called diet and lifestyle diseases and if you change your diet and/or lifestyle these diseases can be reversed or cured without prescription medication. There is no reason or excuse for Christians to take prescription drugs other that They have allowed their taste buds to allow them to become addicted to certain chemicals in food.

Dr. Robert H. Fletcher M.D. and Kathleen M. Fairfield, M.D., Ph. D. of the Harvard Medical School and the Harvard School of Public Health, who site in their research, in an 2002 article entitled "Vitamins for chronic disease prevention in adults" states: "most people do not get an optimal amount of nutrients by diet alone. Suboptimal intake of nutrients are associated with increased risk of chronic diseases, including cardiovascular disease, cancer, and osteoporosis. Their findings definitively confirm that all diseases find their roots in nutritive poor and specifically poor mineral nutrition. This lack of minerals in the body manifests itself as diseases.

These finds confirm two time Nobel Prize winner Linus Pauling's earlier statement "Every element, every sickness, and every disease can be traced back to an organic trace mineral deficiency" (categorical statement).

In an article from Time Health, dated May 1, 2014 written by Alice Park, entitled "Nearly Half of U.S. Death can be Prevented with Lifestyle Changes." In the article it states: "We have known now for decades that the 'actual' causes of premature death in the United States are not the diseases on death certificates, but the factors that cause those diseases," says Dr. David Katz, director of Yale University's Prevention Research Center. And now we have even more national data to prove it.

The data continues to grow concerning diet and nutrition, read this next article.

Poor diet is the biggest cause of early death across the world - with red meat and sugary drinks responsible for one in five deaths

- Poor diet had the greatest cumulative effect on worldwide deaths in 2013
- Unhealthy eating leads to more deaths through heart disease and diabetes
- Top risks for early deaths globally were high blood pressure and smoking
- Next top risks were high body mass index and high blood sugar levels

By Madlen Davies for MailOnline

PUBLISHED: 11:13 GMT, 11 September 2015 | **UPDATED:** 15:55 GMT, 6 October 2016
Read more: http://www.dailymail.co.uk/health/article-3230568/Poor-diet-biggest-cause-early-death-world-red-meat-sugary-drinks-responsible-one-five-deaths.html#ixzz522IsdcHz
Follow us: @MailOnline on Twitter | DailyMail on Facebook

THE BIGGEST CAUSE OF EARLY DEATH IN THE WORLD IS NOT SMOKING OR ALCOHOL - IT'S WHAT YOU EAT

Poor diet is the biggest contributor to early deaths across the world, a study has warned. Experts said 21 per cent of global deaths can be attributed to diets high in red meat and sugary drinks, and lacking in fruit, vegetables and whole grains. Eating unhealthily contributes to the most deaths worldwide by triggering ailments including heart disease, stroke and diabetes.The top risks associated with the premature deaths of both men and women are high blood pressure, smoking, high body mass index (BMI), and high blood sugar levels, researchers found. But the greatest cumulative effect on health comes from poor diet, they warned.

Read more: http://www.dailymail.co.uk/health/article-3230568/Poor-diet-biggest-cause-early-death-world-red-meat-sugary-drinks-responsible-one-five-deaths.html#ixzz522Jxr3PJ
Follow us: @MailOnline on Twitter | DailyMail on Facebook

Now, let's apply a biblical principle or two to the issue of diet. When God created the world, specifically mankind He gave dominion to Adam, Genesis 1:26, 28. God even allowed Adam to name the creatures created by God, Genesis 2:19. Now, follow me closely, God placed Adam as His representative of the human family but restricted his diet (food), Genesis 2:16, 17. Another example of diet is the night of the Pass-over when the children of Israel were preparing to leave Egypt. God instructed His chosen people to eat a lamb, roasted with

173

fire with unleavened bread and with bitter herbs, Exodus 12:5-11. God was very specific of what to eat and what not to eat, as he was with Adam. When the children of Israel were in the wilderness God chose to feed them for forty years with manna and for a very good reason. God could have feed them with whatever article of food He chose, but He chose to feed them with a grain, Exodus 16:15, 31, and 35. There are many of examples of God feeding His children, like the raven that fed Elijah by the brook Cherith, 1 Kings 17:4-6. I have said all that about God being particular about man diet because it is a salvation issue. Let's look at Jesus Christ our example, before He started His ministry He fasted 40 days.

"With Christ, as with the holy pair in Eden, appetite was the ground of the first great temptation. Just where the ruin began, the work of our redemption must begin. As by the indulgence of appetite Adam fell, so by the denial of appetite Christ must overcome. "And when He had fasted forty days and forty nights, He was afterward an hungred. And when the tempter came to Him, he said, If Thou be the Son of God, command that these stones be made bread. But He answered and said, It is written, Man shall not live by bread alone, but by every word that proceedeth out of the mouth of God." White, DA, p. 117.3.

From the time of Adam to that of Christ, self-indulgence had increased the power of the appetites and passions, until they had almost unlimited control. Thus men had become debased and diseased, and of themselves it was impossible for them to overcome. In man's behalf, Christ conquered by enduring the severest test. For our sake He exercised a self-control stronger than hunger or death. And in this first victory were involved other issues that enter into all our conflicts with the powers of darkness." White, DA, p. 117.4.

Because of mans perverted appetite, Christians believe that the New Testament is saying that they can eat what they want, when they want and how they want. The Lord says: *"For I am the LORD, I change not; therefore ye sons of Jacob are not consumed,* Malachi 3:6. Remember, God has commanded" *Whether therefore ye eat, or drink, or whatsoever ye do, do all to the glory of God,"* 1 Cor. 10:31. You can only do to the glory of God by doing it His way and not your way. With the events of Daniel 11:45, Rev. 13 and on about to break upon the scenes as an overwhelming surprise, do you really believe you can eat and drink what you please? The standard has been set, the bar has been raised, and God requires that: "Man shall not live by bread alone, but by every word that proceedeth out of the mouth of God," Matt. 4:4.

From SAD (Sad American Diet) to GLAD (God's Life Activating Diet) "Ye cannot drink the cup of the Lord, and the cup of devils: ye cannot be partakers of the Lord's Table, and of the tables of devils." 1 Corinthians 10:21.

It is vital to understand that eat is 3/5 d**EAT**h. "So they poured out for the men to eat. And it came to pass, as they were eating of the pottage, they cried out, and said, O thou man of God, there is death in the pot. And they could not eat thereof" II Kings 2:40.

Food is vital to your health. It provides the building blocks for growth and repair and fuel for energy. It is a key element in the length and quality of life. Poor diet contributes to weight gain, heart disease, cancer, and a host of other diseases. Our bodies are built from the food we eat. There is a constant breaking down of the tissues of the body; every movement of every organ involves waste, and this waste is repaired from our food. Each organ requires its share of nutrition.
The brain is supplied with its portion; the bones, muscles, and nerves demand theirs. It's a wonderful process that transforms food into blood and uses this blood to build up the varied parts of the body; but this process is going on continually, supplying with life and strength each nerve, muscle, and tissue. Those foods should be chosen that best supply the elements needed for building up the body. "He that is faithful in that which is least is faithful also in much" Luke 16:10. How can God trust you with a glorified body, when you don't take care of this human body?

The SAD diet is high in fat and protein, and low in fiber and nutrients. While Christian debate the value of a vegetarian diet, consider the restrictions God has placed on eating flesh foods; "No blood in the meat-Lev.17:10-14, No fat-Lev.7:23, and eat in two days-Lev. 19:7. It is the fat: which gives meat its flavor, and the blood that gives the look of still being fresh while in the store. If you truly cut away the fat and drained the blood you would be eating a product similar to jerky. Bottom line, the animal is to be eaten the same day or the next or it is an abomination, and that soul shall be cut off from among his people" Lev. 19:6-8. Man shall live by every word that proceedeth out of the mouth of the Lord.

Study Links Hot Dogs to Cancer: "Children who eat more than 12 hot dogs a month develop leukemia more than 9 times above normal. Children who ate hot dogs once a week double their chances of brain tumors; twice a week they doubled it" The Recorder, June 4, 1994. Liquid Meat. Cow's milk and other dairy products are high in saturated fat and cholesterol. The dairy industry has cleverly expressed fat content as a percentage of weight. Using this system, 2% milk, which is 87% water by weight, sounds like a low fat product. Expressed as a percentage of total calories, 2% milk is in fact 31% fat. Whole milk is 49% fat, cheese is 60- 70% fat and butter is 100% fat. John A. McDougall, M.D., calls dairy foods "liquid meat" because their nutritional content are so similar. Eating foods high in fat contributes to the development of heart disease, certain cancers and stroke – America's three deadliest killers. Milk protein may confuse children's immune system.

Diabetes and Infants: A recent study of milk drinking patterns concluded that drinking cow's milk during infancy may trigger juvenile diabetes. The study suggests that the consumption of milk triggers destruction of insulin producing pancreas cells by the body's immune system. The study was conducted jointly by researchers in Toronto and Finland. A link between diabetes and cow's milk has been suspected because populations with high rates of milk consumption (such as Finns) also have high rates of diabetes. Also case studies of identical twins have shown that if one twin gets type-I diabetes, there is only a 50% chance of the other twin having it as well. Since identical twins have the same genetic makeup, this suggests that diabetes cannot just be due to genetics.

Got milk? Get allergies, asthma, diabetes, kidney stones, osteoporosis, and sinusitis! Karjalainen J. Martin JM, et al. A bovine albumin peptide as a possible trigger of insulin-dependent diabetes mellitus N Journal of Med 1992 Jul 30; 327(5):302-307.

Tryamine, which is found abundantly in cheese, wine and other rich foods, confuses brain cells. Finberg JP, Seidman R, Better OS. Cardiovascular responsiveness to vasoactive agents in rats with obstructive jaundice. Clin Exp Pharmacol Physicol 1982 Nov-Dec; 9(6):639-643.

Arachidonic acid, which is found abundantly in meat, decreases ability of Frontal Lobe function. In fact, arachidonic acid is found almost exclusively in animal products. Boksa P, Mykita S, Collier B. Arachidonic acid inhibits choline uptake and depletes acetylcholine content in rat cerebral cortical synaptosomes. J Neurochem 1988 Apr; 50(4):1309-1318.

Go back and read the section on the frontal lobe of the brain in chapter VI, then ask yourself, would God want me to eat something that impacts the only place in the human body that He communicates with us and the Holy Spirit Convicts us of sin? God's Life Activating

Diet is low in fat and protein and high in fiber and nutrition. These include fruits, nuts, grains, and vegetables, which are the only food groups not linked to any major disease.

Quotes from Famous Historical Vegetarians:

"Nothing will benefit human health and increase the chances of survival of life as much as the evolution to a vegetarian diet." --Albert Einstein 1879-1955.

"The average age of a meat eater is 63. I am on the verge of 85 and still work as hard as ever. I have lived quite long enough and I am trying to die, but I simply cannot do it. A single beef steak would finish me; but I cannot bring myself to swallow it. I am oppressed with the dread of living forever. That is the only disadvantage to vegetarianism," --George Bernard Shaw, prior to his 85th birthday.

"I have, from an early age, abjured the use of meat, and the time will come when men such as I will look on the murder of animals as they now look on the murder of men." -Leonardo Da Vinci 1452-1519.

"Whenever I injure any kind of life, I must be quite certain that it is necessary. I must never go beyond the unavoidable, not ever in apparently insignificant things. That man is truly ethical who shatters no ice crystal as it sparkles in the sun, tears no leaf from a tree." -- Albert Schweitzer.

In 1968 one of the great minds of the 21st. Century, two time Nobel Prize winner Linus Pauling, Ph. D, coined the term Orthomolecular Nutrition. "Orthomolecular" is, literally, "pertaining to the right molecule." Dr. Pauling proposed that by giving the body the right molecules (optimum nutrition) most disease would be eradicated. He went on to say, *"Every element, every sickness, and every disease can be traced back to an organic trace mineral deficiency."* (Categorical statement).

To substantiate Linus Pauling's statement, I quote *"It is a fact that 99% of Americans are deficient in organic minerals because 'inorganic (i.e., toxic, synthetic, dead, and inert) chemicals, pesticides, and herbicides have destroyed nearly all the critical organic complexes, elements, and minerals in our soils."* 74th. Congress, second session regarding organic minerals (categorical statement).

Remember Dr. Robert H. Fletcher M.D. and Kathleen M. Fairfield, M.D., Ph. D. study results, *"Their findings definitively confirm that all diseases find their roots in nutritive poor and specifically poor mineral nutrition. This lack of minerals in the body manifests itself as diseases."*

C. Everett Koop, M.D., Sc. D, former two times Surgeon General of the United States, produced the first Surgeon General's Report on Nutrition and Health in 1988. It was based on an exhaustive review of the scientific literature. He concluded that "dietary excess and imbalance" contributed significantly to eight of the leading killer diseases in the United States. Dr. Koop highlighted six areas where dietary excess and imbalance were contributing factors in death:

1. Diet has a vital influence on health.
2. Five of the ten leading causes of illness and death are associated with diet (coronary heart disease, cancer, stroke, diabetes and atherosclerosis).
3. Another three have been associated with excessive alcohol intake (cirrhosis of the liver, accidents, and suicide).
4. These eight conditions accounted for nearly 1.5 million of the 2.1 million total deaths in 1987.
5. Dietary excesses or imbalances also contribute to other problems such as high blood pressure, obesity, dental diseases, osteoporosis, and gastrointestinal diseases.
6. It is now clear that diet contributes in substantial ways to the development of these diseases and that modification of diet can contribute to their prevention and control.

Just to drive the point home, I will quote another credible source. The World Health Organization (WHO) commissioned a panel of nutrition experts from around the world. The result, a 200–page technical paper titled, "Diet, Nutrition and the Prevention of Chronic Diseases," was published in 1990. In addition, an executive summary was published in 1991. It concluded: Medical and scientific research has established clear links between dietary factors and the risk of developing coronary artery disease, hypertension stroke, several cancers, osteoporosis, diabetes, and other chronic disease.

Finally, I will share the information produced during the China Study. Drawing on the project's findings in rural China, but going far beyond those findings, the China Study details the connection between nutrition and heart disease, diabetes and cancer. The report also examines the source of nutritional confusion produced by powerful lobbies, government entities, and opportunistic scientists. The New

York Times has recognized the study (China-Oxford-Cornell Diet and Health Project) as the "Grand Prix of epidemiology" and the "most comprehensive large study ever undertaken of the relationship between diet and the risk of developing disease."

In 1995, Time magazine introduced the world to phyto-chemicals. Today, more than 100,000 such disease fighting nutrients have been discovered in fruits and vegetables. Agriculture, especially organic farming, is an integral component of the wellness program. Fruits and vegetables are loaded with compounds called phytochemicals and antioxidants that demonstrably lower the risk of cancer and fight other diseases. As few as twenty years ago, you could discount the diet and nutrition link to optimal health, but today with all the scientific data available, one would only hasten their death by ignoring it.

5. Temperance

Genesis 2:16, 17 And the Lord commanded the man, saying, "Of every tree of the garden thou mayest freely eat: But of the tree of the knowledge of good and evil, thou shall not eat of it: for in the day that thou eatest there of thou shalt surely die." Paul tells us the "Every man that striveth for the mastery is temperate in all things" I Corinthians 10:25.

"In order to preserve health, temperance in all things is necessary; temperance in labor, temperance in eating and drinking" How to Live, Pacific Press Publishing Association, E. White, p. 57.

"True temperance teaches us to abstain entirely from that which is injurious and to use judiciously only healthful and nutritious articles of food" Health Reformer, Review & Herald, White, April 1, 1877.
"Let your moderation be known unto all men" Philippians 4:5.
It was headline news: Carrots may prevent head and neck cancer. New research suggested that eating five or six of the crunchy tubers a day appeared to reverse leukoplakia–a precancerous lesion occurring in the mouth and throat. A friend of mine promptly purchased a machine that turned fresh vegetables into juice. She began to drink five or six pounds of carrot juice a day!

It is true that vegetables are an important part of a healthful diet. It's also true that they are increasingly being valued in their role in preventing disease. My friend's body eventually rebelled. Her skin took on a sickly yellowish color. Fearing hepatitis, she rushed to the doctor. He explained that carrots contain an orange-yellow dye known as beta-carotene. The body handles reasonable quantities of this substance, but excessive amounts are stashed away in the liver, skin, and mucous membranes, turning them the color of a carrot.

Carrots and other yellow fruits and vegetables are rich in beta-carotene, which the body turns into vitamin A, it is also a substance that appears to protect the body against certain cancers. Vitamins can be divided into two basic types — those that are water-soluble (dissolve in water) and those that are fat-soluble (dissolve in fat). Water-soluble vitamins (B-complex and C) are not a special concern, because excess amounts can usually be washed out through the kidneys. But fat-soluble vitamins (A, D, E, and K) are another story. Any excess cannot be eliminated except as it is used.

In excessive amounts, vitamin A begins to act like a toxin (poison) and may cause headaches, joint pain, damaged skin, and hair loss.

Because of this potential toxicity, laws now limit the amount of vitamin A and other fat-soluble vitamins that can be put into supplements. Beta-carotene apparently doesn't have such limits. When the body receives beta-carotene it can make as much vitamin A as it needs and use the rest in other ways. That's why the trend these days is to substitute beta-carotene for vitamin A in vitamin capsules and tablets. This distinction is important because it illustrates how the body uses food. Vitamins, minerals, and other nutrients in natural food occur in exactly the right forms for the body to use. It can pick and choose what it needs. But when we consume one food or nutrient in excess, or tamper with the makeup of food, the whole balance can be upset. This is a hard message for today's world. People do nearly everything to excess-they eat too much, drink too much, smoke too much, spend too much, party too much. Moderation is about as popular as wholesome. Then too, we live in an instant society with a quick-fix mentality, and it's difficult to accept that instant health is not a reality. The human body is able to tolerate excesses of one kind or another for a long time-even six pounds of carrots a day! But the bottom line is that balance, not only in what we eat, but in our total lifestyle, is the key to enduring health and happiness. Too much of a good thing is a bad thing when your health is involved. Common sense and moderation will do more for you than any health fad or miracle cure. Balance is the key to good health-learn to apply it in all areas of your life.

"I have never seen a person who died from old age. In fact, I do not think anyone has ever died of old age yet. To die of old age would mean that all the organs of the body had worn out proportionally, merely by having been used too long. This is never the case. We invariably die because one vital part has worn out too early in proportion to the rest of the body. There is always one part that

wears out first and wrecks the whole human machinery, merely because the other parts cannot function without it. The lesson seems to be that as far as man can regulate his life by voluntary actions, he should seek to equalize stress throughout his being. The human body-like the tires on a car or a rug on a floor, wears longest when it wears evenly." --Dr. Hans Selye.

6. Exercise

Genesis 2:15 "And God took the man and put him into the Garden of Eden to dress it and to keep it." "*The more we exercise, the better will be the circulation of the blood. More people die for want of exercise than through over fatigue; very many more rust out than wear out. Those whom accustom themselves to proper exercise in the open air will generally have a good and vigorous circulation.*" Ellen White, Counsels on Health, Pacific Press Publishing Association, pg. 173.

"Morning exercise, in walking in the free, invigorating air of heaven, or cultivating flowers, small fruits, and vegetables, is necessary to a healthful circulation of the blood. It is the surest safeguard against colds, coughs, congestion of brain and lungs, inflammation of the liver, the kidneys, and the lungs, and a hundred other diseases." My Life Today, Review & Herald Publishing Association, pg. 136, Ellen White.

The quality of life in your mature years depends largely on how well you take care of your house (body) when you are young, as you have to live in it when you are old. To maintain youth and optimal health you need a well-balanced combination of exercise and proper nutrition. Regular exercise improves digestion and elimination, increases endurance and energy levels, promotes lean body mass while burning fat, and lowers overall blood cholesterol. Exercise also reduces stress and anxiety, which are contributing factors to many illnesses and conditions. In addition to the physical benefits, studies have shown that regular exercise elevates mood, increases feeling of well being, and reduces anxiety and depression.

God designed that the living machinery should be in daily activity, for in this activity or motion is its preserving power. Action is the law of our being. Inactivity is a fruitful case of disease. Exercise quickens and equalizes the circulation of the blood, but with idleness the blood does not circulate freely, and the exchanges in it that are so necessary to life and health do not take place. There is no exercise that can take the place of walking. Walk in all cases when possible. It is the best remedy for diseased bodies, because in this exercise all the organs of the body are brought into use. This is not the case in most exercises.

"To have optimal health, you have to have perfect circulation of the circulatory system, so oxygen, water, and nutrition can reach every organ of the body, especially the vital organs, i.e. the brain, liver, Kidneys, heart, etc. "You'd have to go a long way to find something as good as exercise as a fountain of youth. And you don't have to run marathons to reap the benefits. Little more than rapid walking for 30 minutes at a time, three or four times a week can provide ten years of rejuvenation" Dr. Roy J. Shepard, University of Toronto.

Take a look at the facts. The adage "Use it or lose it" applies not only to muscles and bones but also to hearts, lungs, brains, blood vessels, joints and every other part of the body. A sedentary lifestyle is a direct route to an early grave. Inactivity kills us, literally! A strong genetic inheritance helps some people survive incredible odds. But just living longer isn't today's only concern.

Today's concern also includes quality of life and the energy, strength, and health to go with it. I have shared with each of my children, that as I played games like tag, hide-and-seek, and capture-the-flag with them, it is my goal to do the same with my grandchildren. Exercise helps us to feel good! Life becomes more fun, and the high that comes from exercise won't let you down later. Moreover, the hormones producing the exercise high are proving to be health promoting, as well. Exercise strengthens the heart. This is important in a culture in which every second person dies of heart and vascular disease. Exercise lowers blood pressure and resting heart rate, protecting the heart and blood vessels. Exercise lowers LDL cholesterol levels in the blood and often raises HDL cholesterol, again decreasing heart and vascular risk. (LDL is the bad part of cholesterol; HDL the good part.). Exercise strengthens bones by helping retain calcium and other minerals. Exercise lifts depression. Outdoor exercise is one of the most valuable tools for fighting this common and disabling malady. Exercise relieves anxiety and stress. In our harried, pressured society, physical activity is proving to be an effective antidote. Exercise increases overall energy and efficiency in all areas of our lives. Exercise helps maintain desirable weight levels. It builds muscles and burns fat. Moderate exercise blunts appetite by temporarily increasing blood sugar levels.

Exercise improves circulation, and that makes for clearer minds, better sleep, and faster healing of damaged body areas. If you have health problems, or are overweight, before you begin any new exercise routine, check with your doctor. Know your target heart rate zone and stay within it. Choose exercises that are fun and enjoyable to you and exercise at least three times a week for a minimum of 20 to 60 minutes.

"Exercise aids the dyspeptic by giving the digestive organs a healthy tone. To engage in deep study or violent exercise immediately after eating, hinders the digestive process; for the vitality of the system, which is needed to carry on the work of digestion, is called away to other parts. But a short walk after a meal, with the head erect and the shoulders back, exercising moderately, is a great benefit. The mind is diverted from self to the beauties of nature. The less the attention is called to the stomach, the better. If you are in constant fear that your food will hurt you, it most assuredly will. Forget your troubles; think of something cheerful." Ellen White, Council on Diet and Foods, Physiology of Digestion, Pacific Press Publishing Association, pg. 103.

7. Rest

Genesis 2:3 "And God...rested from all His work which God created and made." And he said unto them, "Come ye yourselves apart into a desert place, and rest a while: for there were many coming and going, and they had no leisure so much as to eat," Mark 6:31.

"Rest is what the human family needs; physical rest, mental rest, and spiritual rest. "The stomach, when we lie down to rest, should have its work all done, that it may enjoy rest, as well as other portions of the body. The work of digestion should not be carried on through any period of the sleeping hours. After the stomach, which has been overtaxed, has performed its task, it becomes exhausted, which causes faintness. Here many are deceived, and think that it is the want of food which produces such feelings, and without giving the stomach time to rest, they take more food, which for the time removes the faintness. And the more the appetite is indulged, the more will be its clamors for gratification. This faintness is generally the result of meat eating, and eating frequently, and too much. The stomach becomes weary by being kept constantly at work, disposing of food not the most healthful. Having no time for rest, the digestive organs become enfeebled, hence the sense of "goneness," and desire for frequent eating. The remedy such require, is to eat less frequently and less liberally, and be satisfied with plain, simple food, eating twice, or, at most, three times a day. The stomach must have its regular periods for labor and rest; hence eating irregularly and between meals, is a most pernicious violation of the laws of health. With regular habits, and proper food, the stomach will gradually recover." Ellen White, Counsels on Diet and Foods, Review & Herald Publishing Association, pg. 175.

With this statement, you come into direct conflict with the Diabetes Association that teaches snacking between meals in order to maintain (manage) normal blood sugar levels if you are hypo-glycemic. As mentioned earlier in the section About the Author, p. 2, in 1982, my blood sugar level went as high as 206 and as low as 38, in a hour six hour time period, see appendix A; Glucose Tolerance Test-Rickey Lee. It wasn't until I read the book "Counsels on Diets and Foods", and especially the above quote that I took God at His word and began to increase the amount of time between meals along with the quality of food that I was eating. Of course this required a change in diet, no more junk food, processed food, etc. It wasn't until I incorporated whole grains, nuts, fruit and vegetables into my diet, along with herbs to help heal my pancreas and other natural remedies. Then God blessed my efforts and today, I fast and do cleanse and detoxification programs without having blood sugar issues.

Recently, new research has shown that a modified fast can regenerate the pancreas. "The pancreas can be triggered to regenerate itself through a type of fasting diet, say US researchers. Restoring the function of the organ - which helps control blood sugar levels - reversed symptoms of diabetes in animal experiments. ... In the experiments, mice were put on a modified form of the "fasting-mimicking diet". Feb 24, 2017. **Fasting diet 'regenerates diabetic pancreas' - BBC News - BBC.com** www.bbc.com/news/health-39070183

Come rest a while. It is one of God's special healing remedies, and it is just for you, right now. Let us look and learn about this important necessity of life and the blessings that rest can bring, blessings that you may very much need. Daily sleep is in short supply with many Americans. Research suggests newborn babies sleep from 16 to 20 hours a day. While young children need 10 to 12 hours. Adults do best on seven to eight hours of sleep per night. In America, it is not uncommon for the people to put in a seven-day work week. The medical evidence suggests that there may be both long-term and short-term consequences to such a practice. Just as the body has a natural daily clock called circadian rhythm, it also has a weekly clock called circaseptan rhythm. Circaseptan rhythms are just that: body rhythms that run about seven days in length. Medical research has demonstrated such rhythms in connection with a variety of physiological functions. Some that have been identified include heart rate, suicides, natural hormones in human breast milk, swelling after surgery, and rejection of transplanted organs. Many cultures have experimented with a weekly cycle, including France during the French Revolution, going to a 7-day work week with disastrous results. Others have pointed to an even more compelling reason for the existence of the weekly cycle: it is the way God created us. Indeed, in the book of Genesis, the seven-day weekly cycle is described as part of God's design in creation. You can take one day in seven and rest for physical health, but the seventh day Sabbath is required for spiritual health. "Let us labor therefore to enter into that rest, lest any man fall after the same example of unbelief." Hebrews 4:11.

Some people over fill their lives just as others overeat. To sleep better, try taking frequent breaks during the workday. Walk around, get a drink of water, and take some deep breaths. Daily engage in 30 to 60 minutes of active exercise. Maintain as regular a schedule as possible for going to bed, getting up, eating, and exercising. The body flourishes on regular rhythms. Eat your evening meal at least four hours before bedtime. An empty resting stomach is more conducive to quality rest. Try taking a lukewarm bath about an hour before bedtime. It is a helpful relaxation technique.

Your last thoughts of the day should be filling your mind with gratitude, thanksgiving, and praising God. A clear conscience and a grateful mind are the best pillows to sleep on.

"As we are not our own, as we are bought with a price, it is the duty of everyone who professes to be a Christian to keep his thoughts under the control of reason and oblige himself to be cheerful and happy. However bitter may be the cause of his grief, he should cultivate a spirit of rest and quietude in God. The restfulness which is in Christ Jesus, the peace of Christ, how precious, how healing its influence, how soothing to the oppressed soul! However dark his prospects, let him cherish a spirit to hope for good. While nothing is gained by despondency, much is lost. While cheerfulness and a calm resignation and peace will make others happy and healthy, it will be of the greatest benefit to oneself. Sadness and talking of disagreeable things is encouraging the disagreeable scenes, bringing back upon oneself the disagreeable effect. God wants us to forget all these—not look down but up, up!" Ellen White, Mind, Character, and Personality Volume 2, Southern Publishing Association, pg. 662.

8. Sunshine

Genesis 1:3, 4 "And God said, let there be light: and there was light. And God saw the light that it was good; and God divided the light from the darkness."

"Invalids too often deprive themselves of sunlight. This is one of nature's most healing agents. It is a very simple, therefore not a fashionable remedy, to enjoy the rays of God's sunlight and beautify our homes with its presence. Fashion takes the greatest care to exclude the light of the sun from parlors and sleeping rooms by

dropping curtains and closing shutters, as though its rays were ruinous to life and health. It is not God who has brought upon us the many woes to which mortals are heirs. Our own folly has led us to deprive ourselves of things that are precious, of blessings which God has provided and which, if properly used, are of inestimable value for the recovery of health. If you would have your homes sweet and inviting, make them bright with air and sunshine. Remove your heavy curtains, open the windows, throw back the blinds, and enjoy the rich sunlight, even if it be at the expense of the colors of your carpets. The precious sunlight may fade your carpets, but it will give a healthful color to the cheeks of your children. If you have God's presence and possess earnest, loving hearts, a humble homemade bright with air and sunlight, and cheerful with the welcome of unselfish hospitality, will be to your family, and to the weary traveler, a heaven below."
Ellen White, Testimonies for the Church Volume Two, Exercise and Air, pg. 527.

Earth is a solar-powered world with 98 percent of its warmth coming from sunshine, the rest from geothermal heat. Solar energy lifts rain clouds, drives winds, and sparks the photosynthesis in plants, which feed all living things. A miracle factory is at work just beneath your skin, and when the ultraviolet rays of the sun touch the skin, the factory gets to work. It is a most marvelous system, and without it, you could not remain alive an hour. There are millions of red corpuscles constantly flowing through very small blood vessels throughout every part of the 3,000 square inches of your skin. And there are also tiny oil glands just beneath the skin which biochemists call sterols. As sunshine strikes them, substances within them, called ergo sterols, are irradiated and transformed into vitamin D. Carried to all parts of the body, it enables you to have strong bones, teeth, nails, and a major benefit for the heart.

Every living thing in the world is dependent upon the sun. Without sunshine, nothing could live. In 1877, two researchers, Blunt and Downes, discovered that sunlight can destroy harmful bacteria. Today, it is used to treat bacterial infections. Sunlight on the body dramatically lowers high blood pressure, decreases blood cholesterol, lowers excessively high blood sugars, and increases white blood cells. Adequate sunlight on your body will lower your respiratory rate and will cause your breathing to be slower, deeper, and even easier. Your resting heart rate will decrease, and after exercise it will return to normal much more quickly. Sunlight increases the capacity of the blood to carry oxygen and take it to your body tissues. Even a single exposure to the ultraviolet light in sunlight will greatly increase the oxygen content of your blood, and this effect will continue for several days. Bronchial asthma patients, who could hardly breathe, were able to inhale freely after a sunbath. It is of interest that many of these beneficial effects of sunlight are heightened if a person combines sunbathing with a regular program of physical exercise. In recent years, melatonin, a natural body hormone, has been found to enhance sleep. Melatonin levels reach a peak in children, then falls slowly and steadily throughout adult life. This may explain why children sleep so much better than older people. The body carefully regulates melatonin production. The process is largely controlled by the light-dark cycle. Optimal melatonin production occurs only at night, in a dark environment. The pineal gland, located in the center of the brain, is the "clock" that regulates this process at the right time. Melatonin is not stored in the body. We need a liberal supply each evening to sleep well. Studies demonstrate that daily exposure to natural sunlight will boost melatonin output. Artificial light is a weak substitute, as well as manufactured supplements.

9. Cleanliness

Deuteronomy 23:14. *"Every form of un-cleanliness tends to disease. Death-producing germs abound in dark, neglected corners, in decaying refuse, in dampness and mold and must. No waste vegetables or heaps of fallen leaves should be allowed to remain near the house to decay and poison the air. Nothing unclean or decaying should be tolerated within the home. In towns or cities regarded perfectly healthful, many an epidemic of fever has been traced to decaying matter about the dwelling of some careless householder. Perfect cleanliness, plenty of sunlight, careful attention to sanitation in every detail of the home life, is essential to freedom from disease and to the cheerfulness and vigor of the inmates of the home. Scrupulous cleanliness is essential to both physical and mental health. Impurities are constantly thrown off from the body through the skin. Its millions of pores are quickly clogged unless kept clean by frequent bathing, and the impurities which should pass off through the skin become an additional burden to the other eliminating organs. Most persons would receive benefit from a cool or tepid bath every day, morning or evening. Instead of increasing the liability to take cold, a bath, properly taken, fortifies against cold because it improves the circulation; the blood is brought to the surface, and a more easy and regular flow is obtained. The mind and the body are alike invigorated. The muscles become more flexible; the intellect is made brighter. The bath is a soother of the nerves. Bathing helps the bowels, the stomach, and the liver, giving health and energy to each, and it promotes digestion. It is important that the clothing be kept clean. The garments worn absorb the waste matter that passes off through the pores; if they are not frequently changed and washed the impurities will be reabsorbed,*" Ellen White, Child Guidance, p. 108.

10. BENEVOLENCE (kindly giving)

"Put on therefore, as the elect of God, holy and beloved, bowels of mercies, kindness, humbleness of mind, meekness, longsuffering." Colossians 3:12

A promise of health ""*Is* not this the fast that I have chosen?... *Is it* not to deal thy bread to the hungry, and that thou bring the poor that are cast out to thy house? when thou seest the naked, that thou cover him; and that thou hide not thyself from thine own flesh? **Then shall thy light break forth as the morning, and thine health shall spring forth speedily:** and thy righteousness shall go before thee; the glory of the Lord shall be thy rereward." Isaiah 58:6-9.

Digestion: One of the Keys to Optimal Health
"*You can do more for your own health and wellbeing than any doctor, any hospital, any drug, or any exotic medical device.*" Joseph Califano, Secretary of Health Education & Welfare.

Why is digestion the key to optimal health? Understanding anatomy and physiology, we know that digestion begins in the mouth and ends with the anus. If at any place along the process digestion breaks down, it sets the stage for the pH to change, affecting body chemistry which leads to dis-ease, resulting in disease. If digestion is sluggish from a high pH (6.8 or higher), toxins build in the colon until they begin to seep into the blood stream, spilling over into the joints of the body causing pain and stiffness. If the condition is not corrected, the toxins will be deposited on the surface of the skin causing rashes, and all sorts of skin conditions. This build up of toxins will affect first the liver and kidneys, then permeating the rest of the organs. Finally once the organs are full, the body dumps the toxins into joints and tissue. The toxicity level suppresses the immune system, giving disease the foothold it needs to take control of your system. If you learn about your body's digestive system and how to protect it, you have control over your health. If the digestion system's pH is to low or acid (6.2 or lower), then food is broken down too fast and mal-absorption leads to the weakening of organs (dis-ease), setting the stage for disease. Unlike the blood's pH of 7.1 to 7.3, the optimal digestion system pH has to be 6.4 in order to have optimal digestion. If you suffer from gas, belching, burping, etc… your digestive pH is out of balance. Very few people understand the significant of the digestive system's pH.

Dr. Carey Reams was right!

Dr. Carey Reams always warned that high urea is an important risk factor, in and of itself for myocardial infarction (heart attack). Recent research from the Albert Einstein College of Medicine confirms the link between urea and heart disease. In the May 10, 2000 issue of the Journal of the American Medical Association, they reported that high serum uric acid is an independent risk factor for death from cardiovascular disease after adjusting for other associated risk factors, including smoking, age, race, body mass index, cholesterol, and hypertension. The relationship was seen in both men and women regardless of race. This finding is huge as Dr. Reams was hassled by the American Medical Association (AMA), and jailed on several occasions for his health care beliefs. Yet, the Albert Einstein College of Medicine proves his research findings, and the AMA has never issued a formal apology to the Reams family. One of the simplest and yet most cost efficient ways you can protect your family members health is to learn the Reams Theory of Biologic Ionization as applied to Human Nutrition. The perfect equation for perfect health is 1.5 (blood sugar) 6.4/6.4 (urine and saliva) 6-7 (salt) .04 (cell debris) and 3/3 (ammonia nitrate and nitrite Nitrogen). We are going to focus on the numbers 6.4 over 6.4. The pH of the digestive system is different from the other pH numbers of the body. The small "p" refers to activity and the capital "H" refers to the hydrogen ion. The ratio between the alkaline and acids in a solution determines the pH value. It will have an effect on the activity of the hydrogen ions. The pH values are not a measurement of the volume of alkaline and acids, but, instead, it is an indication of the resistance between them. Technically, the pH value is the negative logarithm of the hydrogen ion concentration in a substance. Never forget the pH values are not a measurement of the volume but a measurement of resistance between alkalis and acids. Stated another way, it is a measurement of resistance between anions (alkalis) and anions, anions and cations (acid), and cations and cations. The pH scale 00 to 14. Pure sulfuric acid has a pH of 00 and pure calcium has a pH of 14. In orthodox chemistry, 7.00 is the neutral point. pH values above 7.0 is considered alkaline and pH values below 7.0 is considered acid. However, within the body chemistry for digestion, neutral is 6.4. Above 6.4 we consider alkaline and below 6.4 we consider acid. Our reference points are different, so do not confuse the two.

Sulfuric Acid	$\longrightarrow$	Neutral	$\longleftarrow$		pure Calcium
acid		x		x	Ca.
H_2SO_4 0		6.4		(7)	14

The better supply of minerals we have in the body, the less fluctuation there will be in the pH numbers. Likewise, the fewer minerals in the body chemistry, the more change there will be, and a greater pH fluctuation will occur. Fluctuations will also be present in the various mineral salts of the body and the sugars. If the urine pH is 6 at 9 a.m. and at 12 noon it is 7.5, this would be interpreted as a mineral deficiency. The better the functioning of the various organs of the body, especially the liver, and the better mineralization of the body, the less variation and fluctuation in pH will be noted. It will gradually change under proper treatment until it reaches 6.4, and this should be the pH no matter when the urine and saliva are taken. In order not to have to take blood every time, Dr. Carey Reams devised this formula for measuring proper pH.

pH of the Urine + 2 times the pH of the Saliva

----

divided by 3 = average pH

The Refractor meter is a meter good for measuring the sugars in urine on the Brix scale. There is also litmus paper which measure pH, which you should be able to get in a drug store. However, please see that these tapes measure over a wide range and that the increments of measurement are not too wide apart. So get a tape which measures one tenth increments if possible and you will be able to be much more accurate. Remember, the urine and saliva must be tested at the same time. Do not eat anything an hour before testing, or wait two hours after eating before testing.

General Stages of Degeneration Shown by Urine & Saliva Patterns

	From ideal $\longrightarrow$ to death				
	(1)	(2)	(3)	(4)	(5)
Urine pH	6.40	Alkaline	Acid	Alkaline	Acid
Saliva pH	6.40	Alkaline	Alkaline	Acid	Acid

A deeper understanding of the significant of urine and saliva pH patterns is when you understand and associate them with pleomorphism as described by Bechamp and proved bacterial and fungal changeability. Both Claude Bernard and Bechamp inspired

190

Enderlein to confirm that germs are symptoms. Germs simulate the occurrence of more symptoms as a result of thriving in an unbalanced terrain. "Terrain," a term brought to the fore by Bernard, is the internal environment of the body. A healthy or diseased terrain is determined primarily by four things: its acid/alkaline balance (pH); its electric/magnetic charge (negative or positive); its level of poisoning (toxicity); and its nutritional status.

French microbiologist Gaston Naessens used the term somatid for a primitive pleomorphic living element. This somatid cycle in an unbalanced body (Terrain), contains 16 stages of bacterial, yeast and fungal forms. By observing these stages in the blood, he can correlate them with the existence or onset of symptoms, such as cancer or degenerative disease.

Over the years the somatids were revealed to be virtually indestructible! They have resisted exposure to carbonization temperatures of 200° C and more. They have survived exposure to 50,000 rems of nuclear radiation, far more than enough to kill any living thing. They have been totally unaffected by any acid. Taken from centrifuge residues, they have been found impossible to cut with a diamond knife; so unbelievably impervious to any such attempts is their hardness. The eerie implication is that the new minuscule life forms revealed by Naessens's microscope are imperishable. At the death of their hosts, such as ourselves, they return to the earth, where they live on for thousands of years! *In the sweat of thy face shalt thou eat bread, till thou return unto the ground; for out of it wast thou taken: for dust thou [art], and unto dust shalt thou return.* Genesis 3:19. The process for returning unto dust already exists within us and we cannot extend the amount of life that has been programmed into our DNA, but we can certainly shorten our life span. The somatid cycle is the true gem of understand pH. Many brush off pH as insignificant to their premature death.

"Be not over much wicked, neither be thou foolish: why shouldest thou die before thy time?" Ecclesiastes 7:17.

In Summary:
From what you have read, it is evident that the pH of the urine and saliva must be kept as close as possible to 6.4 if one is to have the best digestion, which contributes to better health. However, for optimal health, the other five numbers that make up body chemistry must be

accurate. Once again, I am not talking orthodox chemistry but rather body chemistry. The 1.5 number listed above refers to blood sugars as read by a Brix, the range is from 1.0 to 2.0 with 1.5 being ideal. The Brix reads all eight sugars not just glucose.

I just discussed the 6.4 numbers. The 6-7 number refers to the sodium content of the body; the .04 number refers to cell debris or toxicity of the body; and the last two numbers in the equation, 3 over 3 refers to the ureas. It is divided into two parts: nitrate nitrogen and ammoniacal nitrogen. The urea numbers are usually looked at together; the total of the two numbers gives the urea reading. If you will learn the principles of body chemistry or go to a Christian Health Restoration Practitioner that does, and apply God's natural laws of health; Trust in Divine Power, exercise, fresh air, sunshine, rest, diet, water, and temperance, along with natural remedies, and leave the outcome with God, you will be blessed far above surgery, chemotherapy and radiation.

It has been emphasized that if the pH is not normal, the body chemistry is lacking in minerals, and especially calcium, usually in the form required to lower the pH. The following are observations which might be valuable to you:

1.   Anytime the pH varies from 6.4, there is a mineral deficiency, especially calcium, and disease is encouraged.
2.   Anyone varying from the normal range needs vitamin A.
3. B_{12} is recommended for pH 6.5 or below, consistently.
4.   When the pH is too low, Vitamin D is needed.
5.   High pH over a period of time may produce constipation.
6.   Low pH or on the acid side may produce diarrhea.
7.   Vitamin C (ascorbic acid) is used to reduce the pH when it is too high.
8.   Calcium carbonate may be used to increase the pH when it is too low. Also, use a non-ascorbic vitamin C when the pH is acidic.
9.   The continued low pH will cause nervousness, irritability, impatience, and, at times, depression. The lower the pH, the more nervous one becomes. A body chemistry analysis should always be a part of marriage counseling.
10.   An out of balance pH activates the somatid cycle which causes premature death.

Now that we are beginning to understand the importance of overall body chemistry, and the pH of the systems, let's enjoy the new birth experience without side effects and symptom management, in order to truly heal.

Make A New You Physically & Spiritually: John 3:3
"Health is a matter of choice, not a mystery of chance." -Robert A. Mendelsohn, M.D.

Humans are composed of about 300 trillion cells. Of these cells, there are millions that die each day and are replaced by the one million cells that are born each and every hour of every day. The complexity of the cellular activities may be better understood by the realization that just one liver cell may contain at least 1,000 enzymes (a protein substance) to assist and speed along reactions which will occur at the rate of over 1,000 times per second. The cell is responsible for everything that occurs in the body. Everything starts at the cellular level, including health and sickness. *"If the foundation be destroyed, what can the righteous do"*? Psalm 11:3. The cell has what is known as "cellular intelligence," and has the ability to sample the entire body environment (Inner Terrain) and determine what type of raw materials and fluids are needed and transport them to that site to be utilized. The cells are also sensitive to the consumption of too much refined or processed foods which may upset the potassium/sodium balance, throwing the cell out of balance and making it difficult to control fluids and to clear toxins efficiently.

How to Build a New and Healthy You

Every 90 days the blood cells renew. Every 3 years the soft tissue renew. Every 7 years hard tissue renews. The quality of the new you depend upon:
- ✓ The condition of the walls of the small intestines.
- ✓ Nutrient bioavailability.
- ✓ The quality and the quantity of the food we eat.
- ✓ The quality and the type of supplements we take.
- ✓ The number of factors that affect our biochemical efficiency.

As you can see, time becomes a very important factor. We must be patient with nature while we continue to do the right things. The X factor makes the difference. At age 20, it takes X amount of minerals to build a cell; at age 40 it takes 2X; age 60 it takes 3X; at age 80 it takes 4X. At age 20 it takes 6 months to restore the body's energy, at age 40 – 12 months; at age 60 – 18 months; at age 80 – 24 months, all things being normal.

Cells do not live forever! They are continually replacing themselves and producing new cells. This means that you are constantly replacing the old worn-out cells with fresh, new cells. The importance of this is quite significant; however, most people rarely think twice about this phenomenon. Your body is actually being reborn piece by piece, or I should say cell by cell. This is true healing, God's way of healing without drugs or side effects. The cells of the bloodstream are capable of replacing themselves every 90 days. They are some of the hardest working cells of the body and tend to wear out faster than other cells. Their main functions are to carry oxygen to the cells, to carry toxins out of the body, and to fight foreign invaders that take advantage of imbalances in your body chemistry. The cells of the soft tissue are capable of replacing themselves every three years. This means that all your organs, i.e. pancreas, heart, lungs, liver, kidneys, etc, are reborn every three years, depending on the cycle the cells are in. Cells are not replaced all at the same time within the three year cycle; every cell of an organ will have replaced itself. The cells of the hard tissues are reborn every seven years. These include all your bones. When you give your body the raw material i.e. minerals, follow God's eight natural laws of health, and balance your body chemistry, then the new cells will be healthier than the cells they replace. Eventually, you will regain optimal health and be restored to the image of God. That is why it took a year and three months to heal my pancreas at age 26.

James says, *"But let patience have [her] perfect work, that ye may be perfect and entire, wanting nothing"* James 1:4. It takes time to heal as the above information points out, but we have been programmed to want instant relief at whatever the cost. God says, *"My people are destroyed for lack of knowledge: because thou hast rejected knowledge, I will also reject thee, that thou shalt be no priest to me: seeing thou hast forgotten the law of thy God, I will also forget thy children"* Hosea 4:6. Christians perish because of a lack of knowledge of anatomy, physiology and God's ten natural laws of health and simple yet very effective remedies.

As you allow nature to heal you, one day you start to notice symptoms like, itching, tiredness, constipation, etc, will be gone. The disappearance of these symptoms is your evidence that your body is in the healing process and if you are patient and help nature and not hinder her, you will recover health. That is why a little pill, which is void of life itself, which has no nutritional value, and turns your pH acid, cannot and will not ever be able to heal.

Even the threatened and dreaded Bird Flu should not cause distress in people's lives. *"If people understood how illness develops and what determines the severity of symptoms, they would not have an irrational fear of Bird Flu. They would know how to build their immunity through diet and lifestyle, and be confident they could properly treat the flu if they got sick. They would also realize that vaccines do not prevent disease."* Dr. Sherri J, Tenpenny, D.O.

WE THE SHEEPLE

We the people, of the United States of America once fought for our freedoms and liberty of conscious. GIVE ME LIBERTY OR GIVE ME DEATH was the motto. Valiant men and women through history have sacrificed wealth, position, and even life itself to defend liberty.

Today, the prediction of Dr. Benjamine Rush has come true: *"Unless we put medical freedom into the Constitution, the time will come when medicine will organize into an undercover dictatorship...To restrict the art of healing to one class of men and deny equal privileges to others will constitute the Bastille of medical science. All such laws are un-American and despotic and have no place in a republic... The Constitution of this republic should make special privilege for medical freedom as well as religious freedom."* -Benjamin Rush, M.D., Signer of the Declaration of Independence, Physician to George Washington, President.

The above statement is very telling. First, the United States is no longer a republic, which has become a democracy and soon to become a dictatorship, Rev. 13:11-17. What is so disappointing is that most Americans do not even care, as long as they can have their entertainment, pleasure and leisure, etc... Secondly Dr. Rush says that all such laws are despotic. The government has incorporated alternative medicine into Integrated Medicine, with the medical doctors as the gate keepers because of the peoples demand for. Also, because the government is looking for ways to lower health care costs. This despotism of laws began with the corporate takeover of medicine (AMA) by the Rockefeller and Carnegie around 1905. Since despotic laws have been pasted concerning the legalization of tobacco, alcohol, gambling (lotteries) and now recreational and medical marijuana. The U.S. government continues to legalize substances that compromises' the frontal lobe of the brain, deadening the spirituality of its citizens, which is leading them further away from God. More despotic laws will be passed until America repudiates every principle of it constitution making way for a national Sunday law, becoming the Image of the Beast of Rev. 13: 14, 15.

It began after World War I, Americans became obsessed with leisure and pleasure, and it was called the Roaring Twenties. It was a time when fun, parties and elegance was the theme. In the 1940s and 1950s opulence was the goal, and it is this time period which today is nostalgic to most Americans. It was the time Americans dreamed of obtaining the American dream, get your slice of the pie, which turned into the keeping up with the Jones', to the current economic policy of eliminating the middle class.

We have set the old against the young, ethnic group against ethnic group, the rich against the poor. Sports, entertainment and the pursuit of pleasure has distracted the American people to the point that they have become indentured servants and most do not even know it or care to know it. However, one day when the luxuries and freedoms we enjoy are taken away, it will be too late, for the enemy is already working within, attacking the constitution and your liberties. These are liberties which our forefathers fought and died for, which we do not value or appreciate because they were given to us on a golden platter.

Chapter VII: The Ultimate Goal is Population Reduction
Vaccinations: the Untold Truth

Among other things, Louis Pasteur is credited with improving and successfully using the technique of vaccination, which was blindly begun in 1876 by Edward Jenner. Jenner took pus from the running sores of sick cows and injected it into the blood of his "patients." Thus was born a vile practice whose nature has changed little to this day, and whose understanding is still clouded by Pasteur's theory. Robert O. Young, Ph.D, D.Sc, Sick and Tired, p. 23.

"Are vaccines safe" ...Or are they? Health authorities credit vaccines for the decline in disease and assures us of their safety and effectiveness. Yet these assumptions are directly contradicted by government statistics, published medical studies, Food and Drug Administration (FDA) and Centers for Disease Control (CDC) reports, and the opinions of credible research scientists from around the world. In fact, infectious diseases declined steadily for decades prior to mass immunizations and doctors in the U.S. report thousands of serious vaccine reactions each year, including hundreds of deaths and permanent disabilities. Fully vaccinated populations have experienced epidemics, and researchers attribute dozens of chronic immunological and neurological diseases that have risen dramatically in recent decades to mass immunization campaigns. A recent outbreak of mumps puts an exclamation point to what I have written.

Harvard University mumps outbreak grows; dozens infected; by Faith Karimi, CNN, April 27, 2016. Paul J. Barreira, director of Harvard University in Massachusetts, USA, health services reports that a mumps outbreak left 40 people sick over the past two months. The university first announced mumps cases in February of 2016, and infections have steadily increased despite efforts to isolate patients. Last month, the public health department in Cambridge, were Harvard is located, said <u>all students affected had been immunized against mumps before they contracted it</u>. Powerful, you are only defiling the human temple with toxic poisons that do not protect, but you have been brainwashed to believe in a failed system based upon disease as a market place.

Much of the American population know firsthand the tragic fact that the resistant bacterium are winning the war as they watch a love one die, or even they themselves die from an enemy disease that was supposed to be conquered 50 years ago. Presently, more than 45 million Americans have no health insurance coverage or are under-insured. Americans spend more than one trillion dollars on health annually. Within the next five years, approximately $300 billion will shift from conventional (allopathic) medicine to alternative healthcare," Estes Park Institute 2000, Estes Park, Colorado.

God has made it very clear that prescription drugs do not heal. In fact, He says in Rev.18:23. "for by thy sorceries were all nations deceived." Remember…"insomuch that, if it were possible, Satan would deceive the very elect." Matthew 24:24

Florida has reported more mumps cases in 2017 than the last five years combined.

The measles, mumps and rubella or MMR vaccine is the most effective way to prevent infection with any of the three diseases, Florida health officials said. The measles, mumps and rubella or MMR vaccine is the most effective way to prevent infection with any of the three diseases, Florida health officials said. But <u>even vaccinated persons can contract mumps,</u> as a recent rise in cases in Florida and elsewhere has shown as a recent rise in cases in Florida and elsewhere has shown. Yet, in at least half of the cases, the infected person had a <u>documented history of the MMR vaccination</u>, according to the December advisory for physicians. http://www.miamiherald.com/news/health-care/article190625819.html

Powerful, did you notice that the vaccine does not prevent the very disease it is created to protect against? Another fact to notice is that not all doctors report which mean that the number of people per incidents of disease, as well as the number of people injured from vaccinations are probably much higher than reported. http://www.miamiherald.com/news/healthcare/article190625819.html

As a Christian you are only defiling the human temple with toxic poisons that do not protect, but you have been brainwashed to believe in a failed system based upon disease as a market place.

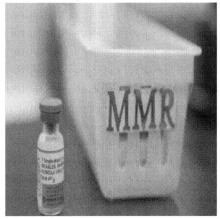

Let's look at the ingredients of the MMR vaccine. God has stated what is clean and what is unclean.
MMR (MMR-II)
chick embryo cell culture, WI-38 **human diploid lung fibroblasts**, vitamins, amino acids, **fetal bovine** serum, sucrose, glutamate, recombinant **human albumin**, neomycin, sorbitol, hydrolyzed **gelatin**, sodium phosphate, sodium chloride.

The Federal government Vaccine Averse Events Reporting System (VAERS) was established by Congress under the National Childhood Vaccine Injury Compensation Act of 1986. It receives about 11,000 reports of serious adverse reactions to vaccinations annually, which includes as many as one to two hundred deaths, and several times that number of permanent disabilities. VAERS officials reported that 15% of adverse events are "serious" (emergency room trips, hospitalization, life-threatening episodes, permanent disability, and death). Independent analysis of the VAERS reports has revealed that up to 50% of reported adverse events for the Hepatitis B vaccine are "serious." While these figures are alarming, they are only the tip of the iceberg.

The FDA estimates that as few as 1% of serious adverse reactions to vaccines are reported, and the Center for Disease Control (CDC) admits that only 10% of such events are reported. In fact, Congress has heard testimony that medical students are told not to report suspected adverse events.

The National Vaccine Information Center (NVIC, a grassroots organization founded by parents of vaccine-injured and killed children) has conducted its own investigations. It reported: "In New York, only one out of 40 doctors' offices confirmed that they report a death or injury following vaccination." In other words, 97.5% of vaccine related deaths and disabilities go unreported there. What about your state? Implications about medical ethics aside (federal law directs doctors to report serious adverse events), these findings suggest that vaccine deaths and serious injuries actually occurring may be from 10 to 100 times greater than the number reported. With the current promotion of vaccinating young ladies and girls, from ages nine to 26 for sexually transmitted diseases in the United States, one should be seriously concerned as you read and learn of the United Nations and other organizations plans and goals of 'population sterilization.'

Vaccines: Are They Really Safe and Effective?

A Parent's Guide to childhood Shots. Neil Z. Miller. Santa Fe, NM: New Atlantean Press, 1996.

Immunization: The Reality Behind the Myth, 2nd Edition. Walene James. Westport Conn.: Bergin & Garvey, an imprint of greenwood Publishing Group, 1995. This is one of the best books due to its range of information, holistic basis, and awareness of Bechamp, but may be difficult to obtain. Call 800-225-5800.

Overcoming Oppressive Laws: The Immune trio. The Humanitarian Society. Richlandtown, Penna. 18955: The Humanitarian Publishing Company, 1995. This book has a section entitled "How to Legally Avoid Unwanted Immunizations of All Kinds." It offers support for standing up for your rights and facing down bureaucrats who wish to think for you, but who are unwilling to take responsibility for their actions. Most states provide waivers for parents opposed to forced immunization.

Be aware that it is not an easy process. The book can be obtained from: The humanitarian Society, PO Box 77, Quakertown, Penna. 18951. Call 800-779-3796. If your doctor or local authorities prove unmovable, the National Vaccine Center may be of help: National Vaccine Information Center, 512 Maple Avenue, #206, Vienna, VA 22180. 703-938-3783.

Vaccines and Eugenics

Every year hundreds of thousands of people in America suffer adverse reactions, especially children from vaccinations. So the vaccine industry went to Congress: #HEALTH NEWS
February 22, 2011 / 10:19 AM / 7 years ago

Supreme Court rules for vaccine makers on lawsuits

WASHINGTON (Reuters) - The Supreme Court ruled that federal law shields vaccine makers from product-liability lawsuits in state court

seeking damages for a child's injuries or death from a vaccine's side effects. The high court on Tuesday ruled for Wyeth, which is now owned by Pfizer Inc, in a lawsuit brought by the parents of Hannah Bruesewitz, who suffered seizures as an infant after her third dose of a diphtheria-tetanus-pertussis (DTP) vaccine in 1992. Pfizer and other vaccine makers had argued that a Supreme Court ruling for the plaintiffs could open the door to a flood of lawsuits -- many by families who believe vaccines cause autism -- and threaten the supply of childhood vaccines. At issue in the ruling was the National Childhood Vaccine Injury Act of 1986, a law that created a special program to handle disputes in an effort to ensure a stable vaccine supply by shielding companies from most lawsuits. The federal program, involving what is known as the vaccine court, has awarded more than $1.8 billion for vaccine injury claims in nearly 2,500 cases since 1989. It is funded by a tax on vaccines. National Vaccine Information Center, Your Health. Your Family. Your Choice.
No Pharma Liability? No Vaccine Mandates.
Posted: 3/2/2011

Vaccines Are Pharmaceutical Products

Vaccines are pharmaceutical products that carry a risk of injury or death, a risk that can be greater for some than others. If a vaccine is effective, then those choosing to use that vaccine will have nothing to fear from those who make another health care choice. If a vaccine is not effective, then consumers are being asked to take two risks: a risk they will be harmed and a risk the vaccine will not work at all. That is not a product that should be legally required, especially when doctors cannot predict ahead of time who will be harmed by a vaccine and there is no civil liability for the company selling it, the person giving it or the government official mandating it. No liability?, No accountability?, No mandates. Against this backdrop, every time you take a vaccine you run the risk of injury or death. Just as disturbing, as of October 4, 2016 the United States Vaccine Court has paid over three billion dollars to vaccine-injured families. The science and medical establishments are working deliberately to exterminate African Americans from this planet, they are committing systematic genocide. NaturalNews.com.

The Vaccine Extermination Agenda

The story begins with Polio and polio vaccines. There are two ways that you can get polio, one is to catch it from a wild circulating virus; the second way is to get it from a polio vaccine. It is a well know phenomenon and it is called vaccine induced polio. Now when they inject children with polio or they do nasal vaccines or other forms of vaccines, not all the vaccines are fully attenuated, which means weakened; some of them have live viruses. So sometimes when they are giving vaccines to children and in large numbers and some small percentage of those children are going to be infected with the disease, with polio. It is called vaccine induced polio. Recently, 355,000 children were vaccinated in Syria, a Middle Eastern country against polio. Why were they vaccinated, because there was a polio outbreak. What caused the polio outbreak? The polio vaccine. This was a vaccine induced polio outbreak that was then treated with more vaccines. Now 355,000 children were then injected, if one out of a thousand children developed polio from a polio vaccine. Then didn't they just create 355 more children with polio? Yes they did, and that will be reported as an outbreak and someone will call for the World Health Organization (WHO) or Unicef to come in and vaccinate a million children, whatever it takes. You see the vaccines are the continuation of the disease that they claim to stop.

Now if you understand epidemiology, statistics, science and medicine, it is true that in a population were you have say a million children; and let's say polio is endemic. Let's say half the children in the country have polio, in that case because the infection rate is so high a polio vaccine can drastically reduce that infection rate and save far more lives than it would terminate. However, that same vaccine when the rate of infection is low, if you give that vaccine to large numbers of children, hundreds of thousands or millions, you will create more disease that you halt. This is what is used in Africa and across the world to keep the disease process going, so they can keep manufacturing vaccines, which are remember made from aborted African American babies. We are talking human fetal cell tissue. They take it from the abortions. Plan Parent Hood cells it to these companies. They put it in large vats and inoculate it with viral strains and they grow and fester a large amount of biomass of disease material. Then they homogenize with tissue homogenizers, they filter it, and put it in the vaccine vials with outer ingredients that are toxic like aluminum, lead, or mercury and then they inject that into other kids.

We are living in a world where they are murdering and grinding up African American babies to feed them to other babies. This is like the Matrix, this is medical cannibalism and it is happening every day. Many of these vaccines are made from human fetal tissue that is harvested from aborted babies. Many of the doctors don't even know it; a lot of the pharmacists don't even know it because they have never read the list of ingredients of a vaccine. All you have to do is go to the Center for Disease Control and Prevention (CDC) or Federal Drug Administration (FDA) website and read for yourself, it is all right there.

A recent study literally ran by the CDC using CDC money and CDC scientist found that vaccines cause spontaneous abortions. So now they are pushing vaccines on pregnant women, you have heard that recently that pregnant are encouraged to go out and get multiple vaccines, which was never taught in medicine until the last twenty years. Before that doctors were told no, no, no, you never vaccinate a pregnant woman you might harm the unborn baby. Oh you are pregnant here get your vaccine, take antidepressants, take chemotherapy, which is poisoning your body but don't worry it does not affect the baby. But it does, because these medical liars are genocidal, homicidal maniacs they are deceiving you; they are lying to you as they know vaccines cause spontaneous abortions. It has just been admitted by the CDC, the study was reported in the journal Vaccine, one more population control mechanism. For more information about population control, go to depopulation.news or genocide.news and eugentics.news and your eyes will be opened and come to see the truth about what is actually happening. To some extent we are all being targeted for extinction, but African Americans are the focal point. Form the article Global 2000 revisited the goal of the elitist is to reduce the global population down between one to two billion people.

Where is Black Lives Matters, why are they not marching concerning the abortion industry? What about the psychiatric drugs being given to young African American children, or the autism epidemic, or the use of African American children for medical experiments. Black Lives Matter does not touch any of those issues and you are still being exterminated because it is in the food, it is in the medicine, the scientific community is working to exterminate you. Your enemy is not the Nazi or even the White Supermist, it the scientist. It's the pharmacology; it's the evil doers the drug companies, it's the vaccine companies, it's the abortion providers that is who is killing you.

Covert Food Sterilization

In November 23, 1969 The New York Times ran an article authored by Gladwin Hill. The article is entitled "A Sterility Drug In Food Is Hinted" Biologist stresses need to curb population growth. The article sited a scientist named Paul Ehrlich who is a depopulation advocate, as well as the chief science advisor for then president Richard Nixon, his name is Dr. Lee DuBridge and he said "population control should be the prime task of every government." Here is how they were going to accomplish this, according to the New York Times article. Dr. Lee DuBridge said "The addition a temporary sterilant to staple food or to the water supply" in order to cause mandatory infertility. Notice that they called for adding this sterilization chemical to the food supply and water supply. What has happened since then, lead poisoning in Flint Michigan that is a damaging chemical in the water supply isn't it? It was taken right out of the play book of 1969, it is part of the plan and that was the one time that they got caught. What about the tetanus vaccines in Africa that were found to be contaminated with a sterilization chemical. Same thing, they were going to hide it in the food and the water and now they are putting it in the vaccines, it is all consistent. Oh and by the way that chemical that they found in the vaccines is call Beta BCG. I am going to describe this to you; Beta BCG causes the female body to have an immune system response that builds antibodies that destroy her own fetus if she gets pregnant. Do you realize that through this chemical that they secretly inserted into the vaccine, they can cause a women's body to turn against itself and to murder its own baby; in absolute violation of natural law, biblical principles, medical morality and everything else.

They were putting this sterilization chemical in these vaccines without the informed consent of the women who were being sterilized. This is evil medicine, this is evil science, and this is genocide in the name of vaccines for public safety. That is what they tell you; oh this is for public safety, while they are making a woman's body murder her own baby before it can be born and they don't tell her about it. Wasn't it Evan Burke who said "all that is necessary for evil to prevail is to let good men do nothing." I am not going to stand here and be silent, I am not going to stand here and be intimidated. Those people out there they can slander, they can defame me all they want, all day and night. Call me anything, fake news, lies, fake accusations; the truth is that you people are genocidal maniacs trying to kill black babies. You turn black women against their own babies; you turn her womb into a murder system through the use of covert sterilization chemicals. That is a scientific and medical fact and that is why I am standing here today, to speak this truth. To pout on the record so that no one can hide from this fact that this genocide is taking place, right now today. It's not 1932 Tuskegee experiment anymore, it is more advanced. Now it is not just one vector killing people, it is five or six different vectors, it's in the food, it's in the water, it's in the vaccines, it's in the medicines, and it's in the psychiatric drugs.

Let's get to the food because it will absolutely shock you. Hopefully you are aware of Genetic Engineering of the food supply; it is called Genetically Modified Organisms (GMOs). This is an advance science technique to alter the DNA of food crops in order to build in certain traits and physical properties and even chemical properties that the scientists want to put into the food. Let me explain to you how your food is now being weaponized as an extermination vector to eliminate black lives. I am a food scientist, the author of the book Food Forensics. It achieved the number one best selling science book on Amazon.com. I am the co-author of science papers that have been published in main stream science journals. I am not just a causal lay person when it comes to food science. I run a Mass Spec laboratory that is ISO 17025 accredited, validated, audited, inspected and have passed many, many tests. Our data can be used in a court of law anywhere around the world. We do food analysis; we can search for complex molecules such as pesticides or elements such as mercury or cadmium. So I run the lab, I am the lab science director; I know a thing or two about food science. Now what they have invented, when I say them, I am talking about the genetic engineers, not only have they found a way to put these genetically engineered traits in to food crops; they have now found a way to cause food crops to grow RNA fragments that can be specifically targeted like bio-weapons to interfere with the physiological processes of targeted species that might eat the food. Now, this technology is called RNA Interference technology and it is relatively new, compared to GMOs. It's being touted now as a tool to eliminate the use of pesticides because what they are saying is that they can for example cause a corn crop to grow RNA fragments that will kill the insects that eat the corn without having to use pesticide like toxic chemicals that overload the insects nervous system and kill it from a nervous system breakdown and so on. This RNA interference technology is a pesticide technology but it does not rely on pesticide chemicals, it relies on RNA fragments in foods. Now, what's disturbing about this is that this technology can be fined tuned to target a specific race of people who eat the food.

Crops that Kill Pests by Shutting Off their Genes

"Plants are among many eukaryotes that can 'turn off' one or more of their genes by using a process called RNA interference to block protein translation. Researchers are now weaponizing this by engineering crops to produce specific RNA fragments that, upon ingestion by insects, initiate RNA interference to shut down a target gene essential for life or reproduction, killing or sterilizing the insects." Science Daily, July 27, 2017.

Now what is disturbing about this technology can be fined tuned to target a specific race of humans who eat the food. I want you to follow me very carefully on this because most people have never heard of this before. They have never heard of this technology, they do not know that they can be targeted by race. Food crops can be engineered right now, based upon existing technology to cause infertility in black people alone, or Mexicans alone, etc... That technology is a reality; actually it is widely covered out there in the main stream science media, RNA Interference technology widely covered. They openly talk about how it can be targeted specific physiological processes of certain insect species. They can interfere with DNA repair or protein synthesis in insects; they can interfere with fertility or reproduction, they can interfere with mobility and nervous system interaction with the muscular skeletal system depending on what insect we are talking about. I ask you does that technology exist, the answer is yes. It absolutely exists right now.

RNA Interference Technology turned out to be a powerful Biological Weapon

In essence, scientist accidently discovered that RNA interference technology, originally pursued to save lives, could be tweaked into a powerful, deadly, biological weapon. With engineering of some precise RNA fragments, almost any race or body organ system could be targeted. Mike Adams, NaturalNews.com.

Are they using that technology, I ask you to do a little bit of research and look at the plummeting sperm production in African American men. Sperm production is precisely the kind of physiological process that can be targeted by RNA interference technology. Now is that the proof that the food crops are being engineered to cause sperm production to plummet in African American males, no it is not proof but when you connect the dots, all the other things that are being done covertly, this becomes something very likely in the realm of possibility. It would take a lot of advanced testing to find this out. Guess who control nearly all the science funding in America today, the federal government. The same government that allows the CDC to cover up the truth about vaccines and the "Racial Differences in Developmental Regression in Children with Autism Spectrum Disorders." The same government that funds

Planned Parenthood abortions. The same government that covers up the Environmental Protection Agency's (EPA) contamination of water ways affecting Native Americans and other populations, including Flint Michigan a predominately an African American community. This government, the same government that runs the Federal Bureau of Investigations (FBI) is at war with you. The government is at war with you and they control the science funding, which means that there will never be money for any genetic science of the food supply to uncover this truth if it were there. It will be covered up like everything else has been covered up, this entire time. You are being targeted, like I said earlier, to a certain extent we are all being targeted but black people are targeted more than anyone else.

So what do we do with all this information, take to the streets and bash heads, no. The problem is consolidation of power in the institutions of science and medicine. The problem is that science has been taken over by globalist agendas, and depopulation agendas with government funding. The problem is that we do not have a decentralization of science. The problem is, if you will even allow me to invoke this terminology, we are all slaves to science tyranny as it is being operated today. We are living under a science dictatorship that refuses to tell us the truth and targets our brothers and sisters, our children and our grand children with extermination agendas through medicine, through food like everything we have talked about. That is the problem, we need independent science, we need decentralization, we need more labs like mine that I operate independently, we don't take any government money and that is why I can tell you this truth. Do you think that if I was on the payroll of some big corporation that uses government money, do you think that I could stand here and tell you this truth, no way. They would yank your funding so fast and cover it up sweeping it under the rug. I can only stand here today because I have no financial ties to the system that is murdering all of you. Nor will I ever have financial ties to that system, I refuse to take money from satanic forces, I refuse to take money from murderous regimes. That is what the United States government is today, a murderous regime and it has been that way under president Obama, President Bush, it is beyond any single president, it has nothing to do with Trump, and it is the bureaucracy. It is the momentum of genocide that is endemic in the culture of the CDC, the culture of the FDA and the culture of the EPA that is beyond the reach of anyone candidate, or anyone politician and it has persisted for generations and it continues to persist and they will continue to target you and murder you. Causing you new diseases, causing you brain damage and cause your children Autism until the day comes that we the people decide to stand up and take back our liberty from this murderous regime that committees murder and genocide in the name of science and medicine and that is what we must do. I don't think that it is a goal that can be achieved through violence, and I don't call for violence because that is being affected against us in far too many ways. It must start with awareness, so the only thing that I ask of you watching to this, listening to this; even if you don't believe every factor of the talk here. Maybe you find some of them hard to believe so far, the only thing that I ask of you is to share this information. Mike Adam, The Health Ranger; NaturalNews.com.

"If people understood how illness develops and what determines the severity of symptoms, they would not have an irrational fear of Bird Flu. They would know how to build their immunity through diet and lifestyle, and be confident they could properly treat the flu if they got sick. They would also realize that vaccines do not prevent disease*."* Dr. Sherri J, Tenpenny, D.O.

*"What? know ye not that **your body is the temple of the Holy Ghost which is in you**, which ye have of God, and ye are not your own*?: 1 Corinthians 6:19.

Many have never considered the ingredients of the vaccines they take or give their children. Because of such ingredients as African Green Monkey Kidney Cells, Fibroblast Cells from Aborted Human Fetuses, Human-Diploid Fibroblast Cell Culture (Strain-38), etc… for a full list of ingredients and excipients go to the CDC's web site at www.cdc.gov/vaccines/pubs/pinkbook/downloads/appendices/b/excipient-table-2.pdf I have listed them for you below but go to the web site to verify but remember, ingredients change from time to time. The ingredients below are from December 15, 2017.

Christians are defiling their body, the temple of the Holy Ghost by injecting unclean animal and human into them. How soon we have forgotten that feeding animals to animals that are herbivore, which I believe created a disease called BSE (bovine spongiform encephalopathy) or Mad Cow Disease. However, the CDC states that "the nature of the transmissible agent is not well understood." What causes mad cow disease and variant Creutzfeldt-Jakob disease (vCJD) experts are not sure what causes mad cow disease or vCJD. The leading theory is that the disease is caused by infectious proteins called prions (say "PREE-ons"). ... People can get vCJD if they eat the brain or spinal cord tissue of infected cattle. God created herbivores to eat plants not animal, so man in his greed for money for corporate profits and arrogance, alters the diet of the animals. Remember before sin, all animals were herbivores. Here are some of God's if you choose to eat animal flesh.

- **NEVER** permitted to consume flesh with blood in it, Genesis 9:4, Leviticus 3:17, Acts 15:20, 29, 21:25.
- The Bible calls consumption of meat with blood in it sin. 1 Samuel 14: 32-34.
- No animal was to be eaten that had died of itself. Lev 17:15; 22:8.
- It was killed in a loving way (humanely). Lev 22:28; Psalms 145:9; Proverbs 12:10.
- The blood had to be drained. It could not be consumed. Lev 7:26-27; 17:10-15; Acts 15:20, 29.
- The fat must be removed; it was not to be eaten. Lev 7:23-25.
- It was to be consumed within three days. Lev 7:18, 22:30.

The worldly system is now directly injecting animal and human tissue directly into the blood stream of human beings, a practice which Antonio Bechamp warned against, and we wonder why humans from infants to the elderly die or have adverse reactions to vaccines. Not to mention the fact that we are defiling the temple of the Holy Ghost and God has promised: **"If any man defile the temple of God, him shall God destroy**; for the temple of God is holy, which *temple* ye are. 1Corinthians 3:17.

If you understood anatomy and physiology and how to apply God's 10 doctors (laws of health) to them, as well as: It is written, Man shall not live by bread alone, but by every word that proceedeth out of the mouth of God. Matt. 4:4; you would not need to be vaccinated. Case in point: "The Black Death and leprosy were the two most terrible plagues of the middle ages. "The principles of public health or hygienic principles given by God and taught by Moses after the Exodus brought those scourges under control. Millions of lives were saved as *worldly* doctors turned to the church for help during those plagues" George Rosen, M.D., History of Modern Health, pg. 63-65. Absolutely amazing! Does man now know more than God?

It is fascinating to note that a total of two hundred and thirteen (213) out of the six hundred and thirteen (613) biblical commandments found in the Torah were detailed Health regulations that ensure the good health of the children of Israel if they would obediently follow the laws of God. These health regulations, the 10 doctors and the healing examples of the Old and New Testament of the King James Bible are better than anything modern medicine has to offer. Because if ignorance and fear Christians who are still in Babylon (Rev. 18) are afraid to trust God, so they are unable to obey Him. Remember the words of the Apostles Peter and John "But Peter and John answered and said unto them, *Whether it be right in the sight of God to hearken unto you more than unto God, judge ye*, Act 4:19. Then Peter and the *other* apostles made their position clear to all so we know for sure where they stand "*We ought to obey God rather than men,*" Acts 5:29. Vaccines are of the world, pioneered by Louis Pasteur so mankind can continue to violate the Word of God and have a false remedy.

Remember, as a Christian God warns "*There are many ways of practicing the healing art, but there is only one way that Heaven approves. God's remedies are the simple agencies of nature that will not tax or debilitate the system through their powerful properties. Pure air and water, cleanliness, a proper diet, purity of life, and a firm trust in God are remedies for the want of which thousands are dying; yet these remedies are going out of date because their skillful use requires work that the people do not appreciate. Fresh air, exercise, pure water, and clean, sweet premises are within the reach of all with but little expense, but drugs are expensive, both in the outlay of means and in the effect produced upon the system.*" Ellen White, Testimony to the Church vol. 5, p. 443.1.

Vaccine Excipient & Media Summary Excipients Included in U.S. Vaccines, by Vaccine. In addition to weakened or killed disease antigens (viruses or bacteria), vaccines contain very small amounts of other ingredients – excipients or media.

Some excipients are added to a vaccine for a specific purpose. These include: **Preservatives**, to prevent contamination, for example, thimerosal.

Adjuvants, to help stimulate a stronger immune response, for example, aluminum salts.

Stabilizers, to keep the vaccine potent during transportation and storage, for example, sugars or gelatin.

Others are residual trace amounts of materials that were used during the manufacturing process and removed. These include: **Cell culture materials,** used to grow the vaccine antigens. For example, egg protein, various culture media.

Inactivating ingredients, used to kill viruses or inactivate toxins, for example, formaldehyde.

Antibiotics, used to prevent contamination by bacteria, for example, neomycin.

The following table lists all components, other than antigens, shown in the manufacturers' package insert (PI) for each vaccine. Each of these PIs, which can be found on the FDA's website (see below) contains a description of that vaccine's manufacturing process, including the amount and purpose of each substance. In most PIs, this information is found in Section 11: "Description."

All information was extracted from manufacturers' package inserts, current as of January 6, 2017.

If in doubt about whether a PI has been updated since then, check the FDA's website at:

http://www.fda.gov/BiologicsBloodVaccines/Vaccines/ApprovedProducts/ucm093833.htm

Vaccine	Contains
Adenovirus	human-diploid fibroblast cell cultures (strain WI-38), Dulbecco's Modified Eagle's Medium, **fetal bovine serum**, sodium bicarbonate, monosodium glutamate, sucrose, D-mannose, D-fructose, dextrose, **human serum albumin**, potassium phosphate, plasdone C, anhydrous lactose, microcrystalline cellulose, polacrilin potassium, magnesium stearate, microcrystalline cellulose, magnesium stearate, cellulose acetate phthalate, alcohol, acetone, castor oil, FD&C Yellow #6 aluminum lake dye
Anthrax (Biothrax)	amino acids, vitamins, inorganic salts, sugars, aluminum hydroxide, sodium chloride, benzethonium chloride, formaldehyde
BCG (Tice)	glycerin, asparagine, citric acid, potassium phosphate, magnesium sulfate, iron ammonium citrate, lactose

Cholera (Vaxchora)	casamino acids, yeast extract, mineral salts, anti-foaming agent, ascorbic acid, hydrolyzed <u>casein</u>, sodium chloride, sucrose, dried lactose, sodium bicarbonate, sodium carbonate
DT (Sanofi)	aluminum phosphate, isotonic sodium chloride, <u>formaldehyde</u>, <u>casein</u>, cystine, maltose, uracil, inorganic salts, vitamins, dextrose
DTaP (Daptacel)	aluminum phosphate, <u>formaldehyde</u>, glutaraldehyde, 2-phenoxyethanol, Stainer-Scholte medium, casamino acids, dimethyl-beta-cyclodextrin, Mueller's growth medium, ammonium sulfate, modified <u>Mueller-Miller casamino acid medium</u> without beef heart infusion, 2-phenoxyethanol
DTaP (Infanrix)	Fenton medium containing a **bovine extract**, modified Latham medium derived from **bovine casein**, <u>formaldehyde</u>, modified Stainer-Scholte liquid medium, glutaraldehyde, aluminum hydroxide, sodium chloride, polysorbate 80 (Tween 80)
DTaP-IPV (Kinrix)	Fenton medium containing a **bovine extract**, modified Latham medium derived **from bovine casein**, <u>formaldehyde</u>, modified Stainer-Scholte liquid medium, glutaraldehyde, aluminum hydroxide, VERO cells, a continuous line of **monkey kidney cells, Calf serum**, lactalbumin hydrolysate, sodium chloride, polysorbate 80 (Tween 80), neomycin sulfate, polymyxin B

Vaccine	Contains
DTaP-IPV (Quadracel)	modified Mueller's growth medium, ammonium sulfate, modified Mueller-Miller casamino acid medium without beef heart infusion, <u>formaldehyde</u>, ammonium sulfate aluminum phosphate, Stainer-Scholte medium, casamino acids, dimethyl-beta-cyclodextrin, **MRC-5 cells** are <u>human cell culture line composed of fibroblasts derived from lung tissue of an 14 week old aborted caucasian male fetus</u>. **normal human diploid cells**, CMRL 1969 medium supplemented with **calf serum**, Medium 199 without calf serum, 2-phenoxyethanol, polysorbate 80, glutaraldehyde, neomycin, polymyxin B sulfate
DTaP-HepB-IPV (Pediarix) *DTaP-HepB-IPV (Pediarix)*	Fenton medium containing a **bovine extract**, modified Latham medium derived from **bovine casein**, <u>formaldehyde</u>, modified Stainer-Scholte liquid medium, **VERO cells**, a continuous line of **monkey kidney cells**, **calf serum** and lactalbumin hydrolysate, aluminum hydroxide, aluminum phosphate, aluminum salts, sodium chloride, polysorbate 80 (Tween 80), neomycin sulfate, polymyxin B, yeast protein.
DTaP-IPV/Hib (Pentacel)	aluminum phosphate, polysorbate 80, sucrose, <u>formaldehyde</u>, glutaraldehyde, **bovine serum albumin**, 2-phenoxyethanol, neomycin, polymyxin B sulfate, modified Mueller's growth medium, ammonium sulfate, modified Mueller-Miller casamino acid medium without beef heart infusion, Stainer-Scholte medium, casamino acids, dimethyl-beta-cyclodextrin. glutaraldehyde, **MRC-5 cells** (a line of normal human diploid cells), CMRL 1969 medium supplemented with **calf serum**, Medium 199 without calf serum, modified Mueller and Miller medium

Hib (ActHIB)	sodium chloride, modified Mueller and Miller medium (the culture medium contains milk-derived raw materials [casein derivatives]), formaldehyde, sucrose
Hib (Hiberix)	saline, synthetic medium, formaldehyde, sodium chloride, lactose
Hib (PedvaxHIB)	complex fermentation media, amorphous aluminum hydroxyphosphate sulfate, sodium chloride
Hib/Mening. CY (MenHibrix)	saline, semi-synthetic media, formaldehyde, sucrose, tris (trometamol)-HCl
Hep A (Havrix)	**MRC-5 human diploid cells**, formalin, aluminum hydroxide, amino acid supplement, phosphate-buffered saline solution, polysorbate 20, neomycin sulfate, aminoglycoside antibiotic
Hep A (Vaqta)	**MRC-5 diploid fibroblasts**, amorphous aluminum hydroxyphosphate sulfate, non-viral protein, DNA, **bovine albumin**, formaldehyde, neomycin, sodium borate, sodium chloride
Hep B (Engerix-B)	aluminum hydroxide, yeast protein, sodium chloride, disodium phosphate dihydrate, sodium dihydrogen phosphate dehydrate
Hep B (Recombivax)	soy peptone, dextrose, amino acids, mineral salts, phosphate buffer, formaldehyde, potassium aluminum sulfate, amorphous aluminum hydroxyphosphate sulfate, yeast protein
Hep A/Hep B (Twinrix)	**MRC-5 human diploid cells**, formalin, aluminum phosphate, aluminum hydroxide, amino acids, sodium chloride, phosphate buffer, polysorbate 20, neomycin sulfate, yeast protein
Human Papillomavirus (HPV) (Gardasil)	vitamins, amino acids, mineral salts, carbo-hydrates, amorphous aluminum hydroxyl-phosphate sulfate, sodium chloride, L-histidine, polysorbate 80, sodium borate, yeast protein
Human	vitamins, amino acids, mineral salts, carbo-

Papillomavirus (HPV) (Gardasil 9)	hydrates, amorphous aluminum hydroxylphosphate sulfate, sodium chloride, L-histidine, polysorbate 80, sodium borate, yeast protein
Influenza (Afluria) Trivalent & Quadrivalent	sodium chloride, monobasic sodium phosphate, dibasic sodium phosphate, monobasic potassium phosphate, potassium chloride, calcium chloride, sodium taurodeoxycholate, ovalbumin, sucrose, neomycin sulfate, polymyxin B, beta-propiolactone, **thimerosal**
(multi-dose vials) Influenza (Fluad)	**squalene**, polysorbate 80, sorbitan trioleate, sodium citrate dehydrate, citric acid mono-hydrate, neomycin, kanamycin, barium, egg proteins, CTAB (cetyltrimethylammonium bromide), <u>formaldehyde</u>
Influenza (Fluarix) Trivalent & Quadrivalent	octoxynol-10 (TRITON X-100), α-tocopheryl hydrogen succinate, polysorbate 80 (Tween 80), hydrocortisone, gentamicin sulfate, ovalbumin, <u>formaldehyde</u>, sodium deoxycholate, sodium phosphate-buffered isotonic sodium chloride
Influenza (Flublok) Trivalent & Quadrivalent	sodium chloride, monobasic sodium phosphate, dibasic sodium phosphate, polysorbate 20 (Tween 20), baculovirus and Spodoptera frugiperda cell proteins, baculovirus and cellular DNA, Triton X-100, lipids, vitamins, amino acids, mineral salts
Influenza(Flucelvax) Trivalent & Quadrivalent	Madin Darby Canine Kidney (MDCK) cell protein, protein other than HA, MDCK cell DNA, polysorbate 80, cetyltrimethlyammonium bromide, and β-propiolactone
Influenza(Flulaval) Trivalent & Quadrivalent	**ovalbumin**, <u>formaldehyde</u>, sodium deoxycholate, α-tocopheryl hydrogen succinate, polysorbate 80, **thimerosal** (multi-dose vials)
Influenza (Fluvirin)	ovalbumin, polymyxin, neomycin, betapropiolactone, nonylphenol ethoxylate, <u>thimerosal</u>
Influenza (Fluzone) Quadrivalent	<u>formaldehyde, egg protein</u>, octylphenol ethoxylate (Triton X-100), sodium phosphate-buffered isotonic sodium chloride solution, **thimerosal** (multi-dose vials), sucrose

Influenza (Fluzone) **High Dose**	egg protein, octylphenol ethoxylate (Triton X-100), sodium phosphate-buffered isotonic sodium chloride solution, <u>formaldehyde</u>, sucrose
Influenza (Fluzone) **Intradermal**	<u>egg protein</u>, octylphenol ethoxylate (Triton X-100), sodium phosphate-buffered isotonic sodium chloride solution, sucrose
Influenza (FluMist) **Quadrivalent**	<u>monosodium glutamate</u>, hydrolyzed **porcine gelatin**, arginine, sucrose, dibasic potassium phosphate, monobasic potassium phosphate, **ovalbumin**, gentamicin sulfate, ethylenedia-minetetraacetic acid (EDTA) **Japanese Encephalitis** (Ixiaro) aluminum hydroxide, protamine sulfate, <u>formaldehyde</u>, **bovine serum** albumin, **host cell DNA**, sodium metabisulphite, host cell protein
Meningococcal (MenACWY-Menactra)	Watson Scherp media containing casamino acid, modified culture medium containing hydrolyzed <u>casein</u>, ammonium sulfate, sodium phosphate, <u>formaldehyde</u>, sodium chloride
Meningococcal (MenACWY-Menveo)	<u>formaldehyde</u>, amino acids, yeast extract, Franz complete medium, CY medium
Meningococcal (MPSV4-Menomune)	Mueller Hinton <u>casein</u> agar, Watson Scherp casamino acid media, **thimerosal** (multi-dose vials), lactose
Meningococcal (MenB – Bexsero)	aluminum hydroxide, E. coli, histidine, sucrose, deoxycholate, kanamycin
Meningococcal (MenB – Trumenba)	defined <u>fermentation</u> growth media, poly-sorbate 80, histidine buffered saline.
MMR (MMR-II)	**chick embryo cell culture**, WI-38 **human diploid lung fibroblasts**, vitamins, amino acids, **fetal bovine** serum, sucrose, glutamate, recombinant **human albumin**, neomycin, sorbitol, hydrolyzed **gelatin**, sodium phosphate, sodium chloride
MMRV (ProQuad) **(Frozen)**	**chick embryo** cell culture, WI-38 **human diploid lung** fibroblasts MRC-5 cells, sucrose, hydrolyzed **gelatin**, sodium chloride, sorbitol, <u>monosodium L-glutamate</u>, sodium phosphate dibasic, **human** albumin, sodium bicarbonate,

	potassium phosphate monobasic, potassium chloride; potassium phosphate dibasic, neomycin, **bovine calf** serum
MMRV (ProQuad) (Refrigerator Stable)	**chick embryo** cell culture, WI-38 **human diploid lung** fibroblasts, MRC-5 cells, sucrose, hydrolyzed **gelatin**, urea, sodium chloride, sorbitol, monosodium L-glutamate, sodium phosphate, recombinant **human albumin**, sodium bicarbonate, potassium phosphate potassium chloride, neomycin, **bovine** serum albumin
Pneumococcal PCV13 – Prevnar 13	soy peptone broth, casamino acids and yeast extract-based medium, CRM197 carrier protein, polysorbate 80, succinate buffer, aluminum phosphate
Pneumococcal (PPSV-23 – Pneumovax)	Phenol
Polio (IPV – Ipol)	**Eagle** MEM modified medium, **calf bovine** serum, M-199 without calf bovine serum, **vero cells** (a continuous line of monkey kidney cells), phenoxyethanol, formaldehyde, neomycin, streptomycin, polymyxin B
Rabies (Imovax)	**human** albumin, neomycin sulfate, phenol red indicator, MRC-5 **human diploid cells**, beta-propriolactone
Rabies (RabAvert)	**chicken** fibroblasts, β-propiolactone, poly-geline (processed **bovine gelatin**), **human serum albumin**, **bovine serum**, potassium glutamate, sodium EDTA, ovalbumin neomycin, chlortetracycline, amphotericin B
Rotavirus (RotaTeq)	sucrose, sodium citrate, sodium phosphate monobasic monohydrate, sodium hydroxide, polysorbate 80, cell culture media, **fetal bovine** serum, **vero cells** [DNA from porcine circoviruses (PCV) 1 and 2 has been detected in RotaTeq. PCV-1 and PCV-2 are not known to cause disease in humans.]
Rotavirus (Rotarix)	amino acids, dextran, Dulbecco's Modified **Eagle** Medium (sodium chloride, potassium

	chloride, magnesium sulfate, ferric (III) nitrate, sodium phosphate, sodium pyruvate, D-glucose, concentrated vitamin solution, L-cystine, L-tyrosine, amino acids solution, L-250 glutamine, calcium chloride, sodium hydrogenocarbonate, and phenol red), sorbitol, sucrose, calcium carbonate, sterile water, xanthan [Porcine circovirus type 1 (PCV-1) is present in Rotarix. PCV-1 is not known to cause disease in humans.]
Smallpox (Vaccinia – ACAM2000)	African Green **Monkey kidney** (Vero) **cells**, HEPES, **human serum** albumin, sodium chloride, neomycin, polymyxin B, Glycerin, phenol
Td (Tenivac)	aluminum phosphate, formaldehyde, modified Mueller-Miller casamino acid medium without beef heart infusion, ammonium sulfate
Td (Mass Biologics)	aluminum phosphate, formaldehyde, **thimerosal**, modified Mueller's media which contains **bovine extracts**, ammonium sulfate
Tdap (Adacel)	aluminum phosphate, formaldehyde, 2-phenoxyethanol, Stainer-Scholte medium, casamino acids, dimethyl-beta-cyclodextrin, glutaraldehyde, modified Mueller-Miller casamino acid medium without beef heart infusion, ammonium sulfate, modified **Mueller's growth medium**
Tdap (Boostrix)	modified Latham medium derived from **bovine casein**, Fenton medium containing a **bovine extract**, formaldehyde, modified Stainer-Scholte liquid medium, glutaraldehyde, aluminum hydroxide, sodium chloride, polysorbate 80
Typhoid (inactivated – Typhim Vi)	hexadecyltrimethylammonium bromide, formaldehyde, phenol, polydimethylsiloxane, disodium phosphate, monosodium phosphate, semi-synthetic medium
Typhoid (Vivotif Ty21a)	yeast extract, **casein**, dextrose, galactose, sucrose, ascorbic acid, amino acids, lactose, magnesium stearate. **Gelatin**
Varicella (Varivax)	**human embryonic lung cell** cultures, **guinea**

Frozen	**pig cell** cultures, **human diploid cell** cultures (WI-38), **human diploid cell cultures** (MRC-5), sucrose, hydrolyzed **gelatin**, sodium chloride, <u>monosodium L-glutamate</u>, sodium phosphate dibasic, potassium phosphate monobasic, potassium chloride, EDTA (Ethylenediaminetetraacetic acid), neomycin, **fetal bovine** serum
Varicella (Varivax) *Refrigerator Stable*	**human embryonic lung cell** cultures, **guinea pig cell** cultures, **human diploid cell** cultures (WI-38), **human diploid cell cultures** (MRC-5), sucrose, hydrolyzed **gelatin**, urea, sodium chloride, <u>monosodium L-glutamate</u>, sodium phosphate dibasic, potassium phosphate monobasic, potassium chloride, neomycin, **bovine calf** serum
Yellow Fever *(YF-Vax)*	sorbitol, gelatin, sodium chloride, egg protein
Zoster *(Shingles –Zostavax* *Frozen*	sucrose, hydrolyzed **porcine** gelatin, sodium chloride, <u>monosodium L-glutamate</u>, sodium phosphate dibasic, potassium phosphate monobasic, potassium chloride; **MRC-5 cells**, neomycin, **bovine calf** serum
Zoster (Shingles – *Zostavax)* *Refrigerator Stable*	sucrose, hydrolyzed **porcine** gelatin, urea, sodium chloride, <u>monosodium L-glutamate</u>, sodium phosphate dibasic, potassium phosphate monobasic, potassium chloride, **MRC-5 cells**, neomycin, **bovine calf** serum

A table listing vaccine excipients and media by excipient can be found in: Grabenstein JD. ImmunoFacts: Vaccines and Immunologic Drugs – 2013, (38th revision). St Louis, MO: Wolters Kluwer Health, 2012.

Global 2000 & Global 2000 Revisited

To truly understand the aims and goals of the New World Order of the so-called global elite, you have to know and understand HR 907 (Congress of the United States, House Resolution 907). What I find very interesting is why the talking heads of radio and television not informing the public about it? With the introduction on January 29, 1981 of HR 907, the Population Act of 1981, sponsored by Rep.

Richard Ottinger of N.Y., Americans are getting their first glimpses of Global 2000.

Global 2000 is a diabolical plan to reduce the world's population by billions, to a manageable 2 billion people. What's going to happen to the other 4 plus billion? Why, according to Mike Kitch of Zero population Growth, Inc., is a private organization pushing the bill, "We have to make people accept some difficult choices as inevitable." Global 2000 advocates say they will use planned famines, pestilence, planned epidemics, planned conventional and nuclear wars, planned energy and water shortages, etc. "I have already written off more than a billion people in Africa, Asia, and Latin America... These people will continue to suffer from continuous cycles of natural disasters, famines, hunger, flood, drought... they can't be saved." Taylor, a Global 2000 Member. The Catholic Church has weight in on the issue. They would like the world population reduced to one billion people, but more importantly, the one billion people to be Catholics. "Vatican speaker and California Governor in push for massive depopulation... talk of 'Planetary Court' and removal of 6 billion people under new 'Earth Constitution' and 'World Government' by Mike Adams, the Health Ranger, Natural News Editor (NaturalNews) The de-populationists are on the move again, pushing hard for the elimination of six billion people on planet Earth in order to bring the planet down to what's being touted as its "sustainable carrying capacity of one billion people."But this time, the depopulation agenda may be codified by the Vatican. Professor John Schellnhuber has been chosen as a speaker for the Vatican's rolling out of a Papal document on climate change. He's the professor who previously said the planet is overpopulated by at least six billion people. Now, the Vatican is giving him a platform which many expect will result in an official Church declaration in support of radical depopulation in the name of "climate science."

"The teaching document, called an encyclical, is scheduled for release on June 18 at Vatican City," reports Breitbart.com. "Perhaps with the exception of the 1968 encyclical on contraception, no Vatican document has been greeted with such anticipation." A new Planetary Court to hold power over all nations... one ring to rule them all. Schellnhuber daydreams about a "Planetary Court" guided by a new "Earth Constitution" which would hold power over every nation and government on the planet. As he explains himself in this document on HumansAndNature.org, he's a proponent of an all-powerful, climate-focused world government that would rule over the planet... a literal "science dictatorship" based on whatever "science" the climate change proponents can fudge together each year. Go to NaturalNews.com to finish reading the rest of the article. However, the following two articles will expose some of the methods, goals and means behind the New World Order. Reprinted with permission.

POPULATION CONTROL; UN Attack on World Population, TNA Vol. 17, No. 22, pp. 33-34
To UN family planners, human life is not sacred but is a plague afflicting "Mother Earth" that needs to be cured by coercive population control programs by William F. Jasper. Decent people everywhere are horrified when they learn of China's indescribably brutal and totalitarian "one-child policy." The United Nations and its supporters, however, have steadfastly backed this program with funding and enthusiastic praise. What's more, they have been pushing relentlessly to export this coercive program from Communist China to the rest of the planet.

In China, the official one-child-per-family policy means that factory committees and village committees are authorized by Communist authorities to keep a detailed record of their female employees' menstrual cycles, and have the power to grant or deny a married couple permission to have children. Women who become pregnant without a permit and women carrying their second child are subject to official harassment and threats until they agree to let the state kill their children through abortion. Many women who resist the official brow-beating are actually arrested, jailed, and forcibly made to undergo abortions. Millions of women are also forcibly sterilized.

This totalitarian program of forced abortion, sterilization, and infanticide, domestic spying, and invasion of the most private areas of people's lives has been generously underwritten by the UN Population Fund (UNFPA) and the UN's World Bank, along with the International Planned Parenthood Federation and tax-exempt foundations like the Ford, Turner, and Rockefeller Foundations. In 1983, UNFPA gave an award to China's Qian Xinzhong for having "implemented population policies on a massive scale." Those vaunted "population policies" include genocide against ethnic and religious minorities in China's occupied lands. This has been most ruthlessly applied in the mountain kingdom of Tibet, which the Communist government of China has occupied since 1949.

Tears of Silence: Tibetan Women and Population Control, a 1994 report by the Tibetan Women's Association in Dharamsala, India, details the oppressive depopulation campaign being waged against the Tibetan people — a campaign receiving assistance from UNICEF and the United Nations Family Planning Agency. The Communist Central Committee and State Council responsible for control of population growth have stated, "family planning should be practiced among minority nationalities to raise the economic and cultural levels of minority areas and to improve national quality." In 1993, the Communist Chinese authorities announced a new law, "On Eugenics and Health Protection," designed to "avoid new births of inferior quality and heighten the standards of the whole population." The threat of "inferior quality," according to this new law, is from those segments of the population coming from "the old revolutionary base, ethnic minorities, the frontier and economically poor areas" — which is to say, the non-Chinese Tibetans.

Witness: In June 1998, Gao Xiao Duan testified before a U.S. congressional committee regarding the horrors of this program. Mrs. Gao was in a position to know. For 14 blood-soaked years, she had been in charge of an abortuary in a city of 60,000 people in China's Fujian province. As The New American previously reported: Legislators listened in horror as Gao, who had recently fled China, described herself as a "monster" and the most hated woman in her city. Besides apologizing to the countless children and mothers whose lives she had destroyed, Gao gave grisly details of her sadistic career, a career she claimed was typical of those working for China's state-sponsored abortion industry. She recalled interviewing a woman nine months pregnant, whose papers had been stamped "no birth certificate allowed." The unfortunate woman was dragged into an adjoining room, where the baby was aborted and injected with poison as its limbs flailed helplessly. It was then tossed in a trash bin. Gao also described jail cells for non-compliant women, and an elaborate informant system complete with boxes for citizens to anonymously deposit cards with names of non-compliant neighbors. According to Gao, the houses of non-compliant women are sometimes wrecked, and detailed records are kept on all women's menstrual cycles, as well as their marital and reproductive histories.

Humanity Is the Enemy

The internationalist utopians who run the United Nations, and those who comprise the membership of powerful, elitist groups that promote, guide, and direct the UN, intend to fasten China's totalitarian population program upon the rest of the world. These elitists, including some of the planet's wealthiest individuals, insist that the Earth is so overpopulated that drastic, tyrannical policies must be adopted. "Lifeboat earth" is so overcrowded, they say, that we must begin throwing some of the passengers overboard. They are not, however, giving up their places in the lifeboat.

The globalists at the elite and very influential Club of Rome, for instance, revealed much about their totalitarian agenda in their 1991 book, The First Global Revolution. Among the many self-indicting admissions in that report, we find this: In searching for a new enemy to unite us, we came up with the idea that pollution, the threat of global warming, water shortages, famine and the like would fit the bill.... All these dangers are caused by human intervention.... The real enemy, then, is humanity itself. One of the prime movers in the Club of Rome is Maurice Strong, the Canadian socialist billionaire who served as the secretary-general of the UN's Earth Summit (UNCED) in Rio de Janeiro. At UNCED, Strong deplored the world's "explosive increase in population," and warned, "we have been the most successful species ever; we are now a species out of control." "Population," he declared, "must be stabilized, and rapidly." How would this be accomplished? A chilling hint is provided by the late Jacques Cousteau, the famed leftist oceanographer.

Cousteau was one of the most enthusiastically received dignitaries at UNCED. Just a few months before the Rio summit, Cousteau told the UNESCO Courier: "Our society is turning toward more and more needless consumption. It is a vicious circle that I compare to cancer.... The damage people cause to the planet is a function of demographics — it is equal to the degree of development. One American burdens the earth much more than twenty Bangladeshes.... This is a terrible thing to say. In order to stabilize world population, it is necessary to eliminate 350,000 people per day. It is a horrible thing to say, but it's just as bad not to say it." At the summit, Cousteau warned, "the fuse connected to a demographic explosion is already burning." At most, he said, humanity has 10 years to put it out. The famed oceanographer urged "drastic, unconventional decisions" if the world is to avoid reaching the "absurd figure of 16 billion human beings" by the year 2070. This theme was echoed by many other UNCED speakers. Agenda 21, UNCED's mammoth environmental manifesto advocating global regimentation of all human society, calls for some $7 billion per year to implement "intensive programs" for population stabilization. What that means, in plain English, is that the UN is demanding a lot more money to expand its population control programs of sterilization, abortion, and universal access of children and youth to contraceptives and exploitive "sex education."

A 1994 report issued by the United Nation's Cairo Conference on Population and Development announced plans to regulate the most intimate of family matters: "The promotion of the responsible exercise of these rights [marriage and child-bearing] for all people should be the fundamental basis for government- and community-supported policies and programs in the area of reproductive health, including family planning." (Emphasis added). Of course, "responsible" is defined by the UN global-crats to fit their agenda. The same UN Cairo report states that "reproductive health care in the context of primary health care should … include … abortion...."

According to Dr. Norman Myers, an advisor to the World Bank, the World Resources Institute, and various UN agencies, the populations of industrial nations such as Britain, Russia, and America should be reduced by nearly one-half. A fan of Communist China's despotic policies, he recommends reproductive licensing: Government population-control policies using strong economic and social incentives have been effective in China and Singapore.... Is it too far-fetched to imagine that one day people might be issued with a warrant entitling them to have a single child — a type of green stamp?

One of the UN's wealthiest and most boisterous private supporters is billionaire "world citizen" Ted Turner, whose United Nations Foundation has donated tens of millions of dollars to UN projects. According to Turner, an avid proponent of global depopulation, "people who abhor the China one-child policy are dumb-dumbs'...." At the 1999 Global Forum for corporate CEOs hosted in China by Fortune magazine and Time Warner, Inc., Turner schmoozed and dined with the butchers of Tiananmen Square and declared, "I am a socialist at heart." If the United Nations is not stopped — and, ultimately, abolished — one-world socialists like Turner, Strong, Myers, and Rockefeller, along with their Communist Chinese comrades, will impose their totalitarian population programs upon the rest of us. (Reprinted with permission from The New American).

POPULATION CONTROL

Wolf in "Humanitarian" Clothing, TNA Vol. 16, No. 14 pp. 35-37
Underneath its sheep's clothing of "humanitarianism" the UN is a ravenous predator ready to coerce sterilization, force abortion, commit infanticide, and execute eugenics programs reminiscent of Nazi Germany — all on a global scale. By Julie Makimaa.

The Holy Bible's Book of Psalms informs us that children are "a heritage of the Lord," a blessing to be cherished. The UN's Earth Charter, a document expressing the world body's pagan world view, treats children — and human beings in general — as a resource to be managed by a global elite. The charter commands that the UN's would-be subjects must "adopt patterns of production, consumption, and reproduction that safeguard Earth's regenerative capacities, human rights, and community well-being." (Emphasis added.) Under this formula, the UN and its administrative agencies, usurping the role of the Almighty Himself, would set and enforce limitations upon the right of couples to enjoy the divinely ordained blessing of children.

The UN's anti-naturalist arrogance was dramatically displayed in the Balkans during NATO's air campaign against Yugoslavia. On April 8, 1999, the UN Population Fund (UNFPA) announced that it was sending 350,000 "Emergency Reproductive Health Kits" to Albania to be distributed among Kosovo Albanian refugees. Joseph Meaney, of Human Life International, who inspected health-care facilities in northern Albania during the air war and refugee crisis, recounts that these kits included "condoms, birth control pills, 'emergency contraception' or 'morning after' pills that is, chemical abortifacients, intrauterine devices (IUDs), and manual vacuum aspirators," which are used for early term abortions. Although the packages were originally labeled "Pregnancy Termination" kits, the name was changed to "reduce the risk of offending sensitivities and possibly make [them] more acceptable," in the words of a UN document on "refugee situations" issued in 1995.

Dr. Enza Ferrara, who works in a hospital in Scutari, Albania, testified that the UN's anti-natal campaign in that nation began in earnest in 1995. "She saw that women were being surgically sterilized without their knowledge or consent after delivering by C-section in the hospital," recalls Meaney, who interviewed Dr. Ferrara at length. "Time and again it fell upon her to inform women coming to consult her that a tubal ligation was the cause of their infection or inability to have children." When Dr. Ferrara protested to Albanian government officials, she received a candid response from a representative of Albania's Ministry of Health: "We have accepted international aid on condition of reducing births." To carry out a similar mission among Kosovo Albanians, UNFPA helped establish an office of the British birth control organization Marie Stopes International in Pristina.

As tens of thousands of refugees were driven out of Yugoslavia's Kosovo province by the NATO air campaign, Dr. Ferrara collided once again with officials from the UN's population control effort. One visiting UN official informed Dr. Ferrara and other health workers that "reproductive health" — meaning abortion and contraception — were an "urgent" priority. When the doctor asked the visiting anti-natalist commissar why it was so "urgent" to carry out population control measures, she was told: "The refugees are too many. We have to stop them from reproducing." Had any official in Slobodan Milosevic's Serbian government expressed a desire to stop Kosovo Albanians from reproducing, the statement would have been branded a "war crime" and the official would most likely have been arraigned before the UN's kangaroo court in The Hague. But for the UN, deceiving displaced refugees into undergoing abortion and sterilization is merely an exercise in "humanitarianism."

Margaret Sanger's Legacy:

The UN's perverse vision of "humanitarianism" is a legacy of one of the 20th century's most influential bigots, Margaret Sanger, the founder of the International Planned Parenthood Federation (IPPF), which essentially sets population control policy for the UN. In her 1920 book, "Women and the New Race," Sanger sounded a theme identical to that found in the UN's Earth Charter — namely, that uncontrolled births are a threat to "community well-being." "The immorality of large families lies not only in their injury to the members of those families but in their injury to society.... The most merciful thing that the large family does to one of its infant members is to kill it."

Two years later, in her book, "The Pivot of Civilization," Sanger introduced the element of eugenics into her anti-natal program. "The emergency problem of segregation and sterilization must be faced immediately," declared Sanger. "Every feeble-minded girl or woman of the hereditary type, especially of the moron class, should be segregated during the reproductive period. Otherwise, she is almost certain to bear imbecile children, who in turn are just as certain to breed other defectives.... Moreover, when we realize that each feeble-minded person is a potential source of an endless progeny of defect, we prefer the policy of immediate sterilization, of making sure that parenthood is absolutely prohibited to the feeble-minded."

It should surprise no one that the April 1933 issue of Sanger's "Birth Control Review" was devoted entirely to the issue of eugenic sterilization. It featured a tribute to Dr. Ernst Rudin, a high official of the German National Socialist (Nazi) regime — which within a few years would stun and sicken humanity with its exploits in coercive eugenics and the "liquidation" of "life unworthy of life." This is not to say that Nazi atrocities left all equally stunned and sickened.

Writing in 1947, when the horrors of World War II were still fresh, Julian Huxley, the first director-general of the United Nations Educational, Social, and Cultural Organization (UNESCO), emphasized that "it will be important for UNESCO to see that the eugenic problem is examined with the greatest care, and that the public mind is informed of the issues at stake so that much that now is unthinkable may at least become thinkable."

To rational people, it is all but unthinkable to believe that the heirs of Margaret Sanger's malignant vision have billions of dollars at their disposal each year to implement programs to eliminate "defectives," free women from the "bondage" of motherhood, and end the "ills" caused by "over-population." Yet this is precisely the agenda being carried out today by the United Nations. Although the UN is careful to cloak its programs in the language of women's "empowerment," promotion of "human rights," and "sustainable development," for women on the receiving end of the UN's "humanitarianism," the grim reality of its agenda can be found in the candid exclamation by the UNFPA worker in Albania: "We have to stop them from reproducing!"

The "Program"
At the UN's International Conference on Population and Development (ICPD) convened in Cairo, Egypt, in 1994, delegates from more than 180 nations approved a 20-year UN "Program of Action" that defined population "stabilization" as a global priority. When asked to define the difference between "population stabilization" and population "control," Timothy Wirth, who at the time was the Clinton administration's undersecretary of state for global affairs (and who essentially ran the ICPD), glibly replied, "Nobody likes to be 'controlled'" — meaning that the difference is entirely semantic in nature. The crucial achievement of the ICPD was to formally commit the nations of the world to a UN-administered plan of population control — however that plan is described. Total expenditures on that plan were projected to reach a cost of $17 billion annually by the year 2000. By the time of the UN's "Cairo plus-5" conference in July 1999, scores of countries had adopted development policies that incorporated the UN's population goals, according to a UN press release.

Under the Clinton administration, the U.S. federal government diligently implemented the ICPD's Program of Action through

226

treaties, presidential directives, and government policies. In late 1999, as part of a budget deal with Congress, the U.S. resumed taxpayer funding of the UNFPA, providing $25 million in assistance. UNFPA Executive Director Nafis Sadik was delighted by this development, observing that "the example set by the United States helps convince other governments to contribute to these programs."

Such "contributions" — which represent wealth forcibly seized from taxpayers, including those whose religious and moral views do not condone abortion and perhaps other forms of birth control — are used to underwrite what Julian Huxley called "unthinkable": forced abortion, sterilization, and infanticide programs in Communist China. According to China scholar Stephen Mosher of the Population Research Institute, "Under the terms of Beijing's one-child-per-family policy, women who have one child must have IUDs inserted. Women who have two children must be sterilized, or their spouses must be sterilized. Women who are pregnant with an over-quota child must be given 'remedial measures', namely, an abortion."

Despite the UNFPA's published assurance that "all couples and individuals have the basic human right to decide freely and responsibly the number and spacing of children," the UN organ has faithfully funded the Red Chinese population control program since 1979. In 1983, when (according to refugee accounts and other independent sources) the Red Chinese program was being carried out with particular ruthlessness, the UNFPA presented a population award to Qian Xinzhong, the minister in charge of the State Family Planning Commission of China, expressing "deep appreciation" for the way they have "implemented population policies on a massive scale." Beijing's State Family Planning Commission proudly pointed out that the UNFPA award "shows that the UN and the countries of the world approve of the achievements we have made." Sanger would certainly approve of Beijing's approach to the "problem" of human population. In her autobiography she described the "incessant fertility" of the Chinese as spreading "like a plague." Her 1934, "Code to Stop Overproduction of Children," decreed that "no woman shall have a legal right to bear a child without a permit" and that "no permit shall be valid for more than one child." In 1969, longtime Planned Parenthood president Alan Guttmacher embellished Sanger's vision by stating that "each country will have to decide its own form of coercion, determining when and how it should be employed" on behalf of population control. Red China is following Sanger's blueprint for coercion faithfully, with the UN's eager support. In light of

Guttmacher's statement that each country must choose how and when to use "coercion" on behalf of population control, it is significant that the ICPD "Programme of Action" states that "it is the sovereign right" of nations to implement the Cairo policies. This is not to say that the UN recognizes the "sovereign right" of nations to resist implementation of the UN's global plan for population "stabilization."

A 2000 meeting of the UN Women's Anti-Discrimination Committee attacked Nepal because its "current law does not comply with the 1994 Women's Convention." Specifically, Nepal's abortion law requires married women to have their husbands' approval for an abortion, and an unmarried woman must obtain the approval of her parents. According to "experts" from the treaty-monitoring Committee on the Elimination of Discrimination against Women, "Nepal's laws must be brought in line with the 1979 Convention."

Nations whose existing laws or policies do not comply with UN treaties will be pressured to "harmonize" their domestic affairs with the UN's global agenda. What of those nations which resist the UN's pressure? A proposal that was seriously entertained during discussions of the UN's International Criminal Court called for the inclusion of "enforced pregnancy" — that is, opposition to, or denial of, abortion — as a crime against "international law." Given the UN's horrific record, is it really "unthinkable" — to use Julian Huxley's word once again — that at some future date the world body would have the means to arrest and prosecute pro-life activists and political leaders for the "crime" of defending innocent human life? (Reprinted with permission from The New American).

THE FENCE AND THE AMBULANCE

T'was a dangerous cliff, as they freely confessed,
Though to walk near its crest was so pleasant
But over its terrible edge there had slipped
A Duke and many a peasant;
So the people said something would have to be done,
But their projects did not at all tally:
Some said, "Put a fence round the edge of the cliff;"
Some, "An ambulance down in the valley."
But the cry for the ambulance carried the day,
For it spread to the neighboring city;
A fence many be useful or not, it is true,
But each heart became brimful of pity
For those who had slipped o'er that dangerous cliff,

And the dwellers in highway and alley
Gave pounds or gave pence, not to put up a fence,
But an ambulance down in the valley.
"For the cliff is alright if your careful," they said;
And if folks even slip or are dropping,
It isn't the slipping that hurts them so much
As the shock down below-when they're stopping."
So day after day when these mishaps occurred,
Quick forth would the rescuers sally
To pick up the victims who fell off the cliff
With their ambulance down in the valley.
Then an old man remarked: "It's a marvel to me
That people give for more attention
To repairing results that to stopping the cause,
When they'd much better aim at prevention.
Let us stop at its source all this mischief," cried he,
"Come, neighbors and friends, let us rally;
If the cliff we will fence, we might almost dispense
With the ambulance down in the valley."
"Oh, he's a fanatic," the others rejoined;
"Dispense with the ambulance? Never!
He'd dispense with all charities, too, if he could:
No, no! We'll support them forever.
Aren't we picking up folks just as fast as they fall?
And shall this man dictate to us? Shall he?
Why should people of sense stop to put up a fence
While their ambulance works in the valley?
Thus this story so old has beautifully told
How our people, with best of intentions,
Have wasted their years and lavished their tears
On treatment, with naught for prevention.
But a sensible few, who are practical, too,
Will not bear with such nonsense much longer;
They believe that prevention is better than cure,
And their party will soon be the stronger.
Encourage them, then, with purse, voice, and pen,
And {while other philanthropists dally}
They will scorn all pretense, and put up a stout fence
On the cliff that hangs over the valley.
--Joseph Malines

Chapter Eight: True Education & Faith in God is the Answer

"The doctor of the future will give no medicine but will interest his patient in the care of the human frame, in diet, and in the cause and prevention of disease"–Thomas A. Edison

George Malkamus, a Baptist Pastor and founder of Halleluiah Acers is correct when he says "God gave the Seventh-day Adventist Church a health message for the world." In 1863, God delivered to His church through Mrs. Ellen G. White a healthcare discipline second to none. You can read the health principles in the book, "Spiritual Gifts," vol. IV, pages 120 to 149; in the chapter simply titled "Health." As a baptized member of the body of Christ, and a Missionary Health Restoration Practitioner, I have to apologize to Pastor Malkamus and the world for the organized church letting you down. The world through caring doctors, nutritionist, scientists, researchers, etc... are confirming the various aspects of God's ten health laws, and especially nutrition is fighting and reversing disease. The scientific data concerning diet and lifestyle as it relates to health is irrefutable so God has taken away that excuse.

Faith-Endurance-Patience

Faith: "Daughter be of good comfort; thy faith hath made thee whole, Matthew 9:22. There are many examples in scripture were Jesus told someone that their faith had healed them. What did Jesus mean by a person's faith healing them? What Jesus is saying is that the individual believed in Jesus Christ as the Messiah-the son of God; and if they died or lived, got sicker or healthier, they were content with the outcome because they trusted God. The individual believed that whatever item Jesus chooses to use to heal someone, i.e. mud and spittle, or just speak the words "rise, take up thy bed and walk" that it was blessed of God to heal them. When it comes to health restoration God's way, you have to believe in God and have faith in His way of healing, which is superior to man's system of sick care and be content with the outcome. Remember, "There are many ways of practicing the healing arts, but there is only one way that heaven approves" 5T, Ellen White, p. 443, (1885). What has God ordained as His remedies? "God's remedies are the simple agencies of nature that will not tax or debilitate the system through their powerful properties. Pure air and water, cleanliness, a proper diet, purity of life, and a firm trust in God, are remedies for the want of which thousands are dying... 5T, Ellen White, p. 443, (1885).

Endurance: "…but he that shall endure unto the end, the same shall be saved", Matthew 13:13. As discussed earlier in the section Physically Reborn, true healing takes time. Most people do not want to put up with the pain or discomfort and immediately reach for the prescription medication, which gives them instant relief, but also lasting side-effects. It takes the right nutrients and the other laws of health to produce the next generation of healthy cells. "And so, after he had patiently endured, he obtained the promise, Hebrews 6:15.

Patience: "But let patience have her perfect work…" James 1:4. God said it and I believe it, therefore it is settled. If you will patiently follow God's Ten Laws of Health, not cheating yourself, then your faith in God and His healing methodology will reward your efforts. "…in which it was impossible for God cannot lie"…, Hebrews 6:18. True health is found by following the prescription for healing found in Isaiah 58:1-8.

History of Hoxsey Treatment: A Documented Cancer Therapy

The cancer treatment practiced by Harry M. Hoxsey (1901-1974) is one of the longest-lived unconventional therapies of this century. It has retained great popular appeal, despite unrelenting opposition by the medical profession; despite 40 years of biting journalistic ridicule by such skilled AMA journalists as Arthur Cramp and Morris Fishbein; despite an unceasing stream of court actions; even despite an unprecedented Public Warning Against Hoxsey Cancer Treatment which the Commissioner of the FDA ordered mounted in 46,000 US post offices and substations in 1956 (Young, 1967, 387; Larrick, 1956). Since Hoxsey's death, his treatment has continued under his longtime nurse assistant, Mildred Nelson, who currently oversees the thriving Bio-Medical Center at Tijuana, within sight of the border between Mexico and the United States. Hoxsey treated external cancers apparently with considerable success, even in the judgment of his critics with local applications: sometimes by a red paste containing antimony sulfide, bloodroot (Sanguinaria canadensis) and zinc chloride; sometimes by a yellow powder containing arsenic and antimony sulfides, various plant substances, talc, and what Hoxsey called yellow precipitate (JAMA, 1951, 253; Hoxsey, 1956, 47).

In 1941 Frederick Mohs, a respected surgeon in Madison, Wisconsin, with the help of the Dean of the University of Wisconsin Medical School and several of its faculty, devised a method of surgically removing accessible cancers under complete microscopic control, Mohs, 1941 Hoxsey vs AMA a battle which attempted to discredit the method and the man.

More recent literature leaves no doubt that Hoxseys formula, however strangely concocted by modern scientific standards does indeed contain many plant substances of marked therapeutic activity. In fact, orthodox scientific research has by now identified anti-tumor activity of one sort or another in all but three of Hoxseys plants and two of these three are purgatives, one of them (Rhamnus purshiana) containing the anthraquinone glycoside structure now recognized as predictive of anti-tumor properties (Kupchan, 1976). Between 1964 and 1968 four articles appeared in Lancet, Pediatrics, and Nature, describing the mitogenic activity of pokeweed, which triggers the immune system by increasing the number of lymphocytes, causing the formation of plasma cells, and elevating levels of immunoglobulin G, Farnes, 1964; Barker, 1965; Barker, 1966; Downing, 1968.

In 1966 two Hungarian scientists, engaged in a screening program at the University of Szeged, published their findings of considerable anti-tumor activity in a purified fraction of burdock, a plant which they included in their project because of its use as a folk remedy for new growths and ulcerations (Dombradi, 1966). In 1972 Kupchan described the growth-inhibiting activity of sesquiterpene lactones, a structural group which includes burdock (Kupchan, 1972). In 1984 researchers at Nagoya University, Japan, found in burdock a new type of desmutagen; a substance uniquely capable of reducing mutagenicity both in the absence and in the presence of metabolic activation. So important is this new property that these scientists named it the B-factor, for burdock factor, Morita et al., 1984.

Two recent studies from the Orient, one Japanese, one Chinese, have established the presence of anti-tumor substances in barberry (which Hoxsey also sometimes called berberis root). Testing tumor size in mice by the total packed cell volume method, Hoshi and his co-workers found strong anti-tumor activity in berberrubine, an alkaloid isolated from Berberis vulgaris (Hoshi, 1976). Also in 1976, Owen et al. derived from berberine a new anti-tumor substance which they have named Lycobetaine (Owen, 1976).

At the University of Virginia in the mid-70s, Kupchan and Karim isolated an antileukemic principle from buckthorn (Rhamnus frangula). Their discovery that the efficacy of this substance in leukemia is vehicle-dependent led these scientists to advise re-testing of other anthraquinone plant substances for similar anti-tumor activity (Kupchan, 1976).

The least studied of Hoxseys herbs to date are stillingia sylvatica and prickly ash (Zanthoxylum americanum), but even these are represented in the scholarly literature.

In 1980 two German scientists discovered several new diterpene-esters (a chemical group known to have anti-tumor activity) in Stillingia root, the portion of this plant used by Hoxsey (Adolf, 1980).

At a symposium on folk medicine in 1986, Varro Tyler observed that, despite the wide use of Northern prickly ash bark in folk medicine, it has been nearly 50 years since any studies were done of its chemical composition and there have never been activity-directed fractionation studies. Noting that pharmacological tests have revealed significant anti-inflammatory and anesthetic properties in several closely related species, Tyler urges scientists to study prickly ash for these and other therapeutic properties (Tyler, 1987, 106).

Sarton had in mind chaulmoogra (for leprosy), cinchona bark (for malaria), and variolation (for smallpox): to these we can now add (for cancer alone) periwinkle, mistletoe (labeled a promotion by Morris Fishbein as recently as 1965), Mayapple, autumn crocus, and chaparral tea. Sarton counseled the profession to exhibit less intellectual arrogance and more open-mindedness: The remembrance of these astounding folk discoveries should sober our thoughts when we

criticize too freely the old pharmacopoeias.

Judge Atwell upholds Hoxsey's cancer remedy as reported December 22, 1966 "...comparable to surgery, radium and x-ray in its effectiveness, without the destructive side effects of those treatments."

It is easy to make fun of mediaeval recipes; it is more difficult and may be wiser to investigate them. *Instead of assuming that the mediaeval pharmacist was a benighted fool, we might wonder whether there was not sometimes a justification for his strange procedure.* (quoted in Hartwell, 1960, p. 24).

How God Healed My Pancreas

I shared with you in the about the author section of the book, my story of how God healed me of my hypoglycemia. I also have provided you with a copy of my Glucose Tolerance Test results in appendix A.

Now I am going to share with you the protocol God showed me that healed my pancreas. Remember, back in the early 1980's, medical doctors knew very little about hypo and hyperglycemia. First, after reading the book Counsels on Diet and Foods, I decided to stop eating every four hours and snacking every two hours as recommended by the American Diabetes Association. If you understood how the stomach and the digestive system works, you would realize in the long term, this is best. The digestive system, like any other organ or system requires rest or recovery time. I started increasing the time between meals by 15 minute increments, then a half hour until I could go five hours between meals without my blood sugar dropping. Realizing that my overall, general health must be improved, I went on a three day vegetable juice fast, cleanse and detoxification program, while changing my diet and lifestyle to conform to God's Ten Health Laws.

The majority of blood sugar issues are because of a person's toxicity level and consumption of bad fats or a high fat diet. The fats coat the cells and the toxins stick to the cell receptors not allowing the insulin to unlock the cell, so to speak, allowing insulin and glucose into the cell where the glucose mixes with the oxygen producing energy. Therefore, a supervised cleanse and detoxification program is essential for eliminating the possible cause of your blood sugar imbalance, as well as assisting you in getting it under control. I stress supervised cleanse and detoxification program because injected insulin is a concentrated salt and the body will store excess salt in the fat and muscles, just like it store's other salts. The supervision is critical because when the body chemistry starts to respond, the pancreas will begin to manufacture insulin and the stored salts (insulin included) will be released from the fat and muscle tissue. This excess insulin can lower the blood sugar level too low, causing black outs or coma.

The role the liver plays in the functioning of the pancreas and how to support the health of your liver is critical to overcoming diabetes or hypo/hyperglycemia. For the liver to function the kidneys must filter properly, therefore the health of both organs is critical. For the liver and kidneys to function optimally they must have a pH of 6.4.

A simple urine sample using litmus paper can gauge liver and kidney function. If the liver pH is 6.6.or higher, use Calcium Lactate to bring the pH down. If the liver pH is 6.2 or lower, use Coral Calcium to raise the pH. A good habit to cultivate is checking your urine and saliva at the same time for a correct pH of 6.4. Check the urine and saliva before eating or two hours after eating a meal and remember, no snacking between meals.

When your liver is healthy, it will manufacture a substance called glycogen. When this glycogen reaches the pancreas, it will manufacture three other substances: Alcohol, Insulin and Thyroxin.

As you know, insulin regulates the sugar levels in the blood and is inversely related. If there is too much insulin, the sugars will be too low and if the is not enough insulin, the sugars will be too high. So part of the solution to overcoming hyper/hypoglycemia or diabetes is a healthy liver, functioning properly. One more interesting fact about the liver is that it requires oxygen (one of the 10 laws of health).

The importance of oxygen to the liver is only second to the brain. The amount of sugar in the blood, too little or too much, regulates the amount of oxygen available to the liver via the blood. If you are tired of pricking your fingers for a blood sample, use a Refractor meter as I did and test your urine. The unit measurement for the Refractor meter is Brix. When using a Refractor meter if the reading is less that 1.0 or greater than 5.0, there is an increased oxygen deficiency. It is important that the liver is healthy and functioning properly so it can provide the pancreas with glycogen to produce insulin.

The major vitamins and minerals the liver needs to be healthy are vitamin A, iron, iodine and calcium. The major vitamins and minerals the pancreas needs to be healthy are, B complex, magnesium, iron and chlorine. Because of the needs of the liver and pancreas, I became to "true vegetarian" eating nothing with a face or a mother, or its bi-products, i.e. dairy or eggs. Every time before you eat, test your blood sugar and then eat according to your blood sugar level.

Below are lists of Nutriments that raise or lower blood sugar levels. Starch and sweet foods can raise blood sugar by 5 to 20 points. Fruit juices, sugar foods, jelly, deserts and pasta all raise blood sugar by approximately 20 points. Green bananas and bananas, plantain, potato, rice, bread, yams, cornmeal, dry fruits, honey, grapes, raisins and sweet fruit, all raise blood sugar by approximately 10 points. While, carrots, oatmeal and grains raise blood sugar levels by approximately 5 points.

Fat and protein foods raise blood sugar levels between 10 and 20 percent. Flesh meats, dairy and soy cheese, fat and oils, fried potatoes, butter, veggie butter, margarine, mayonnaise, oil in vegetables and soy meats fried, all raise blood sugar approximately 20 points. While, dry beans, nuts and seeds, cow and soy milk and soy foods raise blood sugar approximately 10 points.

It is just as important to know which foods lower blood sugar as well. Below is a list of foods that lower blood sugar from 5 to 20 points. Cabbage, greens, Broccoli, vegetable salad, vegetable juice and millet lower blood sugar levels approximately 20 points. Green beans, vegetable soup, Jerusalem artichokes, garlic, string bean juice and cucumbers lower blood sugar levels approximately 10 points.

While buckwheat lowers blood sugar approximately 5 points. Therefore, it is important to eat some whole grains especially buckwheat and millet, raw vegetables and citrus fruit are beneficial. The key is eating a large vegetable salad twice a day. For a salad dressing, use an olive oil mixed with lemon juice and a touch of basil and garlic and other low fat dressings, but watch out for the added sugar.

Now, let us look at the affect of herbs, constipation and walking on blood sugar. If you have three bowel movements a day, you can expect to lower your blood sugar by 20 points. . If you have two bowel movements a day, you can expect to lower your blood sugar by 10 points. If you have only one bowel movements a day, you can expect to raise your blood sugar by 10 points. The herbs goldenseal, fenugreek and comfrey lower blood sugar approximately 10 to 20 points. While, licorice root raises blood sugar. Green drinks are used to help the pancreas regulate blood sugars. Green drinks are also used to rebuild the pancreas. Original Healing Ministries has an excellent green drink/super food available called "Cellular Nutrition" formulated by Dr. Lee, which he used to help heal his pancreas. To learn more about Cellular Nutrition, contact Original Healing Ministries. Cedar berries are excellent nourishment for the pancreas. There are other herbs that are good for the liver, pancreas and kidneys. However, you should research them for your specific situation and/or condition.

If you walk in the fresh air and sunshine you can lower blood sugar from 5 to 10 points. If you drink 50% of your body weight, in ounces, of distilled water, you can lower blood sugars by 10 points. If you drink less than the recommended amount, you raise blood sugar by 10 points.

If you would trust God and apply His 10 Natural Health Laws to your specific disease/symptom, your next generation of cells will be healthier than the ones they replace and you will begin to experience God's healing ways.

A School & Lifestyle Center Built Upon the Blueprint:
"God has revealed to me that we are in positive danger of bringing into our educational work the customs and fashions that prevail in the schools of the world. If teachers are not guarded, they will place on the necks of their students worldly yokes instead of the yoke of Christ. The plan of the schools we shall establish in these closing years of the message is to be of an entirely different order from those we have

236

instituted. There is too much clinging to old customs; and because of this we are far behind where we should be in the development of the third angel's message. God has been waiting long and pleading long for us to believe in His way of education, and practice it 100% in our schools." Counsels to Parents, Teachers, and Students, White, p. 532.

"The drug science has been exalted, but if every bottle that comes from every such institution were done away with, there would be fewer invalids in the world today. Drug medication should never have been introduced into our institutions. There was no need of this being so, and for this very reason the Lord would have us establish an institution where He can come in and where His grace and power can be revealed. Ellen White, Spalding and Megan Collection, p. 137.

Original Healing Ministries (OHM) operates the Original Healing Wellness Center and the Institute of Original Healing. The goal of Dr. Lee is to raise the level of education and training currently available by non-governmental accredited organizations and schools. Neither Dr. Lee or any of his ministries knowingly accepts funding directly or indirectly from any federal, state or local governmental agency.

The OHM, has established such a school which will help to raise the credibility of the Health Restoration Work. God has to reestablish the right arm of the message, which is health, the entering wedge to reach people with the gospel of Jesus Christ. The state has the right to review what the students are being taught to make sure the curriculum meets certain requirements, but it does not have the authority to usurp the church's authority, or impose any requirement not related to the quality of the curriculum.

The name of the school is the Institute of Original Healing (IOH). IOH will offer courses in Missionary Health Restoration, Christian Nutrition, Herbology, Reams Theory of Biological Ionization and Missionary Health Restoration Practitioner (Naturopathic Doctor).
We need your prayers and financial support to make the lifestyle center a reality.

Anatomy and physiology of the human body has not changed since God created Adam. So whether you are an M.D., N.D., D.O., LMT, D.C., etc the human anatomy is the same. The differences in the disciplines are based upon the methodology and ideology of what you give the body and how you treat the body for it to properly heal. It is the fear of losing prestige, one's job, family, the fear of going to jail, and especially death that keep people, Christians from trusting God and use His healing methods. God said it best, "There is no fear in love; but perfect love casteth out fear: because fear hath torment.

He that feareth is not made perfect in love. 1 John 4:18.

Mrs. White in her letter to Dr. Kellogg stated that "*the medical missionary work might better be named the "Missionary Health Restoration Work*" Letter 77, 1900, pg. 5, To J.H. Kellogg, December 1899. [MR No. 56—20] page 242. God showed Sister White what was soon to come to pass and warned His people. Five years after recommending the name change, the history of the A.M.A., shows that it launched its vicious attack on the other healthcare disciplines in America, and continues to attempt to bring them under their control through government sponsored healthcare programs and integrated medicine.

Contact the Institute of Original Healing (IOH) for a school catalog at IOH@originalhealing.org.

God has sent you his word and can heal you, and deliver you from destruction, Psalms 107:20.
MARANATHA!!!

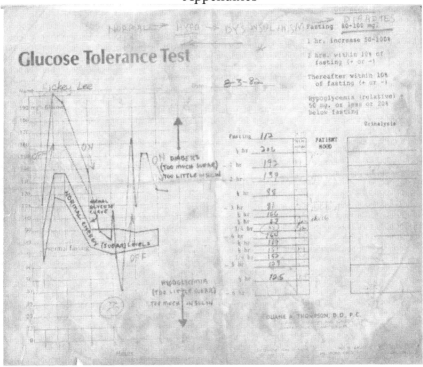

Appendix A – Glucose Tolerance Test Results

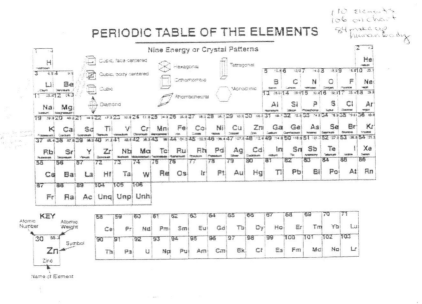

Appendix B – Periodic Table of Elements

Appendix C – Abraham Flexner

Flexner, Abraham, (1866-1959), American educator and author who significantly advanced medical and science education in the United States. Flexner was the founding director of the Institute for Advanced Study at Princeton University. His older brother, Simon Flexner, helped isolate the polio virus and was the first director of the Rockefeller Institute for Medical Research.

Flexner was born in Louisville, Kentucky. After receiving his Bachelor of Arts degree at Johns Hopkins University in Baltimore, Maryland, in 1886, Flexner taught high school in Louisville. He opened a college preparatory school but closed it after several years. Flexner entered Harvard University in Cambridge, Massachusetts, and was awarded a Master of Arts degree in 1906. He continued his studies in Germany at the universities of Berlin and Heidelberg, where he wrote his first book, "The American College: A Criticism" (1908).

The same year, Flexner joined the staff of the Carnegie Foundation for the Advancement of Teaching. Its director, Dr. Henry S. Pritchett, commissioned Flexner to write Medical Education in the United States and Canada (1910) and Medical Education in Europe (1912). Flexner's books inspired a revolution in teaching in American medical schools. In 1916, Flexner wrote a pamphlet titled, "A Modern School," that resulted in the establishment of the Lincoln Experimental School of Teachers College at Columbia University in New York.

For three decades, the experimental school offered pioneering programs in secondary education.

In 1917, Flexner was appointed secretary of the General Education Board of the Rockefeller Foundation, and in 1925, became the director of the foundation's division of studies and medical education. While working for the General Education Board, Flexner guided many of the charitable gifts of the Rockefellers, the Carnegie trusts, George Eastman, the Whitney family, John Pierpont Morgan, and other American business leaders. Over the course of a decade, Flexner helped distribute a $50 million gift from the Rockefeller family to reorganize American medical education.

After his retirement from the General Education Board in 1928, Flexner became the first director of the Institute for Advanced Study at Princeton University in Princeton, New Jersey. The institute became internationally renowned for its research in mathematics and theoretical physics, with a faculty that included Albert Einstein, John von Neumann, and J. Robert Oppenhemier. Flexner retired as director of the institute in 1939 and devoted himself to writing.

In 1940, he published his autobiography, "'I Remember' (published in 1960 as Abraham Flexner: An Autobiography)."

Appendix D – The Honorable Katherine Langley; Congressional Record, Proceedings and Debates of the 76th. Congress, Third Session.

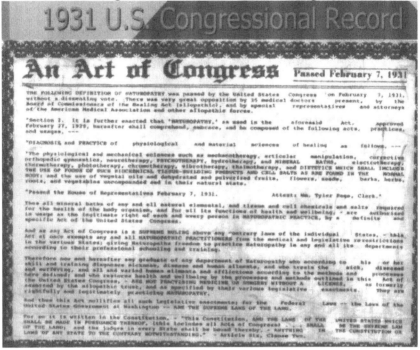

Appendix E - Dr. Alice Stewart

Dr. Alice Stewart was an epidemiologist who proved links between exposure to radiation and cancer, and forced the authorities into greater openness. For more than 40 years, the epidemiologist Alice Stewart challenged official estimates of the risks of radiation. Her research in 1956 and 1958 alerted the medical profession to the link between fetal X-rays and childhood cancer. Two decades later, in her seventies, she again called for a change in working practices when she published a study showing that workers at nuclear weapons plants are at greater health risk than international safety standards admit. In 1974, having officially retired and moved from Oxford to Birmingham, where she had accepted a research appointment, the 68-year-old Stewart received an unexpected phone call from America. Dr Thomas Mancuso, who had been at work on a government study of the health of nuclear workers at Hanford, the weapons complex that produced plutonium for the Manhattan Project, wanted her to "take a closer look" at his data. Mancuso's study had been going on for more than a decade, and was not expected to turn up anything troubling, since workers' exposure at Hanford, the oldest and largest nuclear weapons facility in the world, was well within the safety limits set by international guidelines. But Stewart and Kneale, her statistician found that the cancer risk to the workers was about 20 times higher than was being claimed, a discovery that put them at odds with the multimillion-dollar Hiroshima and Nagasaki studies on which international safety guidelines are based.

The American Department of Energy dismissed Mancuso and attempted to seize the data. But Stewart and Kneale took their work back to England, and, together with Mancuso, published a series of studies which continued to corroborate a cancer effect considerably higher than the Hiroshima studies indicated. The Energy Department denied the scientists further access to the workers' records and kept research under strict government control.

Although the statistical methods of the study were criticized by the Oxford epidemiologist Richard Doll (who had been one of the first to prove the link between smoking and cancer), the Mancuso findings attracted public attention and provoked congressional investigations in 1978 and 1979.

The accidents at Three Mile Island in 1979 and Chernobyl in 1986, while the British and American governments were trying to expand nuclear facilities and weapons production, brought the anti-nuclear movement back to life, and Stewart became one of its heroes. She found herself much in demand, called on as an expert witness to testify against the building of nuclear facilities and dumps and to testify in compensation cases by veterans and victims who had lived downwind of various plants.

In 1986, when she was 80, she received the Right Livelihood Award, the "alternative Nobel" as it is called, which is awarded in the Swedish Parliament the day before the Nobel Prize to honor those who have made contributions to the betterment of society. The British Embassy, however, refused even to send a car to the airport to pick her up. In 1992 she was awarded the Ramazzini Prize for epidemiology.

Even in the years when Stewart was making dozens of public appearances on behalf of activists in Britain and America, she always insisted that she was a scientist, not an activist, and that she did not have a political program. She published more than 400 papers in scientific journals. However, although she could deliver her findings in person with exceptional clarity, her publications were often very hard to decipher.

Also in 1986, Stewart received a $1.4 million grant to study the effects of low-dose radiation. This came not from a government agency or academic institute, but from activists, and derived from a fine imposed upon the Three Mile Island facility.

To undertake the study, Stewart needed access to the nuclear workers' records, but the American government refused to release them. It took several years and several Freedom of Information suits to get at them. When in 1992 Stewart was finally granted access to the records of one third of all workers in nuclear weapons facilities in the US, the front page of The New York Times called it a blow for scientific freedom.

Appendix F – Tri-State Leukemia Study:

Between 1959 and 1962 over 1200 families in Maryland, Minnesota, and New York were part of a large research project called the Tri-State Leukemia Study. The purpose of this study was to identify risk factors for childhood leukemia. At that time, scientists at Roswell Park Cancer Institute asked mothers of children with leukemia and mothers of healthy children about a number of factors that may be linked to a greater risk of leukemia.

These mothers also provided very specific information about each of their pregnancies. This earlier study identified several important risk factors for leukemia. These study findings have been published in many scientific journals and made important contributions to scientific knowledge. We would be happy to send you a copy of the report. To request copies please call 1-877-ASK-RPCI (1-877-275-7724) and mention the Tri-State Health Study. Note the size of the study. It was no small sampling. Note the words "prominent and proven."

Not surprisingly, Dr. Bross lost his funding from the National Cancer Institute when his study was published in the respected American Journal of Public Health. This despite the fact the Dr. Bross is an eminent researcher who has held prestigious positions at major medical centers including Roswell Park and John Hopkins.

JAMA®

The Journal of the American Medical Association

December 16, 1998

Appendix G – Lifestyle Heart Test Trial

Appendix H – Senate/House Bill Back - Session

"*Multitudes remain in inexcusable ignorance in regard to the laws of their being. They are wondering why our race is so feeble, and why so many die prematurely. Is there not a cause? Physicians who profess to understand the human organism, prescribe for their patients, and even for their own dear children, and their companions, slow poisons to break up disease, or to cure slight indisposition. Surely, they cannot realize the evil of these things or they could not do thus. The effects of the poison may not be immediately perceived, but it is doing its work surely in the system, undermining the constitution, and crippling nature in her efforts. They are seeking to correct an evil, but produce a far greater one, which is often incurable. Those who are thus dealt with, are constantly sick, and constantly dosing. And yet, if you listen to their conversation, you will often hear them praising the drugs they have been using, and recommending their use to others, because they have been benefited by their use. It would seem that to such as can reason from cause to effect, the sallow countenance, the continual complaints of ailments, and general prostration of those who claim to be benefited, would be sufficient proofs of the health-destroying influence of drugs. And yet many are so blinded they do not see that all the drugs they have taken have not cured them, but made them worse. The drug invalid numbers one in the world, but is generally peevish, irritable, always sick, lingering out a miserable existence, and seems to live only to call into constant exercise the patience of others. Poisonous drugs have not killed them outright, for nature is loath to give up her hold on life. She is unwilling to cease her struggles. Yet these drug-takers are never well.*" Selected Messages Book 2; White, Disease and Its Causes, p. 453.

References:

Mendelson, Robert S. M.D.
   Confessions of a Medical Heretic,
   pp. 16, 17.

Dr. James Balch, M.D. and Phyllis Balch. Rx Prescription for Cooking.
   Nutrients Targeted for Specific Body Parts, pp. 18-26.
   PAB Books Publishing, Inc, 1991.

George Alexander. Readers Digest Article
   How Life Began on Earth, pp. 116120.   November 1982.

Moodie, R.
      Antiquity of Disease.
      University of Chicago Press

Thorwald, J.
      Science and Secrets of Early Medicine,
      pp. 39, 1962; Ucko, D.P.
American Review of Respiratory Disease,   pp. 90, 1964.

"International Standard."
      Set by the EU Codex Alimentarius Commission.
      http://www.cfsan.fda.gov/~dms/dscodex.html.

White, Ellen. Patriarchs and Prophets:
      The True Object of Education, pp.595, 596.
      Pacific Press Publishing Association, Mountain View, California
      1958.

White, Julius G. The Christian Experience: The Place of Physiology in
      Christian Education and in Christian Experience, pp. 168-176.
      Northwestern Publishing Association; Sacramento, Calif., 1945.

Thiel, Robert J. Ph. D.
      Naturopathy for the 21st Century.

Major, Ralph.
      A History of Medicine, p. 28.

Garrison, Fielding MD.
>An introduction into the History of Medicine.
>pp. 61, 62, 161, 162

Major, Ralph. A.
>History of Medicine, p. 28.

Lois, Wagner N.
>A History of Medicine, pp. 19,20.

Jobes, Gertude.
>Dictionary of Mythology, Folklore and Symbols.
>pp. 266, 267.

Arnold Whittick.
>Symbols, Signs and their Meaning,
>1961, p. 40.

E.A. Walls Budge.
>Amulets and Superstitions.

Moodie, R.
>Antiquity of Disease, University of Chicago.

Thorwald.
>Science and Secrets of Early Medicine.
>1962, p. 39.

Harris, J.E. and K.R. Weeks.
>Second X-Raying the Pharaohs; Charles Scribner & Son.
>New York, N.Y., 1973.

Rosen, George, M.D.
>History of Public Health, pp. 63-65.

Gibson, Rosemary and Janardan.
>Wall of Silence: The Untold Story of the Medical
>Mistakes that Kill Millions of Americans.

The Journal of American Medical Association,
      July 26, 2000, pp. 284(4):483-5

Lapp'e, Marc, PH.D. When Antibiotics Fail.
      University of Illinois, College of Medicine

Buhner, Stephen Harrod. Herbal Antibiotics:
      The End of Antibiotics? pp 4-5.
      Storey Books; Pownal, Vermont. 1999.

Estes Park Institute 2000.
      Estes Park, Colorado.

White, Ellen. Council on Health:
      A Warning Against Spiritualistic Physicians, pp. 454.
      Pacific Press Publishing Association, Mountain View,
      California. 1923.

Vasquez, Manuel. The Mainstreaming of the New Age.
      Traditional Chinese Medicine, Including Acupuncture; Other
      Occult Therapies,
      pp. 131, 142, 155, 157. Pacific Press Publishing Association,
      1998.

Journal of Cancer.
      Cancer Research 44, [pp.1735-1742, May 1984]

Black, Dean. Health at the Crossroads:
Taking Healing from Natures' Hands, pp. 9-11, 23-25, and 29.
      Tapestry Press, Springville, UT. 1988.

White, Ellen. The Ministry of Healing.
      Coworking of the Divine and the Human; The Use of
Remedies, pp.112, 237.
      Pacific Press Publishing Association, Mountain View,
California 1909.

Sagan, Carl. The Skeptical Inquirer Journal.

White, Ellen. Spiritual Gifts Volume 4
      Health, pp. 120-151.

Review & Herald Publishing Association, Washington, D.C., 1945.

Nedley, Neil, M.D. Proof Positive:
　　　　The Frontal Lobe, pp. 260.
　　　　Neil Nedley, M.D., Ardmore, OK, 1998.

White, Ellen. Desire of Ages:
　　　　Calvery, pp. 746
　　　　Pacific Press Publishing Association, Mountain View, California, 1940.

White, Ellen. Council on Health:
　　　　The Christian Physician; City Conditions, pp. 34, 55, 61, 272-274, 356, 746.
　　　　Pacific Press Publishing Association, Mountain View, California. 1923.

American Journal of Public Health. 1996,
　　　　Mar;86(3): pp. 341-346

　　　　2 Selected Messages, Review & Herald Publishing Association, Ellen White, p. 458.

Levin JS, Vanderpool. HY. Is frequent religious attendance really conducive to better health, towards an epidemiology of religion?
　　　　Soc Sci Med 1987; 24(7): pp. 589-600.)

Levin JS, Chatters LM, Taylor RJ.
　　　　Religious effects on health status and life satisfaction among Black Americans.
　　　　J Gerontol B. Psychology, Science, Sociology. 1995 May; 50(3): 154-163.

Ellison CG.
　　　　Religious Involvement and Subjective well-being. J Health Soc Behav. 1991 Mar; 32(1):80-99.

Journal of Longevity.
Vol. 9/No 7, p. 3, 5

White, Ellen. Testimonies for the Church, Vol. 1
Sympathy at Home, pp. 701.
Pacific Press Publishing Association, Mountain View, Calif., 1948.

White, Ellen. Counsels on Diet and Foods.
Physiology of Digestion, Regularity in Eating, pp. 103, 173, 419.

Review & Herald Publishing Association, Takoma Park, Washington, D.C. 1946.

The Journal of American Medical Association. Hard vs. Soft Water: Monroe County, Florida, October 7, 1974.

White, Ellen. 2 Selected Messages, Book 2:
Disease and its Cause, p. 458.
Review & Herald Publishing Association, Washington, D.C., 1958.

White, Ellen. Counsels on Diet and Foods:
Beverages, pp. 420.
Review & Herald Publishing Association,   Takoma   Park, Washington, D.C. 1946.

White, Ellen. The Ministry of Healing:
Diet and Health, pp. 295.
Pacific Press Publishing Association, Mountain View, Calif., 1909.

Journal of the American Medical Association (JAMA):
Intensive Lifestyle Changes for Reversal of Coronary Heart Disease, pp. 2001.
JAMA, December 16, 1998.

Karjalainen, J. Martin JM, et al.
A bovine albumin peptide as a possible
trigger of insulin-dependent diabetes mellitus.
N Journal of Med 1992 Jul 30; 327(5):302-307.

Finberg JP, Seidman R, Better OS.
  Clin Exp Pharmacol Physicol, Cardiovascular responsiveness
  to vasoactive agents in rats with obstructive jaundice.
  1982 Nov-Dec; 9(6):639-643.

Boksa P, Mykita S, Collier B.
  Arachidonic acid inhibits choline uptake and
  cortical synaptosomes. J Neurochem 1988
  Apr; 50(4):1309-131.

White, Ellen. How to Live: pp. 57.
  Pacific Press Publishing Association, Mountain View,
  California.

White, Ellen. Health Reformer: Review & Herald, April 1, 1877.

White, Ellen. My Life Today: pp. 136
  Review & Herald Publishing Association, Takoma Park,
  Washington D.C.

White, Ellen. Mind, Character, and Personality Volume 2:
  Thought Habits, pp. 662.
  Southern Publishing Association, Nashville, Tennessee. 1977.

White, Ellen. Testimonies for the Church, Volume 2:
  Exercise and Air, pp. 527.
  Pacific Press Publishing Association, Mountain View, Calif.
  1948.

White, Ellen. Child Guidance:
  Cleanliness, p. 108-9
  Southern Publishing Association, Nashville, Tennessee. 1954.

Tenpenny, Dr. Sherri J, D.O. Newsweek:
  The Bird Flu

Young, Robert O., Ph.D., D. Sc. Sick and Tired:
  How the "Lost Chapter" Was Lost p. 23.
  Woodland Publishing, Pleasant Grove, UT. 2001.

Miller, Neil Z.
  Vaccines: Are They Really Safe and Effective?
  A Parent's Guide to Childhood Shoots.
  Santa Fe, NM: New Atlantean Press, 1996.

Walene, James.
    Immunization: The Reality Behind the Myth,
    2nd Edition. Westport Conn.: Bergin & Garvey,
    an imprint of greenwood Publishing Group, 1995.

Taylor, Global 2000 Member

The New American. Population Control:
    UN Attack on World Population.
    TNA Vol. 17, No. 22, p. 33-3

 The New American. POPULATION CONTROL:
    Wolf in "Humanitarian" Clothing
    TNA Vol. 16, No. 14 pp. 35-37

Ferrell, Vance. The Broken Blueprint:
    Harvestime Books. 2003
    Box 300, Altamont, TN. 37301

White, Ellen. Counsels to Parents, Teachers, and Students:
    A Missionary Education, pp. 532.
    Pacific Press Publishing Association, Mountain View, Calif.,
    1943.

White, Ellen. Spalding and Megan Collection:
    Drug Science has been Exalted, pp. 137.

Made in the USA
San Bernardino, CA
18 January 2018